HOW TO BE AN MP
PAUL FLYNN

\B^b\

Biteback Publishing

First published as *Commons Knowledge* in 1997 by Poetry Wales Press Ltd

This revised edition published in Great Britain in 2012
Biteback Publishing Ltd
Westminster Tower
3 Albert Embankment
London
SE1 7SP

ISBN 978-1-84954-220-3

10 9 8 7 6 5 4 3 2 1

A CIP catalogue record for this book is available from the British Library.

Set in Dolly by Namkwan Cho
Cover design by Namkwan Cho

Printed and bound in Great Britain by
TJ International, Padstow, Cornwall

Dedicated to the honoured memory of the late David Taylor,
MP for North West Leicestershire 1997–2009.

'The best of us'

CONTENTS

TEN BACKBENCHERS'
COMMANDMENTS

1. Value the role of a backbencher as a high calling.

2. Serve constituents, the weak and the neglected.

3. Seek novel remedies and challenge accepted wisdom.

4. Attack opponents only when they are wrong.

5. Never covet a second income, honours or a retirement job.

6. Value courage and innovation above popularity.

7. Honour the party and extend its horizons.

8. Use humour and colour to convey serious ideas.

9. Fortify the independence of backbenchers against the Executive.

10. Neglect the rich, the obsessed and the tabloids and seek out the silent voices.

ACKNOWLEDGEMENTS

The Expenses Scandal, the Wright Reforms and the Bercow Speakership have transformed Parliament. This new volume attempts to wrestle with the bewildering problems ahead while retelling some of the best-loved lessons from the past.

Thanks to Madeleine Moon and other colleagues who have persistently encouraged me to write a new edition of *Commons Knowledge*. My team – Jayne Bryant, Lisa Eynon and Sam Flynn – have inspired with fresh ideas and wise advice. Parliament has been a great teacher for this backbencher. There is much still to learn.

Paul Flynn

FOREWORD

By background a chemist in the steel industry, a community broadcaster, a political researcher and a councillor, Paul Flynn has proved to be a tenacious, resourceful and independent minded Member of Parliament for Newport West. Always a supporter of, but never a slave to, his beloved Labour Party, Paul is one of those MPs who entertains a wide range of political interests and has pursued them unwaveringly according to his own lights, irrespective of the received wisdom of the Government or the Official Opposition at any particular time. Health, drugs policy, social security, animal welfare, constitutional reform, Afghanistan and opposition to the Trident missile system are but a few of the issues on which he has been an outspoken and passionate campaigner. Following a brief spell on the opposition front bench, which ended over two decades ago, Paul Flynn has devoted himself to being an effective backbench parliamentarian. He has acquired significant experience on parliamentary committees and continues to serve with the Public Administration Select Committee and the Political and Constitutional Reform Committee. Yet he is best known for his witty, incisive and often provocative questioning in the Chamber of the Commons of ministers in successive governments.

Few people can be better equipped to write on how to be an MP. Using a combination of anecdotes drawn from personal experience, historical references and astute perceptions, he manages to capture the practical issues and challenges of political life with good humour, affection and insight. He has seen it all, said it all and done it all in his time and can pass on many clear-sighted words of wisdom to others who want to enter the political fray at Westminster. For those that don't, this book is an entertaining and fascinating account, giving the unvarnished truth about life for an MP and all the compromises and difficulties that entails. His thoughts on the impact of the new intake of MPs since the 2010 election and the reforms that have helped breathe new life into parliamentary scrutiny are an encouraging indicator that we are heading in the right direction.

He tackles many of the challenging issues head on, such as in his sections on 'How to Restore Trust', 'How to Switch on Young Voters' and 'How to Deal with Disaster'. But perhaps his greatest skill is to convey the complex, infuriating, exhausting but ultimately compelling life of an MP. I thoroughly recommend this book with one exception, because a Speaker cannot possibly commend a section entitled: 'How to be a Hooligan'!

I trust you will enjoy what should be a stimulating and rewarding read.

John Bercow
January 2012

FIRST STEPS

How to Arrive

'MP'

You have earned two vibrant letters that inspire pride, hope and trepidation.

Once they were an accolade. Now they can be an albatross.

They are your 'Open Sesame' into a privileged freemasonry of 650 legislators who are loathed and loved in unequal measure – post-expenses scandal now more loathed than loved – by the rest of the population. Difficult choices are ahead. Will you be a 'Tiger' or a 'Bagpuss'? A Roundhead or a Cavalier?

Heart a-flutter you journey to Westminster. Family, friends, your adoring constituency party, purring happiness, waved you off on the odyssey they believe will eventually lead you in triumph to No. 10. Or not. You are about to enter a monastery with glass walls through which the jackals of the tabloids will watch your every twitch and sniff. Following the expenses scandal, ignominy and prison are terrifying alternative destinations.

In your previous career you may have enjoyed high status. Here, captains of industry, acclaimed academics and lions of charities or trade unions are all reduced to apprentice sprogs. It's up to you to adorn your blank page.

It can be an intoxicating experience. After the giddy whirl of the election campaign's adrenalin, sleep deprivation and fatigue, the mood swings into breathless bewilderment and euphoria.

There are consolations. Gone is the past indifference and even hostility that once cold-doused arriving parliamentary virgins. The massive 232 in the 2010 intake have been the first generation of new MPs to be cosseted and cuddled into Parliament. They were ushered up to the first floor of Portcullis House and given their parliamentary pass, a laptop, a Blackberry and a twenty-minute induction on the new expenses system. First contact with the scary Independent Parliamentary Standards Authority (IPSA) is at hand as MPs are walked through the bewildering online claim forms and given detailed explanations of parliamentary etiquette.

A guidebook reveals all, including how to order stationery, 'make friends with the Order Paper' and what to do in case of a chemical or biological attack. Soon the weight of information-overload baffles. The sense of an out-of-body experience wilts the spirit.

A common mistake is to drop into the Commons Post Office and ask if there are any letters. There will be hundreds of constituents eager to test the mettle of new MPs. A high proportion will be hopeless cases that have sought solutions for their intractable problems for years.

A new MP is a celebrity in their constituency; in the Commons a mere insignificant one amongst 650. One Member of the 2010 intake described the frustration she felt during her first few weeks at having to negotiate 'labyrinthine corridors' that all look the same and work from 'a table in a cafe' until she was finally given an office. Old lags will endlessly droll on about how they had to put up with a desk in the corner of the Library for their first ten years. But it has improved. Now, all new MPs will have an office, probably shared at first. The omnipotent whips distribute space. The pinnacle of office accommodation is Portcullis House, only accessible to frontbenchers or senior MPs, but it is a trade-off between proximity to the Chamber and size. A broom cupboard without a window above the Commons Chamber is the equivalent of an office the size of a double garage in far-flung Norman Shaw. Those who fall for the lure of space may regret it. On countless future occasions the penalty will be a breathless dash in the rain from an outbuilding to reach the division lobby in the eight minutes allowed. The airless padded cells above the Chamber are tempting.

Empty, they may look adequate but the free space will shrink to Lilliputian dimensions when the furniture, files and staff move in

How to Take the Oath

The first task is to take the oath. This is not the time to display good manners. Scheme, elbow and cheat a path to the head of the queue. The rule is 'No oath: No pay' – until the traditional rigmarole has been endured, no pay packet will arrive. Pity the by-election winners who have to wait through the long summer recess before they get on the payroll. The place in the queue may determine whether the junior Member will make it as Father/Mother of the House in fifty years' time. Seniority is reckoned according to the position in the queue taking the oath. Bernard Braine owes his spell as Father of the House in 1987 to his industry in 1950. He organised his way to the pole position in the queue ahead of courteous gentlemanly Ted Heath, who was of equal seniority. Braine swore the oath at 5.45 p.m.; Ted at 6.50 p.m. From 1987 to 1992 Heath smouldered as Father-in-waiting. He would have used the weapon of prime seniority to add weight to the bludgeon he used to repeatedly thump Thatcher.

For republicans the oath is tricky, but there is now a precedent for attaching your own conditions to the official wording to weaken or nullify the full meaning. Dennis Skinner in 1992 declared his loyalty to an 'income-tax-paying monarch'. Tony Benn began his oath with the words, 'As a convinced republican and under protest...' The clerk who acts as Master of Ceremonies will not argue with any additional words. The oath is valid as long as the core promise to the sovereign is made. This is the first taste of Parliament's infantilisation before royalty. Instead of standing tall as proud elected citizens, MPs abase themselves as humble subjects. Worse is to come.

Disappointingly, oath-taking is rarely a moving solemn moment. With a queue of hundreds, it is usually a brisk garbled mutter: 'Hold the Bible/Koran/Torah; read the words; swiftly exit left.' Very few Members have taken advantage of the television cameras that are silently recording all 650 oaths. To stir the pride of the electors of Votingham, deliver the oath in a great declamatory voice appropriate for a Nuremberg rally. Let the perfectly formed words reverberate around the Chamber in a sonorous crescendo. The rest of the queue will not understand and they will fret. But on regional television, it will sound Prime Ministerial to the Votingham folk.

Many have regretted their frankness in revealing their full names. After taking the oath they are all published on the Order Paper. Baptismal names that MPs may prefer to forget include Gideon, Aylmer, Knatchbull, Scrimgeour, Choona, Wyvill, Le Quesne, Roffen, Bosco, Pelham, Crolus, Thain, Daubeney, Hendrie, Hannibal, Hadrian, Guinness, Gurth, Haggit, Islay, Egerton, Heneage, Cresswell, Ducane and Flasby.

How to Cohabit with IPSA

The hideous screaming nightmare of the expenses scandal shamed and scarred MPs. We should have raised the alarm earlier. The dishonesty revealed was on a scale that few expected. Some have been justifiably punished. Other lives have been destroyed unfairly.

One may have attempted suicide. A strong minded Tory MP burst into tears when he described to me the insults he and his family had suffered. A Labour MP's hands trembled uncontrollably when the subject was raised. He died prematurely.

None of these three were crooks or dishonest. The scalding abuse of the papers wounded three conscientious MPs deeply. They all eventually blamed themselves for destroying their self respect at the deepest level of their beings.

Mortified by guilt and shame the Commons gripped IPSA in an embrace of revulsion. There is no other solution. A malign beast invaded and occupied MPs' territory. It has little sight or hearing and communicates in incomprehensible jargon and hieroglyphics. It must be kept docile and not aroused too often from its lair. Its irrationality must be learned, imitated and practised.

IPSA was convinced that all MPs would steal their grannies' last pennies given half a chance. IPSA's task was to trust no one and disbelieve everything. Tory commentator Iain Dale described IPSA as 'a quango feathering its own nest and delighting in forcing MPs to wear hairshirts'.

They re-invented a discredited but efficient wheel and came up with a square one with spikes. A simple five-part claims system was atomised into a hundred headings and sub-headings. A monthly thirty-minute chore was complicated by IPSA into endless hours of tedious frustrating trawling through a bureaucratic morass of irrational rules. The nerve-jangling frustration and petty-fogging jobsworth quibbles robbed MPs of their most precious possession – time.

IPSA were merciless in publishing MPs' alleged mistakes. Almost all were the results of failures to obey incomprehensible IPSA rules. The demoralised mood of MPs inhibited criticism of IPSA's failings. In May 2009 one MP was told that £2,500 in pension contributions had been wrongly deducted from him. IPSA promised to repay the sum in June, July and then August. Finally they coughed up in September. In December IPSA told him they had repaid too much. Could they have £500 back?

MPs would embrace a new system without claims or the expensive IPSA. It could be based on an allowance calculated on average expenses and paid automatically. It would be acceptable even if it meant a substantial reduction in the amounts that MPs receive. They would be liberated from the tentacles of the beast. MPs would gain time, IPSA's costs would disappear.

A day of consensus will dawn. IPSA will have served its purpose. It should then be humanely put down, buried under a slab of concrete never to rise again from its dishonoured grave. But until that happens, you'll just have to live with it.

How to Find a London Home

The present crop of MPs are being punished for the excesses of their predecessors. Public scrutiny is sharply focused on MPs' homes.

I regret contributing to a television programme on expenses. My comments were intended to balance wild press exaggerations on alleged extravagance. All in vain. The broadcast programme purported to show a typical MP's balcony flat overlooking the river Thames. They omitted to mention that the £2m purchase price was impossibly excessive on MPs' allowances. But the myth is more powerful than the truth.

The affordable choice is modest, especially since many of the running costs are now not reimbursable. The principal need for the hermitage is proximity to the parliamentary workface. Generations of novice MPs have been first lured by the distant leafy suburbs. Inexorably traffic jams, the congestion charge, high taxi fares and the uncertainty of late night transport have forced them back into the parliamentary square mile.

Many share a mortgage or rent on a flat. The advantages are not just financial. It is useful for sharing cars, taxis and supplying a companion for the bus journey. Ideal MPs' flats have a bathroom for each bedroom. MPs have a monastic unchanging ritual of leaving every morning at 8 a.m. and returning at 11 p.m. The demands on the bathrooms usually coincide. Often a living room and kitchen are rarely used.

The village of the House of Commons provides all the day's comforts from the first beverage of the morning to the midnight nightcap. For the majority of out-of-London MPs the only essential purpose of a flat is to provide a place to sleep. A relative of mine stayed for a weekend in the London flat I shared with another MP for the previous seven years. When he turned on the oven smoke poured out. He was cooking the operating instructions inside. The oven had never been used.

A great scattering of MPs nest in the cheaper properties south of the river, principally in Kennington. MPs may only claim for accommodation expenditure in relation to a property at one location, which may be either in the London Area, or within the MP's constituency, or within twenty miles of any point on the constituency boundary. Mortgage interest payments are being phased out but payments can be claimed for hotel accommodation, rental costs including utility bills, council tax, ground rent and service charges.

IPSA will fund only rented properties. This is now under review. MPs must also repay to IPSA the public share of the notional gain accrued in purchased properties. When property appreciates the taxpayer gains. When property value depreciates the MPs loses. It's rough injustice but it's the public's excessive vengeance for past sins. The London Area Living Payment is limited to £3,760 per financial year. All MPs are eligible for Office Costs Expenditure, whether or not they rent a constituency office. The rates in 2011 are £24,000 for London MPs and £21,000 elsewhere.

How to Appoint Staff

Cautiously.

IPSA has produced job descriptions for staff that have only slight relevance to the real demands of an MP's workload. All must be described as Office Manager, Senior Parliamentary Assistant, Parliamentary Assistant, Senior Caseworker, Caseworker, Senior Secretary or Junior Secretary. There is no choice but to adjust their jobs to fit the parameters of IPSA's Procrustean rules.

Though work can be generally divided into research, secretarial and casework, it's inefficient and disruptive to confine staff to strict silos of work on IPSA lines. If a defined 'Caseworker' or 'Researcher' is absent, the demand for their work continues. While some specialisms are useful, all staff should be able to undertake any task when required. Their job descriptions and titles should be general and embrace every eventuality.

The total allowance appears to be generous. £115,000 translates roughly into three to four full time staff, who must be paid in accordance with IPSA's salary ranges. Adjusting the annual budget is tricky and the temptation to spend up to the limit at the start of the year must be resisted. The nightmare of forgotten additional costs such as pension contributions, employer's National Insurance contributions, overtime, and for any pooled or brought-in services frequently breaks the bank at the year's end. IPSA might ride to the rescue as they feign humanity.

The best place to find new staff candidates is on the splendid website www.w4mp.org. Prepare for at least fifty applications in the first two days after your advert is published. All will have impressive CVs: writing them is now an art form. Be impressed by candidates who have studied your interests and personality and will bring added value to your work. The beast's metamorphosis may be at hand. Generally, secretaries are long-term, while researchers last a few years before they venture into new pastures.

There is no guaranteed formula for recruiting staff. Selecting from known candidates shrinks the gene pool; advertising widely will attract many hundreds of applicants, all but a handful doomed to disappointment. All should receive acknowledgements and, if possible, a few words of helpful encouragement or advice on deficiencies. The work of sifting through CVs and arranging interviews is immense.

The shortlist should not be determined by qualifications alone. One astute candidate boasted that she was 'IPSA literate' – that is now the equivalent of two honours degrees. Choice should be determined by the skills exercised by candidates in observing MPs' individual work. Applicants' letters should be the result of research that informs a carefully crafted re-working of the MPs' own words and fresh re-presentation of personal campaigns.

The perfect secretary has impeccable computer skills, runs a well-organised filing system and is discreet and resourceful with an elephantine memory. The secretary is often the first point of contact. Intelligence and tact of a high order are vital. The perfect researcher should have similar skills, but with an added dash of curiosity and the persistence to find solutions to seemingly intractable problems. The ability to scan vast acres of material and isolate the killer points is vital. Good caseworkers, meanwhile, are born generously endowed with empathy. They have naturally thick skins combined with the sensitivity to detect injustice. For office harmony the individual interests and ambitions of staff should closely match the constituency and campaigning work of the Member.

At least one MP lost his seat because of the collapse of good relations with his staff and the resultant chaos of his constituency office. He set up an over-ambitious high street local office, which became overwhelmed with constituents' drop-in queries. Staff could not cope with both callers and correspondence. Replies to letters were delayed, some for months. His diary became disorganised. Appointments were missed. A bad reputation for constituency work is as contagious as a good one. In spite of his good work in Parliament the MP was doomed to defeat.

One-issue campaigners may seek to use the MP as a conduit for their passions. In the 2005–10 parliament one MP asked only a tiny percentage of his many Parliamentary Questions on matters relating to his constituency. The rest probed the specialist interest of his researcher. Opponents exploited this perceived distortion of priorities, which appeared to neglect the constituents. This probably contributed to his massive electoral defeat.

The work of many other Members is marred and disrupted by rapid staff turnover. Never employ anyone only because they are owed a debt of gratitude for political work or loyalty. Even worse is to pick staff because they are beautiful, a relative or have aroused sympathy because of personal calamity. Permanent commitments should not be made until the final day of a six month trial period.

Under the present system of allowances it is possible to contrive an escalating level of pay and all employees should at least be guaranteed the same inflation increases that MPs have. Researchers understand that their career structure is greatly influenced by their MP's climb up the greasy pole or successful backbench campaigning. Increased allowances from Short Money can be used to increase salaries for rising Opposition frontbench spokespeople. Sometimes it is used to employ more people at depressed rates. The insecurity of the job is exacerbated by the possibility of replacement by civil servants when governments change. The fortunate few can switch employment and land the security and status of special advisers.

The once informal employment of interns is now a bureaucratic minefield. Strict rules apply to wages and conditions for interns or apprentices. Interns must have a job contract and can now be paid a reasonable salary from the staffing allowance. Expenses can be paid to casual 'Volunteers'. Thanks to Tory MP Robert Halfon it is now possible to fund apprenticeships from parliamentary allowances under terms that are reasonable and fair. Halfon was determined to introduce a genuine apprenticeship, consisting of three days in Parliament, one in the constituency and one in the college. He coaxed funding out of Essex Council and Harlow Greyhound Stadium. 'The apprentice is not a general "dogsbody" and does real work,' Robert states. 'This includes research, e-mails, the drafting of EDMs and help with constituent tours of Parliament.' It's a strange concept because there is unlikely to be a job at the end of the apprenticeship. Nevertheless the work and experience gained would be as good as or superior to that achieved by a politics graduate.

There has been adverse publicity for past harsh practices of MPs as employers of volunteers. Lower standards are often demanded of unpaid staff. For a small minority it leads to full time jobs. The majority have no chance of full employment. It is a hateful system. Many became embittered when no real job is offered. All staff should be warned of the precarious, exploitative nature of work in the Commons.

Privileged youngsters will have many other chances in life. Positive discrimination for those from under-privileged backgrounds should be deployed in awarding the rare opportunities to work in Westminster. Wage-less internships unfairly discriminate against those who cannot afford to work for nothing. Reasonable wages can be afforded and must be paid. Parliament's conscience has been aroused by our past neglect of impoverished aspirant interns.

The best applicants will prompt MPs to ask themselves, 'How have I managed to run my office without this person?' The final choice is usually one based on gut instinct. Good luck!

How to Vote

It looks easy but it can be a trap. Outsiders guffaw at the possibility of MPs voting the wrong way. After all the choice is simple, yes or no. Those present who abstain are not recorded.

Gwynfor Evans, Richard Taylor, Martin Bell and Caroline Lucas have all been distinguished one-person parties. They confessed that one of their greatest problems was discovering which way to vote. Commons language and procedure are virtually unintelligible. There is little guidance from the Order Paper. MPs from the major parties are grateful for the sheepdog herding of the whips who direct them safely into the lobby of righteousness and truth. When the MP arrives with seconds to spare before the Speaker's dreaded 'Close the Doors' commandment an instant decision is necessary – sometimes without the guidance of whips. It happened to me on one unforgettable occasion. I had dropped off to sleep in my office and heard the division bell late. I arrived in the nick of time and asked a teller, John McDonnell, for guidance. He pointed to the 'No' lobby. I made it with seconds to spare. The lobby was deserted. As I walked through the teller announced the total of votes as 'One'. On this occasion, however, what appeared to be a major blunder paid dividends. To this day, I have no idea what I had voted against. But it was a cause that was opposed by the *Big Issue*. For weeks they printed photographs of me and lavish praise as 'the only principled MP to oppose this damaging piece of legislation'. I modestly accepted their plaudits. My street credibility soared among the street people.

Ten Minute Rule Bill votes are dangerous. Choosing the sheep's lobby from the goats' lobby can be a gamble if you have missed the debate. The agreed procedure when a Member votes the wrong way is to vote again in the other lobby if time allows. It's a legitimate practice to vote for and against. It's better than voting against the party line for no purpose The Member's name will appear on both published division lists. When it happens, pray that nobody notices. There is only one way to explain this to the people of Votingham: that is to say that this is the only way to register an abstention. It is. On occasions when there is real doubt, it makes the point that the MP is present but is genuinely undecided. David Taylor, former MP for North West Leicestershire, would vote 'No' and 'Aye' when faced with such a situation. The 'David Taylor Vote' is now a legitimate weapon in the parliamentary armoury. It also defuses criticism that the 'MP could not be bothered to turn up'.

Deliberately abstaining is sometimes the worst possible option. An MP who was passionately lobbied by both sides on the feared abortion issue decided to be absent on the day of the vote. He hoped to avoid the wrath of both sides. It was double trouble. The ferocious liberated women of his patch and the Little Sisters of Mercy blasted him from two directions for months. Their resentment was long-lived.

The nightmare that haunts all Members on voting disasters involved Billy Bunter lookalike and former Twickenham MP Toby Jessel in a vital vote on VAT that the Government was about to lose because of a revolt by some of its backbenchers. Normally divisions are over in twelve minutes. This one was being watched by millions live on the main ten o'clock television news bulletins. It dragged on for eighteen minutes. Toby had voted with the Government, then nipped into the 'Labour' lobby to the Gents that were located a few yards beyond the door inside. The Speaker ordered the doors to be closed. Trapped! Aghast, he ran to the glass-panelled locked doors, spread-eagled himself Garfield-like and begged to be let out. The rules dictate that the lobby must be cleared. The only exit was to pass the clerks at the other end and thereby vote against the Government in the most important vote of the Parliament. Word spread around the Chamber that Toby had retreated to the toilet and was refusing to leave. The Speaker's job then is to send in the Serjeant at Arms to prod the Member out with his sword. The Government had lost by eight votes. Mercy was shown. The Serjeant at Arms put his pig sticker away and Toby was allowed to slink off – deflated but not unrecorded.

How to Find a Role

There is no job description and little benign advice. If they choose, MPs can go off and live permanently in the USA or the Channel Islands. Some have. The pay is the same if you choose to smother yourself in overwork or choose absence and idleness. However, the press will not allow serial truancy to pass unnoticed in our modern transparent monastery as they did in the past. The miscreants will be excoriated.

The choice of roles is almost infinite. These are some of the more popular ones.

Sleaze Buster

The cleansing of the stables in Parliament is principally the job of the Standards and Privileges Committee, aided in recent times by the *Daily Telegraph*. With the exception of a few expenses angels, all pre-2010 old lags suffered the hideous trauma of intrusion and exposure resulting from the expenses scandal. The shock therapy of IPSA has been applied. The shock was profound, the therapy protozoan. Some suffered cruel and undeserved torments; others were justly exposed and punished. There is still work to be done to expunge the final remnants of that bad old world where MPs were protected by the myth of being perpetually 'honourable': the revolving door to retirement riches is still an antiquated old-boys mechanism that is potentially corrupting; a few expenses can still be claimed without receipts, though admittedly only within strict, reasonable limits. We are still some way from the puritan perfection of an efficient system that is fair to the public and parliamentarians. It will take a generation to restore the trust of the populace. Those who continue to eliminate the final remnants of sleaze can justly call themselves honourable.

Commons Fixture

Careful positioning is the secret to maximise doughnutting opportunities. At Prime Minister's Question Time a glance at the Order Paper will identify those with a question. Some chronically peripatetic MPs vary their seats in order to appear regularly in the corner of the television screen when the lucky questioners are called. Hone the doughnutting skills. It's helpful to say something now and again, but not essential. 'You're always there,' the grateful constituents will purr as proof of your eternal vigilance on their behalf. Speakers reward regular attenders. The frequency of catching the Speaker's eye is proportional to the frequency of being in 'your place'. Speaker Boothroyd once slapped down a Tory who complained because Dennis Skinner was always being called with the rebuke, 'But he's always here.'

Campaigner

The Commons is a launching pad for crusades. Every word spoken is magnified and broadcast, sometimes into millions of homes. A well-equipped office, intelligent staff and immediate access to the media can all be deployed to begin and sustain a crusade.

Backbenchers have a wonderful record of reforming campaigns. The canard is that elections are won in the marshy middle ground of political consensus, where a harvest of votes comes from the politically ignorant who lack all conviction. Campaigns are the task of the innovative, unorthodox, unusual suspects. All governments are ultimately conservative and reluctant to challenge the ignorance and prejudice of the popular media. It is backbenchers who champion the major reforms and hold the Executive to account.

International Statesperson

MPs whose best friends confide to them that their talent is zero and prospects nil still have a role. A dozen parliamentary organisations will value Members who are ability-free zones. The Council of Europe, the International Parliamentary Union, the Commonwealth Parliamentary Association, all seek MPs with time and unused brain cells to employ. The only qualification is a willingness to devote an extravagant amount of time to travelling and spending hours in airport lounges and hotels. Life is exotic, shared with strangers in a fog of badly translated, confused, imprecise conversations. The main comfort is that the audience will not be listening to the statesperson in his mother tongue. Even vacuous inanities that stun the House into boredom may sound statesman-like when translated into Estonian or Mandarin. It is the death knell for parliamentary ambitions, but great for air miles. As almost all travel expenses are now published, enthusiasm for visits abroad has faded. The folk of Votingham accept that parliamentary business may be possible in Strasbourg, but any trip to Paris must be ooh-la-la. Very few new MPs are prepared to risk accusations of junketing. Now, the worst motives are attributed to all parliamentary activities. This is unfortunate. Foreign excursions have their place as part of the warp and weave of the parliamentary experience. Serious work is undertaken by all these bodies and international contacts provide a wealth of information, especially on different approaches to shared problems. The penalty is to become a forgotten non-person in Parliament and dangerously absent in Votingham. But it is a prized eventide consolation for MPs in their final term, especially those that have given up or never really got started. One cautionary tale involved a newspaper report on a senior MP who had been de-selected by his party because of his alleged excessive absences abroad. 'This is untrue and unfair,' he told the *Guardian* from his hotel in Kathmandu.

Legislator

The most distinguished role for backbenchers is to push laws through Parliament. Only those who win one of the first six places in the raffle have any chance of getting their bills on the statute books. They are happy to unload bills on to more energetic colleagues. Some lottery losers have created several new laws by taking over the bills of colleagues. Bills introduced 'behind the chair', Ten Minute Rule and Ballot Bills can be levered into committee and even into law. Seven hundred and twenty three have made it to the statute book since 1948. But steering a private bill requires parliamentary skills of the highest order. Legislators are the aristocrats of backbenchers. A renaissance of backbench power and innovation is happening. The politics of ideology is being replaced by the politics of reason.

Select Committee Loyalist

Governments need the ballast of the stodgy-brained to pack out Select Committees. Objective truth is a constant threat to the comfort of ministers. Any such outbreak from a lively Select Committee must be smothered by loyalist votes. It is an ideal role for those who are mentally paralysed or impotent. All information and questions necessary to feign competence at public sessions of the committee are supplied by political parties, charities and commercial or trade union interests. The flow is two-way. The loyalist may be called on to leak committee secrets back, including questions provided by advisers. The demands are attendance and constant party loyalty on all votes. The reward is the peace of undisturbed brain receptors that need never be jerked into life. The votes of these pre-programmed minds are perpetually determined. There are also some opportunities for character-building foreign travel and much television exposure as a thoughtful silent doughnut. Happily, some Select Committee loyalists go native. Objective evidence shifts their convictions and rational thought triumphs. Their hold on the job may then be in peril from anxious whips. In opposition there is greater competition for places because fewer frontbench jobs means talent is abundant and underused.

Thorn in the Party's Flesh

Those who are sickened by party timidity or political correctness can still be a valuable irritant and serve the common weal. The easiest way to win notoriety and attention is to be independent of the party catechism of changing rules. There are endless opportunities for subversion. The media has an insatiable appetite for internal attacks. However, some MPs manage to get away with treachery. The trick is to disguise it with the claim that the Member is being 'reasonable and fair minded'. For a few with highly marginal seats this role is a calculated ploy for survival. Attracting votes across the political divide is their only hope. This will understandably infuriate the party attacked. But it will not bear a grudge forever. All will be forgotten and forgiven in perhaps twenty or thirty years.

Euro-Crusader

The Europhobes and Europhiles appear divided but are in reality a priesthood of zealots who communicate in a common language alien to others. During the eternal debate on Maastricht, a prize was awarded to anyone who could understand three consecutive sentences in speeches in Euro-lish by Phobes William Cash and Nigel Spearing. Europhiles Giles Radice and Geoff Hoon claimed that they occasionally understood two; three was asking too much. Euro-fascination is all-consuming. Both sides delight in each other's company. Most MPs during the weary torment of Maastricht would have happily allowed the Phobes and Philes to lock themselves in a padded cell and thrash out the argument. Their final deal would have been gratefully accepted by all.

Euro-crusaders are likely to have a restricted circle of friends who Euro-torture each other without mercy. It's a matter of deep dismay that the 2010 intake contains a determined group of Europhobes on the wilder wing of the Conservative Party who are fanatical and organised. Euro-loathing may lose its bijou minority appeal if tabloid hysteria succeeds. The 2010 parliament swelled the numbers of Euro-crusaders. They have increased interest in their arcane deliberations.

The biggest rebellion by Government backbench MPs took place in October 2011. Tory Euro scepto-realists flaunted potentially self-destructive divisions. A healthy spirit of independent confidence jerked timid new MPs into blinking self awareness. A harbinger of hope.

Sleaze Monger

The crude 'money-in-brown-envelopes' days have passed. Two MPs who were Parliamentary Private Secretaries (PPSs) were expelled from the House in 1994 when they fell for a newspaper sting and grabbed £1,000 to ask Parliamentary Questions about a non-existent product. Following allegations, the extremely insulting charge that MPs could be hired like taxis deeply wounded. But the manipulation of greed still seeks to corrupt the power of Parliament. Successful 'cash for influence' stings caught four noble Lords in 2009 and exposed nine

MPs in 2010. The fumigation of the Palace cannot prevent re-infestation.

Past successful trough-divers plunged their noses so deep that the only parts of them visible were the soles of their Gucci shoes. The foolhardy may still be at it. Little talent or qualification is required, only guile and a thick skin. The job is to ask the questions, fix meetings with ministers and make speeches prepared by Avarice Unlimited plc, Despot-stan or Pharma-larceny. New evidence suggests that an exceptional mental flexibility is required to pile up private riches while posing as the servant of the masses: damaging legal drugs are pushed on the grounds of civil liberties; murderous regimes are defended in the interest of hearing both sides of the argument; lying tabloids are backed in the name of free speech. Self-deception is a potent force when lubricated with money. There are a few new rules. The House is now wiser. The stables are cleaner. But the beast sleaze is ever-present, ravenous to re-infect. The media is always ready to expose the tempted.

Constituency Evangelist

'She/he's a good constituency MP' is the parliamentary equivalent of saying that someone has nice eyes but (it's understood) is not beautiful. The hint is that an exclusive devotion to constituency matters means the Member is incapable of more taxing work. Low-level constituency work can be little more than shifting paper. Complaints are passed on and replies returned without any significant intervention by the Member. Specialist pro-active constituency evangelists throw themselves into advocacy for their constituents. Complaints are pursued with phone calls, delegations and a refusal to take no, or even maybe, for an answer. It is a worthy calling for a Member who may achieve more in his minute local pond than others do thrashing about without a rudder in the national ocean. Constituency work is essential, but it's a sub-plot not the main drama.

Extreme Wing Irritant

To the right and the left there are groupings of like-minded, constructively destructive troublemakers. They share a pathological distrust of current party establishments. The Legislature is stirring. The crash trolley has arrived ready to defibrillate into new vigour the sleeping giant of backbench power. Labour rebels may boast of adherence to every word of the Labour Party Manifesto – of 1945. Tories are enslaved to punishment fetishes. At their most lethal, both are consumed by the backbenchers' disease of jealousy and loathing of frontbenchers. Indifference to career prospects makes them fearless. Advantages: fun, lots of flattering publicity, hero worship from bands of zealots across the nation. Disadvantages: no political future/honours/favours/promotion to the board of Freeloaders plc.

In-Flight Fueller

Known as Parliamentary Private Secretaries (PPSs), they are the bag carriers, the message bearers for the Great Ones. Their prime task is to sit behind the minister in the House and provide in-flight fuelling. This takes the form of notes scribbled by the 'invisible' civil servants who sit in the theatre-like box in the Chamber. Officially they do not exist. But in the Chamber and the committee rooms the minister has a life support system of civil servants a few yards away. The PPSs act as the umbilical link with them. Ministers know that when asked impossible questions in debates, stalling will allow time for the civil servants' notes to reach them.

One Prime Ministerial PPS and occasional minister, Keith Hill, told me that there was nothing in life that he was ever likely to do that was as interesting as his work as PPS to Prime Minister Blair. The qualifications for the task are a readiness to postpone ambition, and the ability to button up and harden the eardrums against a ceaseless barrage of complaints from moaning colleagues. On their minister's subject they are denied the right to speak. Hope must be freeze-framed until the call comes to higher office. It frequently never does.

Protracted silence is a cruel torment for politicians. Sometimes it is terminal, and ex-PPSs and whips have been known to lose altogether their speaking talent and confidence. Constituents are baffled and justifiably angered by what they perceive as indolence or timidity. The excuses of backstage influence or the prospects of future power jobs are thinly plausible.

The aristocrats of the PPSs are those who serve party leaders. All parties use leaders' private secretaries as lightning conductors to divert or channel backbench fury. Ed Miliband has appointed the resourceful and talented Michael Dugher and Anne McGuire. Cameron has the adventurous choice of Desmond Swayne. Swayne has robust views on his fellow Tories, describing one as a 'mincehead', another as 'Mr Angry' and a forum of grassroots party members as 'stooges'. He has also said that Francis Maude is 'not yet trusted by the parliamentary party', and that Theresa May is 'neither liked nor trusted across the party'. The lightning conductor may self-combust.

For those confused by the proliferation of secretaries, Sir Humphrey explains all in *Yes Minister*:

James Hacker: Who else is in this department?

Sir Humphrey Appleby: Well, briefly, Sir, I am the Permanent Under Secretary of State, known as the Permanent Secretary. Woolley here is your Principal Private Secretary. I too have a Principal Private Secretary and he is the Principal Private Secretary to the Permanent Secretary. Directly responsible to me are ten Deputy Secretaries, eighty-seven Under Secretaries and 219 Assistant Secretaries. Directly responsible to the Principal Private Secretary are plain Private Secretaries, and the Prime Minister will be appointing two Parliamentary Under Secretaries and you will be appointing your own Parliamentary Private Secretary.

James Hacker: Do they all type?

Sir Humphrey Appleby: None of us can type. Mrs McKay types. She is the secretary.

Deputy Speaker

Deputy Speaker is now a fresh career path. In 2010, for the first time, they were elected by MPs. It was democracy at its most surreal. I asked the first question at the Hustings. So long and tortured were the replies from the nine candidates that there was very little time for another question.

Out of genuine puzzlement, I wondered why any MP who had just spent months fighting to be elected would want to abandon three quarters of the job. What advantages does the position offer that compensate for the loss of the ability to vote, speak, ask questions and initiate legislation? The answers were unconvincing. They talked of greater access to ministers (how?) and ability to hasten reforms (again, how?). Very significantly, no one mentioned that the job carries an additional salary of up to £40,000. It also comes with faux-prestige, plus some dollops of guilt-free foreign travel and elegant dining. Occasionally major debates are chaired by Deputies. But the cost of presiding over oceans of procedural conundrums and oratorical dross is an excessive one for most MPs.

Speakers-in-Waiting

Unnoticed are thirty senior Members who toil on the Chairman's Panel. They chair Public Bill Committee meetings and play the role of Speaker. With the aid of a clerk, they determine the sequence of debates on bills and keep order. Mute in debate, they can vote only when the committee's vote is tied. Even then they are powerless and must vote for the Government.

The job is tedious, demanding and exhausting with only a few rare flutters of interest. Throughout the long barren hours Members on the panel stare out of the committee room windows. There is ample opportunity to watch the drama of the rise and fall of the Thames, or to admire the architecture of St Thomas' Hospital on the opposite bank of the river. The never-changing view is more diverting than much of the business. But there can never be the distraction of escape to the real world via a BlackBerry or an iPad because the business demands the chair's constant vigilance.

A few may gain embryonic satisfaction through show-ing off their knowledge of the minutiae of Erskine May rules. Occasionally there are chances to slap down disagreeable Members with niggling points of procedure. Most Members on the panel are in their final parliament and have given up on ambition or personal aggrandisement. A few regard the role as important and mildly enjoyable.

There is one flickering hope. Membership of the Chairmen's Panel can lead to a post as Deputy Speaker with a chance of the glittering prize of becoming Speaker. It's a very long shot, but a dream to soothe the mind during those eternal empty hours.

Single Issue Eccentric

Select a neglected issue. It can be anything: sun spots, the art of diamond cutting in ancient Crete, non-ferrous metal-welding, the natterjack toad, human rights in Peru.

Make well-informed, unexciting speeches with an air of authority. The trick is to be identified as that rare MP who knows everything about 'something or other'. It is a hard road. Repeated speeches bore friends and will empty the Chamber. But one day it will all happen. The issue will dominate the day's news. The bore becomes the hero and a respectful House listens in awe. An indefatigable bore on Romania found himself catapulted to fame when the revolution took place there. The hacks sought him out as the only one who knew how to pronounce and spell the names of Romanian cities. Another long-serving MP never stirred a ripple of interest in the UK when he asked a monthly question about an obscure African country that he had once visited. His speeches were ignored here but they regularly made headline news in Africa: 'Fred Nobody challenges British Government on Obscurestan.' Members of a visiting parliamentary delega-tion were astonished to be greeted in villages across the country with banners bearing his name and crowds chanting, 'Welcome Fred Nobody.'

It pays to specialise.

Gullivers

The lure of faraway places is a constant temptation – especially for cosseted parliamentary delegations.

Some trips are good value for taxpayers. Human rights or anti-famine forays into third world countries are gruelling. They bring the House into direct contact with the cruel realities of international tragedies. Occasional visits by those with specialist knowledge of a country or as election observers are worthwhile, sometimes essential where democracies are embryonic and fragile.

But there is little respect for the Gullivers. They are travel gluttons who are consoled by long hours in the sun at the poolside of a luxury hotel. Often Mega-Greed plc, an oppressive regime or environmental polluters lay on the hospitality.

Bophuthatswana was the irresistible destination for a dozen Honourable Members in the 1980s. They proved it by the considerable achievement of pronouncing the name of the country faultlessly. The House was perplexed by the incurable fascination with and loyalty of MPs for this far-distant land. Even more baffling was the advocacy of this oppressive regime by otherwise fair-minded Members. Is is the lure of exotic places, alien concepts or colourful personalities that distorts judgement?

Nothing had changed in 2011, when three Tory MPs embarked on a trip to the hell-hole of Equatorial Guinea. They flew business class to the oil-rich African country and the total cost of the visit was almost £25,000. The biggest fact that the naive trio found on this jaunt was their own ineptitude.

The regime has a human rights record half-way between those of Adolf Hitler and Attila the Hun. The President is proclaimed as a God and his predecessor was a sorcerer who collected human skulls. Even events in Libya did not dissuade the MPs from cosying up to a corrupt dictator. Seventy per cent of the nation's 680,000 people live in poverty without access to electricity or clean water while new hospitals and mansions stand empty.

Inaugural flights have been put on for large groups of MPs. They were persuaded that it is a sensible use of their time to invest fourteen hours flying to the other side of the world, briefly plunging into five star luxury and then flying back. One flight was to Indonesia. Recently the unpleasant, oppressive regime of Azerbaijan has attracted its own admiring all-party group who visited the country. Devotees make a case for the investment and job opportunities of this oil-rich semi-tyranny. The voters of Votingham may not be persuaded on the purity of their motives.

Frontbench Scourge

Reputations have been built by junior Members through their studied attacks on the parliamentary stars. Aneurin Bevan made his name by skilfully savaging the reputation of Winston Churchill.

The victim should be a carefully selected rising or risen star. Acquire an encyclopaedic knowledge of the weaknesses of the quarry. Google and parliamentary sites will reveal all about the vices and vanities of the prey.

Read their speeches; learn their well-trodden paths of thought and speech. They will re-visit them. Anticipate the jokes and bellow the punch line a second before they do. The successful scourge must be omnipresent at committee and Chamber appearances of the victim. Those who show no mercy win the big prizes.

Media Tart

For a Member with the intelligence and sensitivity of the saloon bar drunk who shouts in faces, the tabloids have a job.

To bloat out a story they often need a supporting quote from an Honourable Member. They cultivate MPs who can be guaranteed to give their imprimatur to a racist, sexist, species-ist, xenophobic or homophobic monosyllabic sneer. The hacks usually provide the quote. All the MP has to do is agree that 'their gibe is my gibe too'. The advantages of this role are a certain squalid notoriety with the masses.

Publicity is no longer judged to be the sure-fire vote-winner in elections that it was once thought to be. Excessive coverage of MPs' statements of the obvious is damaging. Hacks now can swiftly trawl through the Googled interests of MPs so the ignominy is spread even more widely.

In March 2010 I predicted that Lembit Opik would lose his seat. He was recklessly over-exposed in vacuous media stunts without balancing attention with his serious persona. He lost with a huge swing against him. He said no one saw it coming. Yes, they did, Lembit. When he came last in the vote for the Lib Dem candidate for London Mayor, Lembit said: 'We have to have some wilderness years; Nelson Mandela did.' Mandela on Robben Island; Lembit in fantasy land. An absence of self-awareness is the problem.

Sell your soul to the constituency not the media.

World Conscience

War in the Sudan and Congo, in which millions of lives have been lost, has never captured the interest of the House, yet conflicts where the number of deaths is far fewer continue to absorb attention.

Iraq and the incursion into Helmand Province in Afghanistan were the major blunders of the Noughties. Parliamentary and public sympathy is aroused only when the horrors are shown on television. There is scientific evidence of the irrational distortion of the Commons' compassion in direct proportion to television coverage.

Heroic work has been done by small bands of Members. Few, if any, are pacifists. The House gave almost unanimous support for the UK's involvement in Sierra Leone, Kosovo, the first Iraq War, the initial invasion of Afghanistan and Libya. Voices of protest denounced the second Iraq War and the Helmand incursion. The full force of media savagery will hit those who oppose war but fail to pay generous tribute to the courage and gallantry of our soldiers. The British psyche is still deeply nationalist with lingering imperial traits. The 'wider still and wider' lobby forget that punching above our weight means dying beyond our responsibilities. Many conflicts end in tragedy and retreat. Vast investments of blood and treasure often merely replace one rotten regime with another rotten regime. The persistence of the peaceniks will be rewarded.

Some Members have bravely visited war zones. Ann Clwyd has the proudest record as a fearless advocate and witness for human rights in danger zones.

The peace-mongers and the truth seekers scored one substantial victory. Government and Opposition were in furious denial on the scandal of 'extraordinary rendition'. The persistence of Swiss MP Dick Marty proved that Western government had lied and fallen from the moral high ground.

Miniaturist

A specialist group of Members delight in the shrunken world of House of Commons committees on domestic matters.

The power wielded on the Catering or the Accommodation and Works Committees is Lilliputian. Decisions on the shapes of desks or the number of spoons to order can create deep schisms among the miniaturists.

Their little world has all the drama, victories and treachery of big time politics in manageable doses. It is real politics. The only difference is one of scale. Many miniaturists are life's model-makers or would-be Jesuits whose careers have been diverted from numbering angels on the head of a pin.

Minister-in-Waiting

Cultivate the virtues of dullness and safety. Be attuned to the nation's lowest common denominators of conscience, idealism and cowardice. At all costs avoid any appearance of humour, originality or interest in your speeches.

Never allow your voice, clothes or gesture to be obviously noticeable in the Chamber. Merge invisibly into all backgrounds. At Prime Minister's Questions, never raise your voice unless all other voices are raised. Study video pictures of your appearance in the Chamber. Ideally the body should have a blurred edge that links you seamlessly to backbench neighbours in a spreading blob of nothingness. Much-larger-than-life character Nicholas Soames was denied promotion for years partly because of his love of psychedelic socks that flashed and dazzled at the extremities of his gargantuan frame.

The qualities that will secure the red boxes are loyalty, earnestness, verbal stamina, personal devotion to the party and its Leader. Sexual activity should cease or be confined within marital boundaries. A safe pair of hands is always demanded. No other bits of the body should ever attract attention.

A partial lobotomy might help.

Procedure Buff
Seasoned politicians and even Speakers can be reduced to nervous fretting by the authoritative buff armed with a copy of Erskine May, Parliament's procedure bible. Acquiring a personal copy costs £267, though there is always one available in the Library.

A deft use of procedural traps and obstacles can delay and frustrate the cunning tricks of opponents. The House will listen admiringly; the television audience will be bored and irritated. The greater televising of Parliament has made procedural warfare unfashionable. It is a turn-off for the broadcasters and the viewer, straining to understand Commons exchanges, is baffled by these erudite wrangles. To the uninitiated, and some of the initiated, the quaint, obscure jargon could be a dialect of Finnish.

Victories great and small have been won by the grey people who have studied Erskine May and know the secret paths through the labyrinth. The 'knowledge' is relatively easy to assimilate and can be shared amongst grateful colleagues. Still, surprisingly few Members, and even fewer hacks, now acquire fluency in the arcane, liberating vernacular.

Comedian

Richard Burton said that if an actor on a London stage announced in a sing-song Welsh valleys accent, 'My father and four brothers were killed down the pit', the audience would laugh.

Clement Freud and other Commons comedians have had similar problems. They are expected to be permanently funny. When Clement lectured the House on the fate of the planet, grinning MPs waited for the hilarious punch-line. There was a sense of anti-climax when it did not arrive. The voice, the demeanour, was the same immutable one Clement used for his funny stories.

The handful of genuine comedians in the House enjoys popularity and media adulation. But many of their political talents are sinfully wasted. They are not taken seriously by their parties or colleagues. Humour rivets them to the base of the greasy pole.

Commons wit supreme the late Tony Banks annually received a poor vote from his colleagues in the shadow Cabinet elections. Yet, he made an indelible impression in all his rare forays from the front bench. When full-time Philistine Terry Dicks moaned about 'arty-farty' ballet dancer types, Tony, as stand-in spokesperson for Labour on the arts, said his speech 'proved that in some parts of the country, a pig's bladder on a stick could be elected as a Tory MP'. Tony was a deeply serious man and made original, perceptive speeches on animal welfare, drugs reform and Chartism. Sadly, so dazzling was his comedy, his serious persona was eclipsed.

Stephen Pound's wit and chutzpah is loved. He is the funniest man in the Commons, endlessly inventive and erudite. He won an award for the best speech of the year, opposing the smoking ban. It was brilliantly persuasive to all except Stephen himself. He ended his smoking addiction the following day. Until 2011 he had been overlooked for ministerial office in spite of his great abilities.

Parliament loves entertainers but rarely trusts them with the serious tasks. The remedy is to lace humour with frequent earnest speeches on dull causes plus a curb on the wilder flights of fancy. Humour is a great leaven in the political pudding but the essential ingredients for promotion are still stodge and caution.

Happiness Creator

Improving well-being is now claimed as a practical political aim. Measuring prosperity is easy but it does not correlate to contentment. Slaves to political fashion are drooling about this rediscovered truth.

In Hungary in 2000 a T-shirt asked the question, 'What has ten years of right-wing Government done that fifty years of Communism could never do?' The answer on the back of the shirt was, 'Made the people love Socialism.'

The equality of poverty is preferred to the inequality of prosperity. The equality of no-choice is better than the inequality of choice. Two of the supreme modern political shibboleths are felled: prosperity and choice. A sense of fairness is the path to contentment.

It's what we used to call Socialism.

Witch Doctor

Providing wildly alternative medical advice is a courageous or foolhardy role for those insensitive to gasps of incredulity and eyes rolled towards the ceiling. One MP has offered a litany of weird remedies. They include homeopathic borax to protect animals from foot and mouth and the 'laying on of hands' to cure cancer. He is also an impassioned advocate of dowsing, kinesiology and crystal therapy – on the fragile scientific basis that 'crystals create a radio signal ... so they are likely to contribute to health and well-being'. His latest enthusiasm is iridology. He explains that this is a 'newer science involving looking into eyes to discover medical problems'. In the past he has advocated the use of flowers to cure fatal illnesses. The same Member repaid £755 that he had spent on astrology software, even though IPSA remarkably told him he did not have to. But they did decline to pay a £125 bill for a seminar on honouring 'the male and female essence'.

He adds to the rich variety of parliamentary eccentricity.

Robot

Those whose cerebral processes were stillborn or have become atrophied can shine as robots.

Robots are anointed with ersatz expertise by the received wisdom of others. Whips and frontbench experts provide carefully composed briefings on all debates or statements. All that is demanded is the ability to memorise (or sometimes just read) a hand-me-down question. In some quiet days whole speeches are provided. Fame can come from a slavish repetition of the words of the wise and witty.

There are hazards in straying from the prepared scripts into the alien quagmires of original thought. Thinking and originality are dangerous when talents are confined to the purely robotic. Care is necessary to avoid repeating a question already asked by a fellow robot supplied with an identical script. Because MPs rarely listen to other MPs' questions, this is a major elephant trap. When it happens, the groans of friends and foes are painfully burdensome.

Divine Messenger

Affect a churchly voice and a monastic life style. Neither drink nor smoke. Be in bed by 11.30 p.m., alone, with a Spartan beverage.

The pinnacle of ambition is the job of parliamentary oracle for the Church Commissioners, known as 'God's MP'. Past models are the saintly Michael Alison, the blessed Frank Field and, most recently, the rotund Tony Baldry. They are disappointingly appointed by the Queen and not by God.

The Church Commissioners' role is to manage the Church's

historic assets, today invested in stock market shares and property, to produce money to support the Church's ministry. They
are questioned in Parliament about 'the church and steeples and
the cash that goes therewith'. Questions are allowed on the appro-
priateness of investing in merchants of death to serve the cause of
the Prince of Peace.

Advantages: a gain in precedence with the Speaker as the
conduit for the Divine Will – the sacred messengers glow with the
halo of moral superiority.

Disadvantages: avoided by sinful colleagues; the prized parliamentary lollipops are denied – they are for those who live in
this world.

Virtuoso Bore

Boredom is a mighty political weapon.

Whips cleverly incite boredom. It lowers the temperature
of debate, infuriates political opponents and exhausts them.
Labour's resourceful Peter Pike was once persuaded to speak
for seven hours in a bill committee. With consummate skill he
avoided saying anything of interest. Henry Brooke was regularly
wheeled out by Harold Macmillan at tricky times in the Chamber
to send MPs scurrying off to the tea rooms.

Brilliant bores meticulously strip their speeches of adjectives,
jokes and colour. They must be stuffed with statistics, complex
sentences and hypnotic repetitions.

Social Security Buff

This much is guaranteed: raising a social security issue with journalists will set their eyes glazing over. They will quickly remember another appointment and scuttle off.

There are more people on benefits in Britain than have mortgages. Almost all hacks have mortgages. None are on benefits.
Social Security is a fearsome, mysterious tangle beyond
their comprehension. Only a tiny number of specialist hacks

understand. They have difficulty in convincing their editors that the plight of millions of people on minute disposable income is of any significance.

One of Parliament's major recent failures has been its indifference to the widening gap in incomes. The prejudices of the over-rewarded fat cats have ruled. The myth of the scrounger has become the accepted wisdom.

When Margaret Beckett, Clare Short and I were responsible for Labour's front bench on Social Security an odd phenomenon was noticed. All Labour Members on the Standing Committee were Catholics, ex-Catholics or had received a Catholic education. The legacy that all can guarantee from a Catholic education is an A Level in Guilt. That's a key qualification for labouring in the social security vale of tears.

Ferret

Those who sniff their way through the tangles of complex statistics can discover the murky truths of fraud and chicanery.

The achievements of the Public Accounts Committee are usually unsung and unnoticed. Their activities are on a stratum of complexity that baffles outsiders. The forensic talents of Alan Williams exposed hidden scandals in the accounts of several public bodies.

Panic seized apologists for the royal family at Alan's relentless campaign to publish the details of the Income Support for royals. Especially wounding was the revelation of the billionaire lifestyle of hangers-on and minor royals who elect to avoid work. As a direct result of his probing, policy was changed, sending the Royal Yacht steaming away from the sun spots to other destinations to try to justify its existence.

David Taylor was an accountant and another devastating forensic revealer of financial scandal. He brilliantly denounced the inevitability of the failure of the Private Finance Initiative (PFI) projects that offered instant political gratification to politicians at vast future costs to taxpayers. Parliament needs restless fearless ferrets. It's a worthy task for backbenchers.

Select Committee Chair

Under new reforms, Select Committee chairs are now elected by MPs. Since 2003 they have been paid a substantial extra amount. In 2010/11 it is around £15,000. Their newly elected authority has greatly enhanced the standing of committees and the legitimacy of their reports.

This is a major personal triumph for retired MP, now Professor, Tony Wright. He was firmly told (presumably by the whips) that he would never chair the Public Administration Select Committee (PASC). But he was a dissident with powerfully held, deeply grounded convictions that could never be undermined by whips' pressure. He went on to chair the committee with flair and distinction. The Wright Reforms are his legacy.

Select Committees have not entirely broken free from the manipulation of the Executive. Unfortunately, the caucus of whips from all parties carves up the choice of committees. This resulted in only one candidate for the Welsh Affairs Select Committee, Conservative David 'Top Cat' Davies (Monmouth). Thirty-two of the forty Welsh MPs of other parties were denied the chance to lead the committee. This is far from a perfect democracy.

Mantra Chanter

A sound rule of modern politics is 'Say the same thing, again and again. Then say it louder.'

Training mantras for each side include 'It's Labour's misman-agement of the economy' and 'The NHS is unsafe in Tory hands'. Mantras are not lethal. They are the tools of the small fry artisan. They irritate and wound by constant repetition. Users must hypnotise themselves into the delusion that the words of the mantra are always vital and potent. The memories of the last hundred times the words have been used must be erased.

Deploying monotony as a political battering ram is an undemanding role, ideal for MPs with brains in perma-coma.

Tantric Teaser

'Nudging' is proclaimed as the new revealed truth.

Manufacturers of damaging food are being 'nudged' into putting their customers' health above their search for profits. The Government wags a finger at them and has faith that their food will become less damaging.

It's a hands-off nanny-denying approach that avoids troublesome regulation. Those with infinite faith in the benign unselfish goodwill of the human spirit joyfully embrace tantric politics. It has the appeal and frustration of unconsummated foreplay.

Cynics foresee failure and shame.

Whip

Whips live a half-life of exclusion and silence. It is only tolerable as a period of penance for past sins or to earn a hoist up the greasy pole. The job has been compared with the position of school prefect. It is closer to that of school sneak.

Now judged to be an essential apprenticeship for future ministerial roles, many suffer for a short while and are promoted; others languish for years in eternal hope. Some are ignominiously found wanting and are dropped from the first rung of the ladder.

The whips are excluded from many of the activities of backbenchers. Meanwhile, constituencies are irritated when their mouthpiece is muffled and becomes a shadowy figure in the Commons.

The satisfaction of the long-term whips is that of the toilers in the boiler rooms. Unseen, grubby, unloved, they keep the ships of Government and Opposition steaming steadily forward.

Mute Witness

Silence is a political device. Those rare beings, the happily silent politicians, are the infantry of the political battlefield. Where would the generals be, blasting off from the front benches, without the ranks of mute admirers?

At committee sessions, Government backbenchers' humble role is to stifle words and thought. Mind games will pass the time. Wallow in enticing thoughts of rewards that will come one day: the ministerial car ... the Cabinet minister's leather furniture ... the team of admiring civil servants ... the trappings of the high office ... hah ... one day ... one day.

Merthyr MP Ted Rowlands broke his vow when Jim Callaghan was leading the Labour Government front bench. The scholarly Ted was holding forth at great length on an amendment of which he had great knowledge. Callaghan had previously agreed with the Opposition to finish the session at 7 p.m. so that everyone could go off to an important dinner.

Exasperated, Jim passed Ted a note: 'What do you think you are doing?' Without halting his staccato flow, Ted scribbled back: 'Legislating.'

Jim's wounding reply was 'Well, stop it.' Ted did. He lapsed back into the mandatory cooperative constructive silence. Ted tells the story to make the point about legislating and the frustrations of the backbenchers. The prime task of Government backbenchers in committee is to remain supine and quiet. Just lie back, empty the brain, think of the purity of the party's policies and let the legislative steamroller flatten thoughts and activity.

Tyranny Smasher
Bernard Braine banged the table. It was his favourite ploy when faced with intransigence. It did the trick. He was arguing for the release from prison of Václav Havel, the future president of Czechoslovakia.

Proving that there is life after the front bench, Bernard threw himself into David-like assaults on the Communist Goliaths. Many more have courageously taken on other tyrannies. My prize for courage goes to Lord Judd for standing up to the abuse, curses and threats of Russians over Chechnya. As Frank Judd, he was a minister in Harold Wilson's Government and later ran Oxfam. In Strasbourg, as a member of the Council of Europe and Rapporteur on Chechnya, he was the truthful voice on the dreadful Russian atrocities in Chechnya. Judd remained steadfast against a united attack from the post-Soviet Commonwealth of Independent States politicians and the Russian media. He was called a liar and accused of taking bribes from the Chechens. While many politicians from Eastern Europe are subtle and of high quality, their politics are still marked by the brutal imprint of their communist past. Frank is known to possess saintly integrity beyond the reach of any form of corruption. In Moscow he became a media hate figure. In Chechnya he will be long remembered as a brave politician whose testimony lightened their terrible burdens.

The tyrants in Belarus and Azerbaijan, not to mention the venerable dictator in Equatorial Guinea, have yet to incite the wrath of tyranny smashers. Career opportunities wait.

Heckler

Essential equipment for this job is a sonorous, bellowing voice, a lively, inventive mind and intimate knowledge of the victim. The voice must amplify itself into every corner of the Chamber without electronic aid. The secret is timing. Aimless bawling when the House is noisy can be heard only by the loudmouth's unfortunate neighbours. Choose, instead, the seconds of silence during ministerial pauses to fire the verbal ammunition. One word is best. Four is an absolute maximum.

Study those speakers who invite heckling. They ask rhetorical questions, then pause. Pauses are begging to be filled with well-crafted interjections. Destructive or funny gibes will de-rail the victim's train of thought. Michael Fabricant once asked, 'Is the Member as disturbed as I am...' Pause. He was about to say, '...about Euro fraud?' 'No, I'm relatively sane,' a heckler intervened.

Sometimes, completely thrown, the speaker will desert the prepared text and answer the heckler. When a verbal interruption is answered by the person speaking, the interruption is recorded in Hansard. Usually a note is sent down from the Hansard writers to make sure the correct sedentary heckler is identified.

Hecklers live dangerously. The Speaker's penalty for venal offences is that the offender will not be called to speak. For mortal offences the Speaker may 'name' the transgressor. This is a terrifying experience. The Speaker will bark out the name of the offender as if the words are obscenities. This extreme punishment is restricted usually to the recidivist offender who is also boorish and cruel. Latitude is shown to gentle and funny interrupters.

Chris Ruane took advantage of Ming Campbell in his brief, unhappy period as Lib Dem Leader. High office reduced Ming from a forceful speaker to a diffident, prematurely aged ditherer. When Ming rose at PMQs he frequently paused, waiting for an attentive silence that never came. One long pause was filled by Ruane with the inquiry 'What are all these people doing in my bedroom?'

Michael Heseltine asked rhetorically in a fox-hunting debate: 'What do we mean by flushing out?' Denis MacShane cried, 'Ask Mrs Thatcher!' Everyone laughed except Hezza.

Harold Wilson was interrupted when speaking about his public expenditure plans. A heckler shouted: 'What about Vietnam?' Harold said: 'The Government has no plans to increase public expenditure in Vietnam.' The heckler hit back: 'Rubbish!' Wilson replied: 'I'll come to your special interest in a minute, sir.'

Clever heckling of party colleagues is sometimes required when they are wrong. A brilliantly effective ploy is to sit next to someone whose question is likely to displease you. Prepare a brief heckle for the pause between the end of the question and the minister's reply. Sitting next to the questioner will ensure the heckle will be heard booming throughout the House and the nation at a similar volume to the original because the microphone will still be live. It happened to me. It was galling and ruined the effect of my carefully planned question.

Committee Time-Filler

Public speaking to most MPs is as natural as an eternal train of thought that is never diverted and never reaches a terminus. The task here is to fill large chunks of time with clouds of words. The gifts are grey and long-lasting. Curb speech rhythms and cadences. Practise by singing on a single note until breathless. Desolation should register on the faces of listeners.

No case is known of brain damage as a result of a boredom offensive, but in one committee an MP suffered a transient nervous breakdown under an avalanche of words. He rushed to open a third storey window after listening to hours of droning monotone on the Cardiff Bay Barrage Bill.

Mistaking his intention, someone asked in a Point of Order, 'Is it in order for an Honourable Member to throw himself from a window while another Member is speaking?'

'It's in order,' the exhausted committee chairman ruled, 'for a Member to leave the room in any way he thinks fit. But in these circumstances, he has my sympathies.'

The Cardiff Bill scaled Olympian heights of boredom. It rattled around Parliament for a longer period than the First World War. Exhaustion has strange effects on the brain. Deranged with fatigue and fed up with repeated appeals to save birdlife abundant elsewhere, I made an impassioned appeal to a frazzled Chamber at 2 a.m. It was for a life form not protected by the Royal Society for the Protection of Birds. 'The permanently high water of the Barrage will drown the mud sewerage sludge that is the habitat of the numerous local rat populations. Not only the Turd-grebe and the Litter-shanks are threatened,' I warned, 'but what will be the fate of the rare Grangetown Barking Rat? This blameless creature has no society to protect it. If there was one, it would not be royal.' Inhibitions stripped away by exhaustion, I reached a depth of bleary rhetorical intensity that surprised me in defence of these mythical creatures.

To my protracted and acute embarrassment, one Tory MP was moved by this appeal. For many years afterwards, and on many occasions, Oliver Heald greeted me with a concerned inquiry into the well-being of 'those rats'. I could never bring myself to explain and confess. To his great credit, in 2011 Oliver re-told the story against himself at a dinner in Strasbourg. He blamed it all on my 'Welsh passion and conviction'. Being persuasive about a mythical beast is probably not an accolade. I should have revealed the truth earlier.

QUESTIONS

How to Ask a Question

Parliamentary questions only rarely seek information. Oral Questions never do. It is usually a mark of incompetence to ask an oral question except in certain knowledge that the answer will be damaging to opponents or helpful to allies.

Written Questions can be used to unearth hidden information or to expose the Government's evasiveness by a public refusal to answer a fair question. If information is being sought a letter should be written to the minister. If the issue is of major importance to Votingham a meeting should be sought.

Prime Minister's Questions

The class act of the parliamentary circus is Prime Minister's Question Time (PMQs). Tony Blair said it was 'the most nerve-racking, discombobulating, nail-biting, bowel-moving, terror-inspiring, courage-draining experience' in his political life. The probability of an MP winning the lottery for the first question is once every six years. The first question sets the mood that runs through the full half an hour. Opposition MPs try to bowl the Prime Minister a googly. The PM wants a slow ball lobbed from his own side that he can smash into the stratosphere.

'Number One' for an Opposition MP is the equivalent of firing the first shot in battle. This is the chance to toss in the verbal hand grenade that will blow away the Government's defences. The cognoscenti craft their supplementaries with the devotion of poets.

Margaret Thatcher spent eight hours twice a week preparing for two fifteen minute slots. Only the foolish never rehearse their questions on others. All questions can easily crash land. The Prime Minister spots a weakness and flays the questioner. Failure at PMQs is profound, agonising and invokes terminal gloom.

As a fellow junior frontbencher Tony Blair advised me when I had my first Number One question. He told me to spend the whole morning preparing it. 'Forget the mail. Forget telephone calls. Work on the question.'

Even then failure is possible. Blair ruefully recalled the time he was 'handbagged' by Margaret Thatcher. He had decided to surprise her with a question on a long forgotten Government report published exactly a year before his question was due. It was bound to be well forgotten, he thought.

He spent the morning with a copy of the report in the Commons Library, fashioning a blockbuster of a question. Confidently he asked the question, certain that she could not anticipate it.

Coolly Mrs Thatcher took a full copy of the report from her handbag and gave a magisterial reply that left Blair wide-eyed and speechless. Was it brilliant foresight? Or did someone see him doing his homework in the library? Whichever, it proves that PMQs is professional warfare and no place for the lazy or amateurish.

The champion questioner knows the key ingredients are preparation and delivery. Devise half a dozen possible wordings before the day on issues that people are talking about on the streets. Be prepared to ditch them all for the news item that breaks at half past eleven on your D day.

PMQs fall into the five categories: shroud-waver, shock and awe, current mania, parish pump and the immediately topical.

Shroud-wavers seize the sympathy of the House in the first sentence. Afghanistan deaths or serious injuries, feared diseases, vulnerable people suffering abuse, cheated pensioners – these are topics that will always silence the Chamber.

John Woodcock asked David Cameron:

> After four years, fifteen-year-old Alice Pyne, who lives in my constituency, is losing her battle against cancer. She has posted online her 'bucket list', a simple wish list of things that she wants to do before it is too late. She wants to meet Take That, to own a purple iPod and to enter her dog in a Labrador show, but at the top of the list is a call for everyone to sign up to be a bone marrow donor. Will the Prime Minister work with the Leader of the Opposition and me to find out why too few people are currently on that life-saving register?

Cameron's answer was serious and detailed, indicating advanced notice of the question. This was a rare civilised and constructive exchange that possibly will benefit patients.

Smart Alec shroud-waving will provoke combative responses. They may be politically gratifying but they are usually destructive. David Cameron once asked a combative and unanswerable one while in Opposition that had a re-usable formula: 'What is the PM most proud of – the £1bn wasted on the Millennium Dome or the £1m bung from Bernie Ecclestone?'

Shock and awe are the questions that cannot be anticipated – even after eight hours of preparation. Labour's Gordon Prentice rocked Blair back on his heels with 'A decade ago the Prime Minister won the Labour leadership on a manifesto promising change and renewal. Now, after seven years of Government, can he think of a single dramatic act that would make the British public sit up and take notice?' Philosopher and lorry driver Tony McWalter established his niche in politics with this brain teaser. He asked Blair '...could he briefly outline his political philosophy?' Blair, the virtuoso of PMQs, was thrown twice.

Latching on to the tabloid issue of the day will guarantee the subject and the questioner a reward of ephemeral publicity. Any issue will do as long as it is likely to be of interest until the next day's papers are written. The tabloids will never let you down with their ceaseless flow of scares and alarms. Hamster flu pandemic terror, EU plans square apples, breathing causes cancer, asylum seekers eat pets – whatever the issue, if it's worrying the papers the PM must have a plan of action to stop it.

The safest and least demanding will be a crisis affecting only the square mile of Votingham. The parochialism should not be revealed until the final sentence, otherwise the Chamber will lose interest and return to hyper-babble that will drown your words. If a half-sensible answer is expected, the PM must be warned in advance. The *Votingham Argus* cannot resist a headline – 'PM acts on Votingham scandal.'

The availability of electronic instant news is a gift for those with strong nerves and skills in impromptu oratory. News will break after the PM has started answering questions. He is likely to be knocked off his perch and baffled by a demand that he provides his detailed policy on an event he does not know about. When Alun Michael resigned as First Secretary of the Welsh Assembly the news was broadcast to all Labour MPs' pagers. Tony Blair was caught out, stating his full confidence in Alun's future in the job. The PM appeared to be the only Labour MP without a pager. Breaking news is now distributed at lightning speed via BlackBerries and iPads.

Meticulous presentation is essential for the television audience of millions. Write the question out. Ruthlessly edit out any syllable that is not crucial. Try out the question on friends. Don't accept polite praise. If their faces do not light up at the final 'punch'-word in the punch-line, start again. Ask them to anticipate the Prime Minister's reply. Then amend your question to crush his answer. If the final version exhilarates them, it will impress the House. Get it right. Your party and voters depend on you. You may not get another chance for many years.

The classic PMQ survives. It has three parts in three sentences. Kerry McCarthy scored with a memorable one just before the student demonstration on fees:

1. Seize the attention of the House:

    As someone who claims to be an avid fan of The Smiths...

2. Make a powerful new point:

    ...the Prime Minister will no doubt be rather upset this week that both Morrissey and Johnny Marr have banned him from liking them. The Smiths are, of course, the archetypal students' band.

3. Pose an unanswerable question:

    If he wins tomorrow night's vote [on tuition fees], what songs does he think students will be listening to? 'Miserable Lie', 'I Don't Owe You Anything' or 'Heaven Knows I'm Miserable Now'?

Another model question was asked by Nick Ainger to John Major, two days after John Redwood's bid to oust Major as Leader of the Tory Party failed. It was the topical issue that was the sure-fire way to grab the attention of a noisy distracted House.

1. Attention:

    Given the description by John Redwood of the Prime Minister's leadership as 'uncertainty based on indecision'...

2. Point:

    ...is it the job of the Deputy Prime Minister now to take the decisions?

3. Unanswerable Question:

Or has the Prime Minister not decided yet?

The Prime Minister's answer to Nick Ainger's question was a rambling prepared attack on the conduct of Tony Blair's election, with two verbatim quotes from Max Madden and John Prescott. The logical link between question and answer was at its most tenuous. Nick Ainger won by a mile.

Ian Lucas says that he also uses this formula, as his question proves:

1. Attention:

The Prime Minister has described hospices as one of the great successes of the big society...

2. Point:

...So why, as a result of his Government's increases in VAT and cuts in gift aid, is Nightingale House hospice in my constituency paying an extra £20,000 to his friend the Chancellor of the Exchequer this year?

3. Unanswerable Question:

Will he give it the money back?

The picador-brief, tweet-length questions are piercingly effective. Tory Michael Spicer plagued Gordon Brown with strikes that left Gordon no thinking time to frame an answer. Spicer asked, 'What is the economic theory behind an end to boom and bust?' Later he queried, 'Now we face stagflation what's he going to do about it?' As Brown's premiership drew to a close, Spicer asked,

'Will the Prime Minister confirm that he will soldier on to the bitter end?' All three wounded.

He is not known for his brevity, but the question that floored David Cameron in his marathon session on the English riots was Dennis Skinner's: 'The Prime Minister has been asked a simple question twice and refused to answer it: as Prime Minister, did he ever discuss the question of the BSkyB bid with News International at all the meetings they attended?'

Usually a PM can forge a mildly convincing link between question and answer from his lengthy prepared notes. Hours are devoted each week to anticipating subjects that will be raised. Manifold damaging facts about the constituency and interests of the questioning MP are assembled for the red folder. The Prime Minister's red book is crammed with annotated information, laced with quotes, witty retorts and killer facts.

The delivery of the question depends on the strength of your natural voice, dramatic timing and, often neglected, positioning your voice immediately under a microphone. Many great questions have been ruined by Members standing equidistant from two microphones. This is a particular problem for female Members and men with weak or shrill voices. The timbre of thin voices cannot be adequately amplified by the sound system. The questions disappear, drowned by the disproportionately loud background babble.

Government backbenchers have a relatively easy task. They can contact 10 Downing Street or the whips at 9 a.m. and ask what question the PM would like to be asked that afternoon. The PM's minions are always pleased to oblige.

It's a simple matter of standing up straight and asking the question nicely. Remember to be awestruck or titillated with amusement when the Prime Minister gives the answer that the same minions have scripted for him.

But it can fall apart. Everyone is subject to a possible three-second seize-up of the brain receptors. Have a parachute handy.

Prop a large lettered prompt on the bench in front of you, have one held up by a friend or write notes on a gesturing hand. The luckless Sebastian Coe endured seconds of hell when he dried up at his first PMQs.

A question may flop in the House but succeed on television and radio. It is easy to become dispirited by the catcalls or indifference of political hacks doing their duty. One former Lib Dem leader, Charles Kennedy, endured a weekly purgatory. He said of his scalding: 'What may seem flat or drowned out in the Chamber can come over as the sole, sane voice in the asylum to the real world outside watching on television.' Iraq gave me my opportunity. We were asking the awkward questions of Tony Blair that the Tories could not. And the House wanted to hear his answers. At one stage I felt dispirited, until a senior Cabinet minister approached me and encouraged me to persist. 'You're asking the questions half the Cabinet would love to ask – but can't.'

The controversy of PMQs continues. John Major announced when he first became PM that he wanted to get rid of the 'Yah/ Boo' at PMQs. It was to be a civilised exchange of views. To my great regret I co-operated with him. I had question Number One drawn for PMQs. In the spirit of the new arrangements, I sent a copy of the question to Downing Street a few days early. It was a reasonable request for action on the then future scandal of mis-sold personal pensions. The answer that John Major gave me was described in a *Times* editorial as 'a typical civil service briefing with a party political sting in the tail'. He gave his 'Boo' when I had not given my 'Yah'.

Speaker John Bercow has called for 'more scrutiny, more civility, less noise and less abuse masquerading as inquiry'. He described PMQs as 'a litany of attacks, sound bites and planted questions from across the spectrum', and proclaimed that 'if it is scrutiny at all, then it is scrutiny by screech'.

Cardiff West MP Kevin Brennan has a recipe for reform: 'If

there was a hooter at the clerk's desk that sounded every time the Prime Minister made a factual error, that might help to prevent the patronising of people who are just putting him straight with the facts.'

Some disagree. Stephen Pound says: 'Never, in my fourteen years in this House, have I ever heard any constituent complaining that they despise shouting at PMQs.' The *Daily Mirror*'s associate editor, Kevin Maguire, ventures: 'I don't think the public would watch it if it were a Socratic debate.'

'Yah/Boo' is the future.

Oral Questions to Ministers

Oral Questions on other subjects are less demanding. The House is a tenth full and the mood is less frenetic. The question may be answered by a very junior sprog minister. If Prime Minister's Question Time is the Cup Final, this is the Zamaretto League.

Still, it has many fans, with an increasing number of parliamentary groupies hooked on their television pictures via cable or satellite. The most obscure questions on the Church Commissioners are watched by more people than would hear an MP at public meetings every evening for a lifetime. Speaker Bercow has transformed Oral Questions. Traditionally only about fifteen were called. Now it's usual to have all reached. That's up to twenty-five. The exchanges are briefer, sharper and better theatre.

1. Attention (less important because the Chamber has fewer distractions):

Wasn't it unfair of Mr Alan Clark to say that the Department of Employment did nothing but concoct useless schemes to con the unemployed off the register...

2. Point:

Ignoring entirely the imaginative, creative work that takes place in the department every month to fiddle the unemployment figures?

3. Unanswerable question:

Shouldn't the Department's HQ be recognised for what it is: the country's biggest, most shameless and disreputable massage parlour?

No Employment Minister anticipated a question on massage parlours. Like the medieval minstrels whose poems were meant to be read aloud, Oral Questions maximise their effects by making the most of silence. Best achieved by a surprise final punch word that hangs in the air at the end of the question, taunting and challenging. Let the brain instruct the voice that the punch-word is glorious and poetic. Don't let it fade or die at the end. It will sound like an apology. It must be loud, confident and resonant.

Ideally, it should leave the minister's gob well smacked. The surprise may force him to rethink the answer that has been prepared. Supreme victory is to induce two seconds of bemused silence or, better still, a laugh from the Treasury bench. Llinos Golding silenced Douglas Hogg and left him mouthing air, repeating 'Madam Speaker, Madam Speaker...' to gain thinking time, when she skewered him with a one-liner: 'On what date did the public lose faith in you as a minister?'

Two days after William Waldegrave said that it was legitimate on occasions for ministers to lie, Social Security Minister Ann Widdecombe was trapped into two seconds of bemused lip-biting silence when an oral question ended, 'Can the minister answer any question without blaming the last or next Labour

Government and confess that her employment figures are a tissue of Waldegraves?'

Tony Newton, when Secretary of State for Social Security, was left momentarily nonplussed the day after Peter Walker resigned as Secretary of State for Wales with a masterful punch-word: 'Is the Secretary of State not also sickened with his duties and tempted to resign, or do a runner? Or, as we say in Wales, do a Walker?'

David Taylor was the supreme oral and topical questioner of the 2005–10 parliament. He has asked more questions than anyone else. They were all lovingly crafted in their language and guile. He was feared and respected by ministers. He would shamelessly disarm his target with flattery in his opening sentence:

> I exculpate the minister, who is a very able man of great integrity, but what should be done about the lamentable failures of that ill-conceived, incoherent and incompetent organisation? Perhaps the guilty parties could be locked up for egregious negligence as a pilot group in one of the minister's fabled titan prisons – if there is one big enough.

The lazy parliamentary foot soldiers are content with the constant repetition of tired themes: 'Will the minister tell the House how brilliant he/she has been/is/will be?' Sometimes a variation: 'Will the minister explain what wonderful things he/she has done/is doing/will do?' A new theme: 'Does the minister agree that the European Union or Socialism will lead to unemployment/world war/collapse of family life/a plague of boils/international Communism?' The inevitable groans from the Chamber for tedious repetition rarely discourage the tabloid politician.

Tony Banks was the Labour champion for irreverence, persistence and originality. One of many examples was a plea to honour a great hero of the House.

1. Attention:

    Isn't it a disgrace the way the House has failed to honour the great
    achievements of Baroness Thatcher?

2. Point:

    We are deprived because there is no statue of her on the empty
    plinth in the Members' lobby along with Churchill, Attlee and
    Lloyd George.

3. Question:

    The citizens of Eastern Europe have enjoyed tearing down the
    statues of Lenin and Marx after the fall of Communism. Let's
    erect a statue here to her, so that we can tear it down, now we
    have got rid of the old bag.

The procedure confuses visitors, especially because the questions
printed on the Order Paper are never spoken. Only their numbers
are called. When a Member has had no luck in the shuffle, ingenuity is required to be called for an opportunist question.

After the name of the MP has been called by the Speaker, the
Member shouts out the number of the question. The minister
replies and the Member asks the supplementary. Then it is open
to Members of the opposite party in the ping-pong calling of
speakers from either side of the Chamber. The best chance of
being called is after a political opponent has asked a selected
supplementary.

Only relevant questions are allowed. A link must be forged
between the question on the Order Paper and the one that the
opportunist backbencher wants to raise. The Speaker will silence
and humble those who fail to make the connection. They are often

brutally cut off in mid-sentence or worse, left to flounder and babble trying to construct a connection on their feet.

Tony Banks got away with a cheeky one on foreign affairs. He stood and was not called on fifteen questions. Banks was greatly agitated about Norway's threat to recommence whaling. Previously he had caught the attention of the Norwegians by suggesting that they should eat one another as an alternative to whale meat. He stood and was not called after mentally rehearsing tortuous links with questions on Papua, Sudan and Israel. Finally the Speaker relented and called him. How was Tony going to link his plea with a question that asked, 'What action does the Government intend to take to increase the imports of bananas from the Windward Isles?' We held our breath. 'Madam Speaker,' he explained, 'the people of Norway are going bananas about the whales.' Speaker Boothroyd was so amused she let him get away with it.

I had a similar problem. I had reworked in my head a question I wanted to ask Energy Secretary Chris Huhne. After failing to be called on seven previous questions, the Speaker was doubtful about the relevance of my question, linked to one from the Harlow MP Robert Halfon about the green deal. I am not sure the Speaker was convinced by my account of my morning's work:

Mr Speaker: With reference to Harlow, England or both?

Paul Flynn: In order to inform myself of the effects of the green deal on Harlow, I researched a website this morning, which states: 'The nuclear industry's key skill over the past half-century has not been generating electricity but extracting lashings of taxpayers' money.'

That was on the website of someone called Chris Huhne. Does this person have any connection with the Secretary of State? Has he sold his principles for a Red Box?

There is a convincing theory that no one listens to the first answer that ministers give to an oral question. The House in general switches off. They know it will be a bland and defensive answer. Even the questioner will not hear it because they will be preoccupied rehearsing the supplementary question they are about to ask.

Proof of this was provided by Plaid Cymru Member Ieuan Wyn Jones on 10 December 1996. He had asked how many representations the minister had received on the threatened closure of benefit agency offices in Wales.

'A number' was Social Security Minister Roger Evans's contemptuous retort. Ieuan responded, 'I am grateful to the minister for that reply.' As the answer was the parliamentary equivalent to 'Get stuffed', it is reasonable to conclude that Ieuan was not listening to Roger's put-down.

Daring Peter Bottomley in May 1986 proved the theory by dragging extraneous information into oral replies to transport questions. Bottomley had a bet with, among others, John Major that he could intersperse unnecessary information into Oral Questions. He had a question on the unpromising subject of 'bus lanes in London'. He gave three supplementary answers to experienced Commons performers, including super backbencher Tony Banks. Incredibly, he weaved into his replies the information that Anne Boleyn had six fingers on her left hand; that Burkina Faso means the land of wise men; that frogs eat with their eyes shut; and that 13 per cent of people share their bath water.

No one noticed. Nobody asked whether he had gone off his rocker. He won his bet. Experienced MPs might offer the explanation that it is often difficult in the House to hear Oral Questions unless your ear is glued to the tiny loudspeaker at the back of the seats – the other explanation is that nothing worth hearing is ever said in the first oral answers and there is no point in listening to them. There are victories ahead for quick-witted MPs who change a hallowed tradition and listen to ministers' oral replies. Then immediately zap back.

How to Ask a Written Question

The purpose of Written Questions is to:

- Put pressure on Government to act.
- Necklace the Executive with ineradicable commitments.
- Reveal opponents' inactivity/neglect/stupidity.
- Advertise and strengthen campaigns with authoritative official facts.
- Induce non-replies that expose Government evasiveness.
- Highlight Votingham.
- Seek facts and bring them into the public domain.

Written Questions are a prime weapon in the parliamentary armoury. Skilfully drafted, they pierce the Government's defences. For a hostile questioner the Table Office, which processes Written Questions, can appear as insurmountable as the old Berlin Wall. The clerks at the Table Office are as unyielding as the shovel-faced guards who manned the barricades at Checkpoint Charlie.

An anodyne question is simple. Scribble it down on a piece of paper and hand it in to the Table Office. It is not even necessary to use the printed pro-forma or to type it. The clerks will ensure that it appears next day on the Order Paper neatly printed, grammatically correct, decently spelled and 'in order'. On the nominated day, three days or more later, a matching anodyne futile reply will arrive from the minister.

Avoid direct confrontation with the highly talented clerks. Their skills are underemployed. A battle of wits with an MP will brighten a humdrum day. It's an unequal contest. They are people of Olympian intelligence operating at the foothills of their careers. They have all the big guns and very few MPs outwit them. There is an appeal against their decisions to the Clerk of the House and ultimately to the Speaker. It's a fight where ultimate defeat is almost inevitable. Know when to surrender.

To continue the fight is to court ignominy. A challenge to Written Questions on the subject of Iraq was made by Blaenau Gwent MP Llew Smith. He raised the 'discriminatory' refusal of his questions in the Chamber. His reward was a searing and patronising rebuke from Speaker Boothroyd. Irritatingly, identical questions refused in Llew's name were accepted when tabled by other Members, including me.

The rules are not always rational or fair. Llew Smith was then the most prolific written questioner. The primary rule of Table Office clerks is that MPs' questions must be rejected in an increasing ratio to the numbers asked. The dozen-questions-a-year MP will be welcomed to the office as a rare visitor, possibly thanked for his custom. The thousand-questions-a-year MP will have his offerings severely scrutinised to detect minor breaches of the Erskine May rules. There are good reasons for this. Outside bodies and one or two hyperactive researchers have deluged the Order Paper with an incontinence of questions in flagrant abuse of the system. If all MPs asked the same number of questions as the five most prolific, costs would multiply and the procedure would collapse.

E-tabling of questions is a drudgery-cutting innovation. There is a limit of five Written Questions but typing them in from your office computer is a joy. Notice will be given by written message when questions are not acceptable. The best way to table is through cultivating the clerks as allies. The MP should adopt the posture of a supplicant. Only those with a perverse, twisted mind will ever understand the Byzantine rules for making questions 'orderly'. Give up. The clerks beam when asked to streamline crude queries into perfections of orderliness. They have the secret knowledge.

How to Answer Answers

Some answers are contemptuous. One Labour MP asked a probing question concerning the Prime Minister's meetings with EDF,

requesting information on the dates and locations of the meetings, the matters discussed, the officials present and the cost of
the meetings to the public purse. David Cameron's non-answer
addressed only the first and least important part of the question:
'I met representatives of EDF on 12 October 2010. The meeting was
held at No. 10.'

This is one of the many ploys used. Every answer will have
been crawled over by expert civil servants at least three times.
An elaborate procedure creates the first tentative answer.
Then it is bounced from section to section to scrape out any
speck of incriminating information, often leaving no information at all. The Executive will triumph unless Members
strike back.

Tory Charlie Elphicke enjoyed a fuller reply when he asked
about an event organised by the previous Labour administration.
There was nothing sinister to report, but the Tory minister's reply
was rich in suggestive detail. Charlie was told that the total cost
of the event was £4,719.21 and that the venue, The Brickhouse,
often features such figures as 'burlesque chanteuse Lady Beau
Peep' and 'showgirl sensation Amber Topaz'. The minister
was keen to reveal that the day concluded with a team building event involving drumming, organised by Poisson Rouge.
It would be uncharitable to suggest that there was any political motivation to the answers. All governments behave in the
same way.

There is a bottomless bag of tricks available to deny information. The following are a few of the popular ones. Responses
should be immediate.

Answer is evaded with reply that answers question not asked.
Table immediate pursuant, rewording original question.

A single omnibus answer to several questions to mask non-replies.
Table questions singly and space dates for replies.

Answer refused because of disproportionate cost.
Ask what costs would be proportionate; question for new period.

Only part of question answered.
Table further urgent separate questions at three-day intervals.

The answer is demonstrably untrue.
Raise a point of order/business question in the Chamber.

Answer crafted to infuriate with non-information.
Re-table similar but not identical question; nail culprit minister
with oral question, a letter or a Point of Order.

'Disproportionate cost' is used daily as an excuse to deny information. It is very difficult to argue because only officials can make a sensible estimate. Harry Barnes was offered a tape as an alternative to a 'disproportionate cost' answer. With the help of a library assistant he abstracted the required information at a cost of £15 – a wholly proportionate and minor cost. The current maximum limit is about £800.

On the tenth anniversary of Thatcher's reign I asked her to list all the failures of her Government. The answer was disappointingly brief and cost about thirty pence. Nicholas Bennett, then Member for Pembrokeshire, asked her later to list her successes. The reply occupied twenty-three columns in Hansard and cost £4,500. Not disproportionate costs?

In February 1997, in pursuit of the cost and use of the politicians' palaces of Chequers, Dorneywood, Chevening, Admiralty House and 1 Carlton Terrace, I had typical rebuffs. These houses cost millions to run and one had just had a £3m redecoration. To judge whether they were good value I tried to discover how frequently they were used.

Malcolm Rifkind, as Foreign Secretary, obligingly said that he spent twenty or fewer days a year at Chevening. John Major said he used Chequers regularly and Kenneth Clarke replied that he was at Dorneywood on 'numerous occasions'. Pursuant questions seeking 'on what dates' they were in residence were brushed aside with answers referring back to the previous non-answers.

I tabled an Early Day Motion to expose the non-answers and persuaded a journalist that this was a fine example of denial of information.

How to Use EDMs

Though weakened by overuse, Early Day Motions are still the best gauge of parliamentary opinion.

Derided as graffiti, they are a daily platform for MPs to sound off on any subject with greater freedom than is allowed in Parliamentary Questions. Some have achieved solid results. A maximum of 250 words is permitted, but the briefest are the best. Most Members will not devote three minutes of their lives to ploughing through hundreds of words of tedious prose. But probably all Members would have read Bob Dunn's simple 'This House loves double decker buses'. Many signed it.

The two techniques for tabling are the 'continuous creation' or the 'big bang'. When submitted with one signature the instant effect depends on the news content of the message. The addition of further signatures, 'continuous creation', will ensure that it is printed on the Order Paper daily for weeks, sometimes months.

A 'big bang' of a hundred plus signatures led by the great and good on its first outing proves widespread support. The disadvantage is that if all backers have been used up on the first printing, the EDM will soon disappear from the Order Paper.

Some party whips demand sight of potentially embarrassing EDMs before they are tabled. The strictures of the past are now rarely applied to the present crop of more independent backbenchers. The pay-roll vote and whips are not allowed to sign them except on matters of vital importance to their constituencies.

To stoke up interest in the subject it is useful to mention the number of an EDM while asking for a debate on the subject at Business Questions to the Leader of the House. All the words of the EDM will then be transcribed in Hansard. The oral question will be broadcast and may helpfully draw fresh attention to the issue.

Subjects range from demands to declare war to congratulations to Fred Bloggs for his work as school caretaker or regrets about the failed beetroot harvest in Uzbekistan. They are a prop to campaigns and vital for ventilating constituency issues. Often they, and Written Questions, are the only immediate actions a backbencher can take to raise a new subject.

EDMs are the best way of drawing attention to the jobsworths and the officious. One bizarre event involving my constituents, which occurred before the Hunting Act, benefited from a parliamentary airing:

Duck Feeders Arrested

That this House notes the arrest by Dyfed-Powys Police of twelve ramblers caught in the act of feeding ducks and their subsequent imprisonment for five hours; notes the comment of the group's solicitor that the police are 'keen to arrest people if there is a fox hunt nearby' even when those concerned are not involved in any protest; is delighted that the ramblers have been compensated with £2,000 each for wrongful arrest; and looks forward for similar diligence from the police in apprehending hunters when their activity becomes unlawful.

Some of the motions are probably sponsored and written by outside bodies in their own interests and tabled by pliant Members. If the MP is an enthusiastic supporter of a campaign, it is usually wise to collaborate fully with a supportive EDM. Often they will drum up support from the constituents of other MPs.

A new EDM can be tabled to counteract a disagreeable one. More destructively, an amendment may be tabled to the original giving alternative facts or arguments. Flat contradictions of the theme of the EDM are not permitted by the clerks, but brief pointed variants can be added.

Powerful amendments can wreck an original EDM. New signatories to the original result in the amendment reappearing as well. It is not unknown for promoters of EDMs to discourage new supporters to avoid wider currency to the message of the amendment. An EDM calling for an increased use of prescribed drugs was exocetted by a detailed amendment saying that 'two thousand people a year are killed by medicines and 400,000 are addicted to them'. The EDM died. Supporters were discouraged from adding new names. The friends of the pharmaceutical industry who probably wrote the original EDM did not want that sort of knowledge getting about.

In the 1950s there were approximately 100 EDMs each session. By the 2010 election this had risen to more than 2,000. The record for most signatures on an EDM was set in the 2001/02 session with Malcolm Savidge's EDM on the need to avoid conflict between India and Pakistan attracting 502 signatures. It was not debated. The most recent EDM debated in the House was sponsored by Margaret Thatcher in 1979, which became a vote of no confidence in the Callaghan Government.

Pressure groups and constituents have an exaggerated opinion of the value of EDMs. They are the important small arms of the political fight. They are visible at first to only a relatively tiny number of people who read the Commons papers, but these are some of the most influential readers in the country.

Tam Dalyell cleverly used EDMs at Business Questions to give wider currency to sections of Peter Wright's banned book, *Spycatcher*. It was a way of putting fascinating information into the public domain. He deployed the full 250 words for quotations in several EDMs. The rules for EDMs were then changed to restrict quotes to a third of the text. This is a continuing and pointless irritation. There is a way around the rule by simply omitting quotation marks.

The clerks are invariably helpful in steering Members through the Byzantine rules. Their first loyalty is to parliamentary tradition. They seek to strip EDMs of unorthodox, poetic or interesting language. I was in dispute with a clerk because I wrote that 'the giant hope of the Big Society had shrivelled into a protozoan nothingness'. 'Protozoan' was questioned as excessively exotic a word. After a 'steward's inquiry' it was permitted. When an impasse is reached, Members can appeal to the Speaker for a ruling over a rejected EDM. They rarely succeed.

How to Do the Business

Topical Questions, Business Questions and Points of Order continue to be useful devices to raise fresh issues without prior notice.

In the Indian Parliament there is a daily 'Zero Hour' at noon when Members can speak for a minute on any subject. By arrangement they can have three minutes and a ministerial reply. It is a safety valve. Issues that MPs have not succeeded in airing at any other time can have their moment. A similar system exists in the Canadian Parliament.

Now, in the UK, recent reforms have shortened the two weeks' deadening delay between tabling Oral Questions and answering them down to a few days. Topical Questions require no notice of their subjects. They have succeeded brilliantly. The Chamber can now concentrate on issues of immediate topicality rather than those that were of interest a fortnight earlier. Past parliaments have been hog-tied by antiquated rules that delayed and silenced topical debate. We are now approaching the immediacy of the demands of the 24-hour news appetite.

A successful use of Business Questions was Gordon Prentice's relentless pursuit of accusations against Jonathan Aitken long after the media lost interest. In his autobiography, Aitken recalls that the persistent Business Questions by Prentice on Aitken's alleged perjury did indeed have an influence. The issue could not be quietly forgotten as many establishment figures hoped. Justice was done thanks to Gordon.

Points of Order and Business Questions continue as an alternative way of raising issues of urgent priority. Under Speaker Bercow their value has been expanded by his emphasis on shorter questions and liberal allocation of time for backbenchers. Business Questions follow the Leader of the House's Thursday announcement of the business of the coming week. Members can then plead that other subjects should be discussed. The essential preliminary rigmarole is 'When can we debate..?' But few subjects have any realistic chance of being discussed. Often the process deteriorates into party political point scoring. Unless there is a desperately urgent debate following, Speaker Bercow is generous in allowing all Members who stand to ask a question. Thursday's business is usually un-whipped, with less pressure on time. The hour of Business Questions continues as a vital relief valve for airing matters of supreme or trivial importance. The continuity of Hackgate was lubricated by being raised at Business Questions.

Speaker Weatherill became exasperated with bogus Points of Order that were being used to wreck business. Skilled operators were hi-jacking parliamentary time, delaying business and stealing the speaking chances of others. They had deteriorated into points of interruption and obstruction. In defiance of all accepted procedure for debate he decided that no Points of Order could be raised until Oral Questions and statements were finished.

This stopped the gross abuse but created a new problem. There is no mechanism for raising a genuine Point of Order in the banned period. One incident proves how it cripples orderly procedure. A few Members were deliberately using unusual words during Oral Questions. Ostensibly it was to win a prize of £1,000-worth of games for their constituencies, but it was a blatant advertisement for a word game involving rarely used words. As it happened between 2.30 p.m. and 3.30 p.m. it was not possible for the Speaker to be told that procedure was being abused for commercial ends.

The success and length of a bogus Point of Order depends on the mood of the Speaker, the urgency of the business of the day and the relationship between the MP and the Speaker. A genuine one should be explained to the Speaker beforehand. But genuine Points of Order are rare. In 'Before Bercow' days, irrelevant points were sometimes unkindly scorned by Speakers. The Bercow convention is one of unfailing courtesy from the Speaker, who treats all points with respect and invariably supplies a considered answer. He has even been accused of encouraging Points of Order so that he can have a chance to say something other than 'Order! Order!'

The Speaker's permission has to be given for an Urgent Question (UQs) or Standing Order 24 (SO24) applications. Applications for these must be registered with the Speaker, along with convincing reasons, before noon. In pre-Bercow days they were often only called annually; now they are called weekly. Issues raised must be urgent, specific and important. A brief note to the Speaker's Office with a fifty-word explanation will suffice for serious consideration. When applications for UQs or SO24s fail, a Point of Order is the best backstop ploy.

For a successful bogus Point of Order, do the following:

- Flatter the Speaker, subtly.
- Appeal to his duties as Defender of Backbenchers/Guardian of the Reputation of the House.
- Be amusing: he will be waiting for the second joke.

- Mention Erskine May; a copy in your hand gives authority.

- Be brief; prepare every word beforehand.
- Be intriguing – full meaning not apparent until final sentence.
- Have a serious point: he may be less tolerant next time.

A Point of Order framed on the above lines was:

On a Point of Order, Madam Speaker can I appeal to you to exercise your role as a doughty defender of the reputations of Honourable Members?

It is many years since anyone was called to the Bar of the House, but Erskine May makes clear your powers to summons here those who besmirch the good names of Members. Have you read, Madam Speaker, the attack on the Secretary of State for Wales in which he was unfairly described as 'deluded' and 'simple' and for his fine work in bringing six thousand Korean jobs to Wales he was accused of 'pimping for Britain'?

Will you now call to the bar and insist on an apology from, the Conservative Prospective Candidate for the seat where those jobs will be located?

In desperation, aggrieved Members use Points of Order as points of interruption in the speeches by others. The Speaker made a remarkable new ruling to this one from Scottish Nationalist Stewart Hosie:

Mr Hosie: On a Point of Order, Mr Speaker…
Mr Speaker: I hope it is a point of order.
Stewart Hosie: The use of this neo-fascist description is absurd, offensive and wrong in every single regard. What powers, Sir, do you have to ensure that this nonsense is not said or repeated?

Mr Speaker: My powers do not extend to the refutation of nonsense.

There was a lively one from Eric Forth:

On a Point of Order, Mr Speaker. You will just have witnessed a disgraceful episode in which the Government Chief Whip hurled a substantial book across the Chamber at my Hon. friend the Member for Rutland and Melton on the front bench. Will you now sort out the Government Chief Whip and throw the book at her?

Adjournment debates

'I will raise this matter on the adjournment' is one of the few threats in the backbenchers' armoury. A conspiracy between press and MPs long conned the public into the belief that adjournment debates are of prime importance. It's only on rare occasions that they excite Government or public interest.

In the past they were held late at night with just a handful of MPs and a single minister present. Now Westminster Hall provides peak morning and afternoon slots when the press and public are awake.

In the 1980s a new Welsh MP had secured a debate on the repair of council house roofs in his constituency. Commons business dragged on. It was 3 a.m. when the MP was called to address an exhausted minister and the empty acres of green leather seats. This was before the cameras recorded the dismal sight but sound cassettes were available. The MP proudly sent one to his mother. She summoned her neighbours in to wonder at her son's command of the House. Over a cup of tea, she excitedly explained, 'Listen to this. When that old Maggie Thatcher or Neil Kinnock are speaking, all the MPs are gossiping and laughing among themselves. But when my boy speaks, you can hear a pin drop.'

Occasionally the debates are still late. I was greatly encouraged at 4 a.m. one morning in 2011 to welcome the Speaker to the Chamber to chair my adjournment debate on the conduct of a member of the royal family. Half a dozen MPs turned up, but inexplicably no media.

Now there are a range of adjournment debates. They include half-an-hour ones daily in the Chamber, as well as one-and-a-half-hour and shorter debates in Westminster Hall, some of which are controlled by the Backbench Committee. The range of subjects is immense. One week's list included the bus industry, care for older people, devolution of Welsh energy powers, specials needs schools, Palestine, disabled young people, Coeliac disease and European institutions.

Before a Backbench Committee debate in 2010, the only discussions of the disastrous Helmand incursion decision were two adjournment debates. Junior ministers are summoned to reply to Members' comments. There is justified cynicism that debates without votes are vacuous talking shops, but they remain the principal chance for backbenchers to air their views.

IN COMMITTEE

How to Sparkle on Euro-committees

A few dozen Members have a bizarre vocation to serve on European committees. The rest of the Commons are content to let them exclusively pursue this un-British, masochistic fetish.

The praetorian guard of sixteen Europhobes and Europhiles serve on the grand Scrutiny Select Committee. Usually reluctant and often mystified spear carriers are now appointed ad hoc to serve on the three committees imaginatively named A, B and C. In earlier years the committees had permanent memberships, so that a handful of MPs did actually develop a glimmer of understanding of some European issues.

These committees are charged with the task of scrutinising European legislation before it becomes law. The Scrutiny Select Committee assesses the importance of the 1,000-plus EU documents and decides which are debated. The committee gets details of each document from the relevant minister. All documents deemed weighty or worthy are discussed by the committees. So far, so fascinating.

Rarely do any of the committees crackle into life from their constant comatose state. The Scrutiny Select Committee has more staff than any other Select Committee, including a first-class team of highly qualified advisers who actually seem to understand Euro-speak and know what is going on in the Kafka-esque world of the European Commission. Its elected chairman from 2010 is the talking database Bill Cash. He has informed, infuriated and bored successive parliaments with his own brand of voluminous Eurotrash. Labour's Kelvin Hopkins rivals Cash, having made 150 speeches on these committees. Their overwhelming command of fine details anaesthetises other committee members into stunned silent compliance. Their monologues are a parliamentary wonder, but not popular spectator material. On the other hand, there are those for whom Cash and Hopkins are the standard-bearers for true democracy and the independence of member states – twin St Georges fighting the Euro-dragon in an unending struggle. The discourse is on a stratosphere beyond the reach of ordinary mortals.

The opportunities to shine are rarely seized by non-members of the committee. But there have been rare excitements. In the spring of 1995 a Conservative Euro-brawl was fought out at committee B. For two and a half fierce hours it was at the centre of the political stage. The late Derek Enright, whose faithful weekly presence was hardly noticed before, had a desperate summons. The whips instructed him to fly home immediately from a Dublin meeting of Irish and British MPs. His presence was vital. But the situation ended in Euro-droop as the threatened rebellion by Europhobe Bernard Jenkins wilted and died.

All MPs can attend the meetings and speak but not vote. The winter of 1996 is recalled because more than a hundred Members turned up. The chairman, Ulster Unionist MP James Molyneaux, had the task of bleakly rejecting all the endless nitpicking procedural pleas from the assembled ranks of Europhobes. A rebellion by one in the form of an abstention caused Tory blushes. Here was a divided party, which led to rows in the Chamber and a full debate.

It is regrettable, but the routine weekly meetings are almost private affairs, disregarded by the press and neglected by the committee members themselves. The debates are often relaxed and erudite. They can be a wonderful arena for fledgling MPs to practise their skills.

Euro-committees are the British foothills of the Euro-waffle mountains. One recent report was flagged alphabetically in sections of about 250 pages. The flags ran to section W.

There are rewards for the persistent penetrators of these acres of Euro-babble. Dedicated prospectors in the wastelands of Eurotrash can discover useful nuggets of political knowledge. It happened once in a session on fraud. On page 68 of Section J it said that trillions of Euros are defrauded by the wine trade. In Section B, page 112, was the news that only one person is employed to control wine trade fraud for the whole of the European Union. Bringing those facts together in one question will fuse the brain of the minister replying.

A hundred pages deeper into the report, it was discovered that Ceuta and Melilla were areas regarded as worthy of European aid. The minister will know a little about France and Germany but will almost certainly be under-informed about conditions in the remaining fragments of the Empire of Spain. The most industrious of ministers will quake at the mention of unknown remote places.

Rumour convincingly claims that hapless junior ministers judge Euro-committee as their major torment. Backbenchers can crucify them with details gleaned from the grossly voluminous reports.

Those with a taste for inflicting pain ask brief questions, the meaning of which is not apparent until the final word. However late the junior minister burnt the midnight oil the evening before the meeting, there is no possibility of mastering the fine print. Joyfully, backbenchers are allowed to put several questions. Unsatisfactory answers can be probed again and again. The knife is twisted in the wound. Government backbenchers should apply the balm of helpful 'dolly' questions that give the ministers healing and thinking time.

In a revealing parenthesis, one Member, Chi Onwurah, asked a key question about an immense Euro financial disaster:

Mr Onwurah: In my previous job with Ofcom I had the pleasure – that is just a term of speech – of contributing to such European documents. Will he say a few words on the Government's view of the Galileo project? I understand that the existing policy is that Galileo should effectively be left half-finished by not putting in place the number of satellites necessary for it to work.

Mr Willetts: This very Scrutiny Committee had a long and thorough debate on Galileo a couple of months ago, led by the minister, and I thought she put the case well. It has not been a well-managed project; it is facing serious cost overruns. We believe there should not be extra money for Galileo; it should be resolved within the existing budget.

'Not well-managed' is a Euro-euphemism for a colossal Euro-billions cock-up. The Euro-panjandrum slowly rumbles on, heavy with words, details and incomprehensible complexities. There is a case for classifying Euro-committees as a blood sport.

How to Live Through Private Bills

They are the most unexpected delights or horrors of Parliament. All MPs are expected to suffer one. Go to any lengths to avoid serving on a Private Bill. They are not Government legislation. Local councils and public bodies need Private Bills to authorise the building of bridges, rail links, barrages and other major projects. They are not to be confused with Private Members' Bills, which have a similar format to bills dealing with Government legislation.

Private Bills are very different. Their role is a cross between a court of law and a public inquiry. They are Parliament's greatest thief of time and energy. Predictably tedious, they can some-times capture Members' interest and divert them from their essential duties. Our great national networks of canals, rail-ways and roads were authorised by Private Bills. Contemporary results are less impressive. Bills include the All Hallows Staining Church Bill, The Kent County Council (Filming on Highways)

Bill and the Transport for London (Supplementary Tolls Provision) Bill.

Private Bills are usually promoted by organisations like local authorities or private companies to give themselves powers beyond, or in conflict with, the general law. Their influence is limited to specific individuals or organisations rather than the general public. Anyone who believes they will be detrimentally affected by the bills can petition Parliament and present their objections to committees of MPs and Lords.

Beware smiling whips. The technique of entrapment comes when the hard-faced snarl drops from their lips. They smile sweetly. A little flattery will lubricate the invitation. A whip who habitually greeted me with a sullen grunt at best, one day hailed me warmly with a hand on the shoulder. 'Sit down, my boy,' he said, 'I've got something to tell you. I'm going to get you a cup of tea.' Disarmed, I heard the invitation.

He explained, 'I've made you chairman of a little bill. It's not anything that is going to take a lot of time. Something to do with an extension to a little railway, somewhere. It could be over in a morning.' He described the absolute power wielded by members of the committee and, even more, by the chairperson. World domination beckoned.

Drinking his tea, it seemed churlish to refuse. At the first session of the Docklands Light Railway Crossing Bill, the clerk told me that it would probably be over 'in six months'. I was trapped and coerced into doubling my already impossible workload.

Private Bills proceed with two daily sessions every Tuesday and Thursday for months. Vast swathes of diary dates must be swept clear. Constituents must be disappointed; campaigns neglected. The Private Bill Members will be out of action for prolonged periods when their presence is in demand in the Chamber or office. The daily timetable has to be reorganised and the working day lengthened to fit in work in the evenings.

In accordance with the rules, the subject of the bill must have no connection with a Member's constituency. The constituents of Votingham will not understand why their MP is devoting a third of their disposable time to a project hundreds of miles distant from their local area and beyond their concerns.

There are some thin consolations. Private Bills provide infinite scope for Members to be bloody-minded. Absolute power is in Members' hands to improve the bill or reject it altogether. The Cross Rail Bill was tossed out by four individual Members for reasons that remain inexplicable to both major parties.

Bill meetings consist of the presentation of the case for a project, argued by barristers in the pay of the promoters. Most committee time is taken up with objectors arguing their case and being cross-examined. The objectors are often unsophisticated members of the public trying to defend their home patch. The barristers will rip their arguments apart if allowed. The committee's job is to hobble smooth, stroppy barristers and boost the confidence of terrified witnesses. The greedy can be humbled; the deserving can be exalted. One happy diversion for bored Members is seeing semi-competent barristers being mangled by unsophisticated but smart witnesses.

Barristers need the Members' votes and they dare not antagonise them. But subtle pressure will be applied when the MPs on their first committees are determined to go their own way. Barristers on their umpteenth bill will grandly explain: 'The usual precedent, Sir, in these situations is...' It is a bullying tactic. The firm answer is that the committee members are not slaves to precedence, but innovative trailblazers.

There are no rules. The committee is supreme and omnipotent. On the one that I chaired, a change of Government policy upset the basis of the bill. We seriously considered abandoning the bill and insisting that a fresh one be prepared. Another course we discussed was to call the Prime Minister as a witness because he had wrecked the original character of the bill. To placate us, two senior ministers, Michael Portillo and Roger Freeman, were summoned to explain themselves. They received a deserved roasting from backbenchers of both parties delighted to have roles reversed and to be in a position to have the last word in a joust with ministers.

Two prominent former parliamentarians, George Galloway and Rhodri Morgan, are dewy-eyed about the time they spent on a bill to build the Queen Elizabeth Thames Bridge in 1987. They were originally reluctant to serve on the committee during their first year in Parliament. But they went native and became enthralled by the technical sophistication of this great enterprise. They remain sentimental about this rich experience. It was not a chore but a stimulating lesson on engineering. That was exceptional.

A service would be rendered by MPs who succeed in modernising the irrational rules of Private Bills. One backbencher remarked that Private Bill legislation was archaic and long overdue for reform.

His name was Benjamin Disraeli.

How to Shine at Select Committees

In a contrast to the show business of the Chamber, the Select Committees are blissful oases of intelligence and calm. Now, chairs and members, elected rather than appointed by whips, work with renewed authority and zest. They are the Forum, the Star Chamber, the Inquisition and the Consumers' Court of the nation – and the media has now discovered them.

The country has been fascinated by the inquiries into 'cash for honours' and 'Hackgate'. Twenty-four-hour news has provided platforms for the interrogator MPs. Select Committees in their present form have been in business only since 1979. Their task is to scrutinise the work of Government departments by hearing evidence and taking reports. They are a worthwhile career speciality for the inquisitive. Tom Watson and Louise

Mensch leapt to fame with their forensic cross-examination of the Murdochs. The performance of the committee as a team flopped and invited questions on the unequal contest between MPs and expensively trained witnesses.

Choose which committee to serve on with care. Chairs of committees are influential, sometimes powerful. Their elections are keenly contested. On popular committees, backbench places are in great demand and the first elections prompt a blizzard of e-mail canvassing. The choice of committee is vital. Avoid those that constantly divide on party lines. They are not taken seriously and their reports carry little weight. Choose one whose chair is not a party hack. The perfect chairs are fair-minded, intelligent and have abandoned hope of promotion or honours.

Some knowledge or interest in the subject is useful but less valuable than forensic interrogation skills and Socratic judgement. Refuse committees on subjects where Profits Unlimited plc or the General Union of Court Wanglers fills the wallet or constituency coffers with sponsorship or consultancy fees. However pure Members' motives are, they will be accused of being the mouthpiece of vested interest paymasters.

There are some Select Committee subjects that will guarantee free travel to a luxury sun spot on the far side of the planet. If that's what your heart desires there are jobs going with Thomas Cook. The Gullivers may be heading for the Seychelles or the Maldives; politically they are heading for oblivion. It's relatively effortless to acquire faux-expertise on foreign policy or defence. The toilers for truth are those who plough through the intricacies of the Public Administration Committee and the Environmental Audit Committee.

Ensure that issues chosen for investigation are ones that the committee can genuinely influence. The choice of advisers is pivotal to the quality of the work. They and the clerks draft the model questions and write the final report. It is a mistake to leave the choice of advisers to the chair. The value of the committee's work would be undermined if it was influenced by political, ideological or fraternal considerations. Study the known enthusiasms and foibles of the chair and fellow Members. This will help in anticipating their strengths and weaknesses

Each investigation follows the same course. The subjects are chosen in private session and the political horse-trading is done. The only subjects worth considering are those of high importance where a unanimous report is attainable. Individual or constituency Members' hobby horses must be resisted.

The evidence arrives in a pile of extensive reports, often a foot high. The Member or a trusted researcher must at least skim read it all. Nuggets of precious information are buried in the tortuous prose. Scour the vital sections. Star the killer points.

Ensure that no key witnesses are ignored by advisers. Challenge invitations to witnesses that may reflect partial interests.

The public cross-examination of witnesses is now broadcast frequently on 24-hour television and can also be viewed on the Parliament website. The aim is to draw out helpful evidence from the benign well-informed, expose the deceivers and crush the crooks. Time is very limited. Carefully plan questions from a detailed study of evidence. Quote vital phrases or induce witnesses to repeat their key sentences. A small number of people will read the final reports; millions may hear the verbal evidence.

Some witnesses are unsophisticated. They deserve gentle handling. Put them at ease. Be courteous. Ask deliberately easy questions. Thank them generously. Compliment them on their answers if nervousness persists. Comfort. Flatter. Seduce.

Civil servants were once trained with a video on how to give evidence. It advised them to make their answers as long as possible to ensure that MPs cannot ask too many questions. Politicians, captains of industry and other well-heeled witnesses are now professionally coached before they appear. They have undergone dummy sessions with skilled advisers who have tried to anticipate the questions. They are instructed on the personalities of Members to second guess likely lines of inquires. Speeches of Members are read; blogs and tweets are trawled.

There is strong evidence that many witnesses have prior knowledge of the questions prepared for committee members by advisers. The committee clerk will have legitimately told them of the general headings of the subjects to be raised, but there are grave suspicions that detailed questions may be leaked by political, business or trade union chums on committees. This is the best reason to ditch the prepared questions, especially for formidable witnesses who probably have been tutored in answering them.

Obstructive witnesses deserve no mercy. They are out to conceal the truth. Try to knock them off their perch with your first question. It should expose a contradiction or falsehood in their evidence. Point out, at first courteously, that they are not answering the questions. One minister, in answer to a simple question of mine, spoke for eleven minutes, making all the points he had previously planned to make and not attempting to answer. It is not the function of a Select Committee to provide an additional platform for ministers who already have the Chamber and press conferences as their pulpits.

If witnesses persist in stonewalling, apologise for being direct and discourteous, then ask a question that is sharply direct and discourteous. Often the only remedy for streams of vacuous verbiage is to interrupt the witness. Tell them that they are not answering the question. If they still evade, repeat the question again word for word.

Richard Branson thought the Transport Committee had been hard on him because he wore a jogging outfit to address the committee. Wrong. Their irritation was roused by his ignorance of railways. When asked in a programme connected with the inquiry what he was going to do to improve the running of his privatised service, Branson said he would urge his drivers to drive faster. 'To overtake the train in front, presumably,' was the mocking, whispered response by a committee member.

Those who ask the first questions have an advantage in gaining media attention. In every other respect it is best to be the final questioner. The obvious and the prepared questions will then have been asked. The witnesses will be relaxed, disarmed, vulnerable. Listen carefully to the answers, spot their weaknesses and leap on them. Note the strong points made in answers to other Members. Use the limited time and insist on a second go to rebut or reinforce contradictions.

The main faults of Members are making speeches or asking vague questions. Matthew Taylor of the Royal Society for the Arts, a witness at a committee on which I serve, complained that Members went off-piste, riding their individual hobby horses. We did. The complaint was justified. Our questions generally missed the target. We fell for the temptation of playing to the gallery when a clutch of newshounds were present.

The most eloquent exchanges are the sharp, single sentences that strike at the heart of the issue. Broadcasters are seeking tiny, fifty-second sound and vision bites to illustrate three hours of evidence.

Most of the useful work is done behind the scenes by the splendid anonymous committee staff. Be hyperactive in the tedious, lengthy private sessions when the report's headings are considered. Prepare detailed amendments to highlight key information. Committed Members should draft their own recommendations and not rely on amending those written by advisers. As elsewhere in Parliament, the spoils are won by the industrious.

To fill the gaps in the evidence, ask written Parliamentary Questions on points not fully developed by witnesses. Although reports are usually confined to evidence received, parliamentary answers can be included.

If the final report is not good, a Member can rewrite it. The committee clerk will help. Seek outside assistance if necessary.

Be prepared for the horse-trading. Reports that carry the greatest authority are unanimous ones. Be prepared to sacrifice and compromise even lovingly drafted prose.

Leaking the report to the hacks who request advance details is always damaging. It will ruin the standing of the leaker with fellow members and blunt the impact of the conclusions. The identity of the leaker, in my experience, is always known to fellow committee members. Trust is lost. Friendships fracture. Parts of the media that are not recipients of the leak will strike back with thin or no coverage and sometimes with hostility towards the committee's conclusions.

Press conferences on Select Committee reports are now rare because of other instant means of communication. Individual interviews with committee members have replaced them. Have sound bites ready for both specialist and general reporters, plus a fifteen-second response for the main television news. The speciality subject reporters will read the details. The rest of the hack pack is searching for a simple sentence headline. Give it to them – brief, punchy, news-rich.

Exploit the value of the report afterwards by raising the issues in questions and debates. If the issue is dying, try an adjournment debate, a Ten Minute Rule Bill or an oral question six months later. If the report has wounded some dragons, be ready with a killer punch. The prize virtues of all politicians are patience and persistence. If the vested interests get away with it, it's the fault of the lazy committee members.

Select Committees' status is growing. They have a major role to play in the Legislature's challenge to the Executive. Unfortunately, the weakness in the implementation of the Tony Wright reforms was allowing the whips to determine the party of the chairs. In some of the 2010 committees docile party hacks were elected as chairs. Their reports are strongly influenced by the need to please the Government. They rarely challenge policy or take on outside vested interests. Several of the committees have deservedly attracted little attention for their repeated statements of the obvious. If individual Members cannot enliven these soporific bodies, they should resign and seek a committee that is doing its job.

Select Committees continue to disappoint. Even the acclaimed questioning of the Murdochs was less than competent. In that case there was advice from a distinguished outside authority. There was little evidence of a forensic team approach by the committee that would have drawn the truth from the witnesses. As usual there was competition from the MPs to chase personal hares. Few capitalised on the weaknesses in the Murdochs's answers.

The Murdochs were trained and rehearsed in their carefully manicured replies by expensive legal experts. This is an uneven contest. There is a strong case for calling in wise QCs to train MPs and committee clerks in the art of cross-examination.

How to Endure Public Bill Committees

The chore of Public Bill Committees is a hideous shock to novice Members. Their current operation demeans Parliament and can lead to the creation of bad laws. But there have been a handful of glorious exceptions where the whips have been out-whipped by secret collaborations between ministers and rebel backbenchers.

The purpose of a Public Bill Committee is to undertake the line-by-line scrutiny of a bill. They are made up of fifteen to forty-five appointed Members, reflecting the party balance in the House. A neutral chairman takes the place of the Speaker of the House. They can take anything from one sitting to several months to get through a bill depending on its length and importance.

A new Member is press-ganged on to one usually within the first few months of arriving in Parliament. Immediately, the already full day's workload is doubled by committees that demand huge chunks of time. Morning sessions run from 10.30 a.m. to 1 p.m., afternoon from 4.30 to 7.30 p.m.; sometimes evening sessions can last from 9 p.m. to an unspecified time.

Government backbenchers are the winners. All that is required of them by the whips is their constant attendance and dutiful voting. Speaking is a time-wasting obstacle to the speedy passage of Government bills, the main task of Public Bill Committees. Government MPs learn how to fill their time productively by opening the mail and writing replies. With slackening rules on electronic devices, dealing with the e-mails is a productive time-filler.

Opposition MPs are lectured that their only influence is the ability to delay Government bills. They are urged to fill time spaces with words whose main purpose is to gum up the works. Improvements are attempted to bills, but rarely are they accepted by the elective dictatorships of governments. Public Bill Committees are often self-indulgent political battlegrounds, not rational instruments of reform.

This is the system that produced the Child Support Agency and the law that allowed a good value state pension scheme (SERPS) to be wrecked in favour of personal pensions that have robbed millions. Minutes from the debates of those Public Bill Committees are shaming to most committee members. Few foresaw the consequences of their decisions.

A glorious exception was a bill in the 2005–10 parliament. The event is too recent and too sensitive for precise details to be published, but it is a wonderful example of creative legislating. It was a bill of supreme environmental importance. The whips demanded no amendments. They were fearful that an already weak bill would be further spavined by the Tories. The minister was instructed to oppose any changes. He secretly co-operated with two Labour backbenchers to table improving amendments. The clever, environmentally sound minister feigned opposition to the amendments he had helped to draft. The Tory Opposition were bemused, ignorant of the origin of the amendments, and supported some of them purely to embarrass the Labour Government. As a former whip, the minister knew that the whips office is an intelligence and subtlety-free zone. The minister expressed dismay that his arguments to reject his own amendments were failing. He urged conciliation. All the beneficial amendments were accepted by the Commons. The whips thought they had intelligently compromised. The minister and the two 'rebels' celebrated their creative secret collaboration. The environment will benefit from this inventive initiative.

A real challenge to backbenchers is the reform of these committees from the arrogance of ideological bullying to the intelligence of enlightened debate. Thanks to the heroic work of Graham Allen, pre-legislative scrutiny now makes a significant contribution to the efficacy of the legislative process. The gestation period of this reform has been prolonged and uncertain. Graham's bold vision of online scrutiny was stillborn.

With some reluctance a small number of bills were subject to early scrutiny by Select and Joint Committees during the Blair–Brown governments. The increased number of challenges to the content of bills has discouraged governments from the wider use of an additional process that they believe clogs up the legislative timetable. Ann Widdecombe complained that pre-scrutiny expanded and limited the role of Select Committees who are using their time to do the governments' work rather than their own. The legislative process is still antiquated, wasteful and imprecise. More reforms should be promoted. Only backbenchers will do that.

THE OFFICE

How to Knock-Out the Mail

E-mails are now the main channel of communication, but still the brown tide of letters flows in two or three times a day. The basic weapons for mail warfare are a paper knife and a large recycling bin – known in the trade as 'the circular file'. Be prepared to be ruthless.

One MP in 1987 explained his enviable but dangerous formula. All letters in large brown envelopes or that have post marks other than Votingham are dispatched unopened to the circular file. He had a majority of 18,000. That would not be tolerated now.

Others sort the letters. The obvious junk advertises itself with a logo on the envelope or now, helpfully, a transparent package. There is no obligation to even skim read your copy of *Concrete Quarterly*, the *Farmer's Weekly Whinge* or the *PR Monthly*.

Staff are guided into instinctively evaluating the mail – bad and good. Bad are lobbyists, tobacco companies, drug firms, annual reports, the petrol-head lobby and campaigns to restore hanging, garrotting and public crucifixions. Good are charities, environmental groups, voluntary bodies and campaigns to ridicule tabloids and end drug prohibition.

The prized letters are handwritten with a Votingham postmark. These are from real human beings, often with serious problems. Generous time is devoted to them. Sadly these are not always what they seem. Cunning lobbyists persuade constituents to use this channel. After two or three identical letters, they are sussed.

Some MPs are still e-mail averse. Anthea Leadsom has a standard dismissive reply that says, 'Due to the large number of e-mails and letters I receive every day please bear in mind it may take up to four weeks to respond.' Four weeks? They send unfriendly automatic replies saying that e-mails will not get precedence over other mail. They resent this newfangled device of instant contact that disturbs their well-ordered, leisurely work programmes. They feel they will be left behind and threatened, competing with a system that they do not fully understand. Possibly with some reason they fear 'hacking' and a loss of confidentiality. The leaking of embarrassing e-mail banter between Derek Draper and Damian MacBride may have been the result of hacking by malign interests. The fear persists.

Electronic mail has been beneficial in improving the immediate responsiveness of the service provided. A rapid ten minute exchange of e-mails can solve problems, allay fears or provide advice that would have taken a fortnight by snail mail. As increasing numbers take to instant contact, they deserve quick replies. Ambitious targets should be set for early responses. They reassure and impress constituents. It's perverse to slot e-mails in a queue with snail-mailed messages. This delays answers for no reason.

Spam filters have reduced the nuisance of much junk mail. Lobbyists have become adept at clever campaigning. The ethical group 38-Degrees used individual varied e-mails sent from named constituents. Their campaigns opposing the sell-off of forests and NHS changes forced MPs into individual replies. The strength and quality of the opposing arguments worried coalition MPs. There is evidence that the Government's resolve was undermined on both issues. The influence of blizzards of e-mails will diminish with over-use.

When my constituency predecessor was first elected in 1965 he composed his handwritten letters from a desk in the corner of the library that was his allocated 'office'. Our facilities and electronic tools now equip us to provide a splendid, improved service.

How to Write a Standard Letter

Standard letters are always second best. They are often the written equivalent of a two-fingered sign. Send them rarely to constituents except in response to a standard letter-writing campaign. Even then a few personal words should be added. However, when the office is overstretched they are the only way to send out information rapidly and efficiently.

If a letter to an MP was written by a computer, an MP's computer should reply. Standard printed cards and messages are available. Their use was justified in the bad old days of mechanical typewriters and few staff. Less so now.

How to Write an Abusive Standard Letter

For those who request that you do something that is light years distant from your political stance a simple, direct message will suffice:

Thank you for your communication, which I placed in my insane letters file.

Lobbyists are more difficult to shake off because they are professional naggers. Generally, they are not deeply subtle and understand only a blunt reply. A formula I have found useful is:

Dear Lobbyist,

I know of no good reason why I should co-operate with your inquiry. Lobbying organisations such as yours are an ugly, anti-democratic and corrupting succubus that haunts the British body politic.

If your client is genuinely seeking information I would be happy to provide it after they have directly approached me. Using you as a conduit only adds to their costs for no worthwhile purpose.

The quicker your malign presence is expelled from Westminster the sooner the cleansing of the parliamentary stables will begin.

Drug companies are difficult to repel partly because they are convinced that all MPs are scientific morons. When Drug Pushers Plc urges backing for their campaign to deluge the country with more expensive, questionable toxic medicines, they should be vigorously challenged.

In reply to one reasonable request I made for scientifically respectable arguments to back a claim, they sent me copies of personal testimonies from individuals that had all the intellectual authority of a baked bean advert. Their transcendent greed jumped from every word of their odious letters.

In one instance I was approached by a public relations smoothie in the pay of a drug company. He was hawking a drug for a cancer that one of my constituents was enduring at that time. He passed on exaggerated claims about the new wonder drug. He could not answer any questions on the evidence of its proven value. Deeper research reveals that the drug costs £16,000 a year, has adverse side effects in 10 per cent of patients, including death, and extends life expectancy by just twelve days. Had I passed on the misleading propaganda to my constituent, I would probably have done her a disservice.

The media is frequently bowled over by campaigns for wonder drugs based on poor scientific evidence. To the tabloids all new drugs are miracle drugs. They can raise expectations that will be dashed when distressing or lethal side-effects are discovered. Beware those who seek to use Parliament as a mouthpiece for commercial greed.

How to Deal with Insane Letters

Those who are slightly mad, eccentric or possessed by demons are magnetically attracted to MPs. The obsessive, the unhinged and devotees of religious cults and conspiracy theorists vent their irrationality at great length and with great frequency to Members. It's an unavoidable burden.

Never give them a morsel of encouragement. Politely and non-provocatively deflect the majority onto their own constituency MPs. Patently unreasonable requests sent to all MPs can be justifiably and wisely thrown out, without acknowledgement.

Among missives received in a brief period are:

- In 2064 the tenth planet, Mardok, will enter the orbit of the earth.
- Jedi-ism is a worthy topic for parliamentary debate.
- Rays are being transmitted into my flat by a specialised computer.
- My neighbour has toxic fungus under her floorboards that releases poison fumes when watered.
- The Gospel of the Flying Spaghetti Monster (Bible of Pastafarians).
- I have experienced 200 helicopters hovering over me as I walk.
- According to Bible prophecy it is not Britain's destiny to be part of a European Superstate.
- I am being poisoned/persecuted/spied on by the Catholic Church/sadists in MI5/Baptists/the Home Office (Various).
- Every asthma sufferer can be cured immediately with six minutes of yoga and a set of magnets.
- In two years I have been bashed in the street over 13,000 times.
- Photographs of Mars reveal urbanisation, factories, rivers, docks, ships etc.
- I am a victim of Mafia oppression in South Hendon.
- This is the world's ONLY perpetual motion invention.
- Almighty God has instructed me to write to all MPs.
- Tobacco advertising cuts tobacco use (The Advertising Association).

- My uncle, a famous actor, made me pregnant when I was two years old.
- Soul Eater Incidents Increase (The Think for Yourself Movement).

The Votingham ones must be handled with care. They will know the home telephone number, possibly even the home address of their MP. One MP has become resigned to having a visit from his tame eccentric at every surgery. For him a firm line is now too late. Most Members regret that early tolerance of the eccentric and the slightly deranged encourages a career-long persecution that becomes inescapable.

Others are possibly mentally ill. (See 'How to allow ventilation'.) Unless they are constituents who can be ushered into situations where they can be advised or cared for, it is generally counter-productive to enter into any detailed correspondence.

How to Cull Invitations

Devise a scientific equation for evaluating invitations. Try asking these questions of all invites.

A = Why me?
B = What's to be gained for me/my constituents/the party/my campaigns?
C = What is the cost in time and disruption to my working day?
D = What will be the damage to my waistline/liver/reputation?
The equation is
$(A + B) + (C + D) = X$
When X is positive, accept.
When X is negative, refuse.

If that is too complex then the following instant reckoner may help.

Receptions

Commercial Bodies: Out to bend the ear through offers of food and drink. They can be mildly enjoyable social events but are guilt-inducing wastes of time. Say no and ask for a written report on the points they want to make. If champagne is mentioned in the invitation, say no. Their business is bribery.

Charities: Sometimes worthwhile if there are contacts that need strengthening, but almost always a phone call or a letter is a more efficient way of gaining knowledge. If financial contribution is asked for to pay for the hire of the room, they are likely to be a serious, cost-conscious body. Accept and write a cheque.

Campaigns: Can be useful if they show a film or convey an inspirational message. Some tired campaigns are vastly oversubscribed by dozens of MPs. Best to try the novel cause with a fresh message that challenges accepted wisdom.

Conferences

Most are all-day affairs outside Parliament. Booking in advance may result in a painful absence from a major but unplanned parliamentary event. Rarely is the windy rhetoric of a conference worth a whole day. Experience teaches that only about a fifth of conference speeches contain new material. Sometimes less. Any valuable knowledge can be gleaned in ten minutes from a written report. Often ludicrously expensive fees are demanded.

Lunches

Journalists: Frequently worthwhile if the journalist's work is known to you. Can be useful in gaining knowledge and are often socially refreshing. Never relax if the journalist is a stranger or from a politically hostile paper. They are working, not relaxing. A common manoeuvre is for the hack to feign indiscretion and confidentiality in order to coax similar responses from the MP. Beware the lie, 'I have never said this before to any MP but...' – it's a trap. Insist on picking up the bill for the first meal. The hack can pay for the second and every alternate one. Avoid lunching with more than one journalist – they will gang up on an MP in their account of what was said. And they will convincingly outnumber the Member – as Steve Byers discovered when hacks followed a meal with him by each publishing a piece on Labour's 'embarrassing' union plans. They conspire together and agree a common line that becomes the proclaimed truth. As Byers discovered, it is very difficult to be convincing in disagreement with unanimity from the hack pack.

Overseas Visitors: A very valuable use of time is to meet visiting parliamentarians from countries of specialist interest. Hassle-free arrangements are made by the Foreign Office. All the time is spent in contact with usually very senior politicians. This is the most amenable and time-efficient way to explore foreign issues. Some are extremely rewarding. I enjoyed a very nice lunch with a young Georgian student in 1992. He was later elected President of his country and continues to be a useful contact. Some knowledge of English is usually universal but variable; use interpreters freely when misunderstandings are suspected.

Constituents and Campaigners: The best way of saying thanks, but can be used only sparingly because of pressures on time.

Meetings

All-Party Parliamentary Groups: The 450 All-Party Parliamentary Groups promise everything that an ambitious MP desires. Fulfilling causes, niche interests, foreign travel, musical joy, exercise and alternative medicine are all provided to the enthusiastic groupie.

Almost every country in the world has its gang of devotees. Many exist to facilitate dinners at the Embassy or to give a leg-up for a place on delegations visiting foreign countries. Some are serious. Groups on issues such as disability or alcohol abuse are dynamic, successful advocates for good causes. Others are commercially based and shamelessly promote self-interest.

Of these groups, 283 get cash from outside commercial bodies. BT coughs up £60,000 for the parliamentary choir; £52,000 from drinks companies funds the beer group; and £16,000 from Siemens makes possible a parliamentary boat race. Is this all selfless philanthropy or commercial lobbying by the back door? Reputations have been built by otherwise useless Members through pontificating in the media as an officer of 'All-Party Cetacean/Vegetarian/Esperanto Appreciation Group'. In common with most groups, it probably meets only once a year for an Annual General Meeting with officers only present.

There are achievements, however, and some groups have produced worthwhile results. Andrew Tyrie's All-Party Group on Extraordinary Rendition was brilliantly successful in overturning claims of Government collusion with torturers.

The Drugs Misuse group, meanwhile, produced groundbreaking reports on drugs in prisons and the perils of medicinal drug abuse. Officers of the group have acted as pundits for alternatives to drug prohibition. Pioneering work has also been done by groups specialising in little known diseases.

The best guide to finding groups worthy of an MP's time is to follow the money. If the piper is paid by lobby or commercial interests, they will call the tune. Rules have been tightened but many groups continue to pursue their paymasters' murky aims. Groups with apparently worthy intentions may be fronts for other interests: the British Nutrition Foundation works with the UK food industry; the Agricultural Biotechnology Council pushes the GM industry; and few suspected that the International Life Science Institute was a front for the international food industry or The Obesity Awareness and Solutions Trust (TOAST).

The example of TOAST is instructive and not unique. It used a PR agency called The Whitehouse Consultancy to recruit parliamentary 'patrons' and to raise the issue of obesity in Westminster. TOAST admitted on its own website that it was engaged in lobbying, noting that it had been 'extremely successful'. As a charity, it claimed to be 'completely independent' and to 'derive its income from individual donations and membership fees'.

The splendid investigative group Spinwatch revealed that almost all of its funding in fact came from a diet company called LighterLife. TOAST was, in other words, a kind of 'front group'. No fewer than nine of the twenty-one parliamentary patrons then went on record stating that they were not told of the links between TOAST and LighterLife. Dr Ian Gibson MP stated, 'I was absolutely not aware of this connection and my initial reaction is to be pretty cheesed off.'

Tory Douglas Carswell said, 'MPs and Lords with a genuine interest in subject gathering and talking to various lobbies is clearly a good thing. But other all-party groups appear to be backed by blatant lobby groups that are effectively a front for lobbies in Parliament.' Melanie Newman of the splendid Bureau of Investigative Journalism raised a pertinent question about an all-expenses paid trip to Azerbaijan for members of an All-Party Parliamentary Group funded by Azeri sources. Some of the people on the visit made speeches favourable towards the oppressive, illiberal regime in a subsequent Commons debate. While nothing improper has occurred and present rules have been followed these links are potentially hazardous.

It's very easy to get suckered into serving unworthy commercial interests. If not already corrupt, many of these groups endanger Parliament's reputation. Beware. They could be the source of the next scandal.

How to Delegate

It is impossible to accept all invitations, even from worthy causes.

MPs' staff must be allowed moments in the flattering lime-light of publicity. Selfishness is a deplorable trait in a boss. Staff appreciate chances to take the place of Members who are asked to parachute, bungee jump or abseil down buildings in support of good causes. Staff are generally younger and cope with physical challenges, while Members should be allowed to concentrate on growing old decorously. One MP did not delegate a parachute jump. He lived (only just) to tell the painful tale.

Researchers should be liberated to pursue their own enthusiasms and attend briefings in place of their bosses. Well-informed and passionately motivated staff will deliver work of high quality. In some offices press feature articles are written by staff with specialist knowledge and published under the name of the Member. Sometimes it ends in tears. The Member's superficial knowledge is painfully exposed by diligent press questioning. Gifted staff write speeches that are sometimes delivered verbatim by Members. It's another dangerous lazy game. Interventions will crack the egg shells on which the Member is treading. It is painful to witness Members floundering, exposed, because they do not fully understand the speech they are making. A thorough knowledge of themes is achieved by slaving over a computer writing speeches and articles from notes gathered by staff.

It can also work the other way around when an MP has specialist knowledge in a subject. Outsiders assume cretin status for all MPs and quiz researchers as the founts of all wisdom. That is not always sensible.

Cabals of researchers gather to exchange horror stories about their bosses. The stereotype is a lazy, vain, overpaid prima donna who feeds off the labours of underappreciated, starving minions. The highest tribute an MP can earn as an employer is the enduring respect of employees.

How to be Reported

The Hansard writers buttress their great skills with uncanny intuition. Never once has a Member made a grammatical mistake. Even hopeless gibberish appears as cogent argument. Missed words and even omitted lines in quotations miraculously reappear. The utterly unintelligible speeches of Tommy Graham were miraculously translated. All MPs owe the Hansard staff a debt of gratitude.

But they are not perfect. Once I said that Welsh ministers and the Welsh Office were moving in contrasting directions. Hansard recorded me as saying, 'The Welsh Office is making concrete erections.'

Nick Ainger praised the Welsh language film *Hedd Wyn*. 'Head wind' was printed. William Mckelvey once sang a question that went: 'You've never smelt the Tangle of the Isles.' To Tam Dalyell's discomfort, it was reported as: 'You'll never smell the Tam of the aisles.'

There have been triumphs. Finishing a speech one day I quoted some obscure lines from Chaucer, 'If gold rusts, what will iron do?' An hour later I called in to check the speech and the verse was printed with correct Chaucerian spelling.

Speeches of any substance are always worth checking. Even the most skilled speakers sometimes say the wrong words, omit a vital 'not' or mumble indistinctly. Corrections to the Hansard text must be swift or the mistake will grow legs.

Copies of speeches are very useful to explain a Member's stance on issues, especially when they are correct in every detail. They are extremely useful in sending to enquirers and constituents and avoid a great deal of unnecessary letter writing.

The UK Parliament website carries MPs' questions and speeches in the Chamber three hours after they are delivered. This is of great value to the daily blogger, who can speedily pass on contributions and ministers' answers.

How to Use the Library

The Commons Library is a life support system, an archive, an inspiration and a place to rest and snooze.

No reasonable request is ever denied. Given time, the band of experts produce detailed briefs, informative press cuttings and past Hansard quotations. When the media are screaming out for urgent interviews, updates on half-forgotten issues can be produced in a few hours.

It's risky to delay queries. Never is it fair to ask for a briefing on a question or a debate with less than three days' notice. There is usually only one member of staff for each specialist subject and ample time must be allowed. The quality of the work produced will depend on the Member's relationship with the librarians. Never commit any of their seven sins.

Seven Deadly Library Sins

1. Asking for information and not collecting it from the tray or opening your e-mail.
2. Demanding more information than necessary.
3. Repeating requests for identical material within a brief period.
4. Not turning up for debates/questions on which you have been briefed.
5. Asking staff to research subjects outside their expertise.
6. Expecting librarians to do the work of the MP's researcher/political party/secretary.
7. Never saying thank you.

Members' offices are plugged into the improving parliamentary and Google databases. Library Fact Sheets and Parliamentary Office of Science and Technology (POST) reports can be read and printed from computers in the Members' offices. No other generation has enjoyed such easy access to vast treasure chests of information. They can add greatly and instantaneously to efficiency and speed of service.

The main library has changed little from its traditional role. The presence of newspapers and banks of computers do not detract from its hushed atmosphere, reminiscent of the libraries of the great universities. For about fifty regular attenders, the library is a peaceful refuge. Before the days of individual offices, Members worked from desks there. Dozens still find it the most congenial, phone-free haven for serious work and study. The many computer workstations allow the most to be made of time spent away from offices and near the Chamber.

The most comfortable armchairs in the Palace are in a semi-circle around the now decommissioned fireplaces. Regulars gather there in growing numbers throughout the tiring Parliamentary day to read and snooze. Only the division bells are allowed to disturb the peace.

How to Allocate Time

Parliamentary time is not equally rewarding in achievement, publicity or benefit to humankind. Long hours of exacting toil on Bill Committees will be rewarded in heaven only. Three sentences of inspiration at Prime Minister's Question Time elevate the unknown Members to heroic status among their peers and quicken the pulses of constituents.

The Votingham Standard Guide to the value of MP time is:

30 seconds of PMQs =

20 minutes of Oral Questions =

3 hours of Select Committee questioning =

28 hours of continuous backbench speeches in the Chamber =

2 months of speaking in Public Bill Committees =

28 years of speaking on European Standing Committee B =

78 years of serving on Committees on Statutory Instruments.

How to Run a Campaign

Out of the dreary mulch of humdrum work a Surtsey of an issue will occasionally arise, dazzling and thunderous. It may be a mountainous injustice, a mire of corruption or a wasteland of stupidity that few have noticed.

A campaign issue must be:

- Capable of practical solution by Parliamentary action or pressure.
- Likely to engage significant public sympathy.
- A slayer of dragons or an uplifter of the dispossessed.
- A boost to the sum of human happiness/safety/ecstasy.

The stages are:

Research: Use the Commons Library and pressure groups to explore the issue. Seek information from allies and foes to test strengths and weaknesses. Write down the case; fashion the sound bites. Interest feature-writing journalists in the fine details. Blog and tweet to seek out additional allies and information.

Launch: A PMQ is a dream chance to launch the campaign. Next best are a Ten Minute Rule Bill or an adjournment debate, especially one on a Wednesday morning when more time is available. Send out an embargoed press release with irresistible tasters that intrigue and excite jaded hacks to find out more. Arrange a press conference in the Jubilee Room (one of the few rooms where television cameras are allowed) with witnesses in attendance. Celebrities are useful, but better are those offering powerful personal testimony to back the cause. A trim message is needed to fit the available time slot. In an adjournment debate enlist speeches from other MPs. Political opponents are useful in adding gravitas. Even a minute's contribution from three or four MPs with high reputations greatly strengthens the case.

Media: Clear the decks of all other commitments to cope with press interest. If overwhelmed, ensure that your secretary has a clear idea of news values. It's a sickening experience to be informed, 'Because you're booked for interviews on Radio Hull and Radio Ceredigion, I told *Newsnight* that you couldn't come to their studio.' If the media want a superstar MP rather than you to present the case, don't stand in the way. The issue is supreme, not your vanity.

Long Haul: After the big bang of the presentation there will be a fading afterglow of interest for a few days. Then the real campaigning starts. Unleash a measured but persistent onslaught of parliamentary speeches, questions, EDMs. Organise a press campaign of news, plus letters seeking information and cases to support the cause. The neglected 500 regional newspapers will often co-operate. Some may adopt your campaign as their own. It's worth setting up a database with the addresses of all regional papers.

Write to ministers and the Prime Minister with requests for detailed information. Make the subject a nuisance that ministers long to expel from their daily red box. Buttonhole them occasionally in the lobbies. Judge success by the hunted look in the ministerial gaze. When they become offensive, or better still insulting, success is near.

Woo support from other MPs, outside organisations, the library and the political party. Persuade them to supply you with news of helpful developments. Bombard the Chamber with Business Questions, Points of Order or opportunistic Oral Questions or Topical Questions contrived to back your campaign.

Hail any partial victories. Chart your weekly 're-launches' of the campaign to coincide with media fallow times – Mondays,

Fridays, recesses and Bank Holidays. Never falter. Frequent knocking splits the stone.

If publicity is carefully targeted and repeated, policy can be changed even if new legislation has not gone through the House. Grow a thick skin – fellow MPs groan in weariness at the repetitions on the theme, but they respect persistence and know its value.

A professional lobbyist commented on one campaign:

> Discounting the role and impact of House of Commons back-benchers is naive and short-sighted. We only have to study the impact one backbencher had on the behaviour of the British motor industry on a 'safety issue'. It would be true to say that whilst Vauxhall acted quicker than most, the whole automobile sector has now moved to tackle the problem without a single new law being passed. Media opinion has also turned against the use of bull bars. Advertising too! The backbencher took a lead. Industry followed. Powerful stuff for a mere backbencher.

The safety measure itself was 'talked out' by a Government minister following by a debate that had all-party support. It looked like a flop. But the political weather had been changed by a campaign that had stirred public opinion. Help came from the EU. They adopted the issue. Legislative failure was translated into a safety success through the parliamentary megaphone of publicity.

Reforms in parliamentary procedure take on a life of their own. Pre-legislation scrutiny both expanded and restricted the work of Select Committees. E-petitions were planned as servants of the Backbench Business Committee. They have become an unruly master. The vain hopes that 100,000 signatures would bring back hanging or exit from the EU were irresponsibly aroused. Sky-high public expectations crashed with the reality that governments did not shift policy on the demand of a six hundredth of the electorate. The Backbench committee has had a splendid honeymoon year. The might of the Executive will fight back.

Growing media interest in Select Committee proceedings has also had a role to play in this phenomenon. The rising stars of Chris Bryant, Tom Watson and Louise Mensch show that with perseverance a backbencher can throw the door wide open on an issue important to the public and can achieve real change. Under Speaker Bercow backbenchers have also had the increased ability to call ministers to the House to answer urgent questions, often on the same day. This session has seen Bercow grant more than one urgent question a week (up from four a year under Speaker Martin).

The Private Members' Bill (PMB) system appears to be the next target for reforms to give backbenchers further influence. They have been neglected in recent years. Their 'golden age' in the 1960s was made possible by the backing of the Government of the day, supporting the initiative of individual backbench MPs, especially Leo Abse and David Steel. Thirty-four reached the statute book in 1963/64 but 60 out of 1,096 became law from 1998 to 2008. The highest number to become law in a single recent year was 1996/97 when twenty-two bills were successful. In 2008/9 just 5 out of 110 Private Members' Bills were successful. Three bills that look like becoming law in 2011 are ones on sports ground safety, on allowing grandchildren to inherit even if their parents have forfeited their inheritance and on dealing with shipwrecks – worthy causes but not the great reforms of the past: legalising abortion, decriminalising homosexuality and abolishing the death penalty in the 1960s. The principal cause of the decline is that Fridays are no longer considered by most MPs to be Westminster days. Diaries are packed with constituency engagements. Fridays have become a playground for bill assassins and the self-indulgent. Chris Bryant says Fridays are 'capricious'. They were too often filled with MPs talking out bills, leaving the general public and many other MPs frustrated. The Hansard Society proposed adopting new sitting times for PMBs and increasing the time allocated from the current sixty-five hours per session to eighty hours.

PMBs need to be revitalised if campaigns are to achieve changes in law. The humble campaigner deserves a parliamentary process that reflects public and parliamentary opinion, not a fragile structure that can be brought down by the first whiff of vexatious opposition in an empty Chamber on a Friday.

How to Deal with Disaster

Local disasters propel obscure backbenchers to immediate fame. Instant authority and pre-eminence in debate is bestowed by a generous House on the local Member. Reputations are made or destroyed.

London's recent riots were sparked by a peaceful vigil outside Tottenham police station that spiralled out of control. Twenty-six years ago, a similar riot in the area generated a lasting debate about policing and social integration in Britain. David Lammy, a life-long resident of Tottenham and its Member of Parliament, became the restrained, reassuring voice of his square mile. His frequent appearances in the media and in his constituency were free of the histrionics and grandstanding of lesser politicians.

The least likely Commons star was the genuinely modest Mark Wolfson. He was one of the most unlikely characters in politics because of his unassuming personality. He has no enemies and was thought to be destined for inescapable anonymity. Britain's worst storm, in 1990, reduced his Sevenoaks constituency to One Oak. It was Mark who emerged from the shadows and acquitted himself superbly.

Peter Hain did not allow his frontbench role as a shadow spokesman to inhibit his skilled, sensitive handling of a constituency crisis. A mining accident at Cil y Bebyll ultimately took the lives of four of Peter's constituents. For a few hours rescue was a possibility. The rolling news networks reported the enfolding drama. Hain was ever-present at the mine entrance, knowledgeable, restrained and sympathetic. He privately contacted the families and won their confidence and trust. His was the voice of restraint and realism in a swirl of speculation that was often wildly optimistic in its rescue hopes.

He spoke with pride of the centuries-long Welsh tradition of endurance and sacrifice in the mining industry. He communicated genuine empathy with the victims and their families. This is only possible for an MP who has deep roots in his constituency.

When the news came that rescue was impossible, Peter captured the mood and the emotion: 'Extraordinary courage was shown by the families right through the night, tortuous hours of waiting. We can't imagine what they have been through.' He said the tragedy had reawakened old memories. 'This has been a stab right through the heart of these local communities. There's a long tradition of mining here but nobody expected the tragedies of past generations would come today.' Subsequently he set up the Swansea Valley Miners Appeal Fund to support the families of the victims. A very large sum of money was collected and distributed to the grateful families. Had Parliament not been in recess at the time of the tragedy, he would have used the Commons as a platform in addition to the rolling news. A month later he continued to press for improved mine safety from the Dispatch Box.

It's easy for the artless or opportunist MP to repeat the Bush calamity of being wrong-footed on the Katrina floods. Politicians who seek political advantage from the misery of others risk exposure and contempt. When Workington MP Tony Cunningham's constituency was hit by severe floods he was asked on live television whether politicians had anything to contribute to relieve the effects of disasters. Quietly spoken Tony gave a long list of practical steps he had already taken, including initiating a relief fund that had attracted donations. He was personally self-effacing and constructive. He proved his serious intent by persisting with his campaign against a threatened 'flood tax'.

These are splendid models for all MPs faced with constituency calamities. Others have failed. Some overplayed minor incidents or downplayed serious ones. Others were caught short on unjustifiable trips abroad when disaster struck.

How to Eat and Drink

Simply. There is a persuasive army of people bent on bloating the bodies and dulling the senses of Members with fine food and drink. They aim to induce states of comatosed receptivity for their blandishments.

An MP's working day is long and exhausting. Over-indulging in food and drink is the enemy of work. The Palace of Westminster is awash with alcohol in the seven bars and countless daily receptions. It's possible to go through the whole day, from a breakfast seminar with Danish pastries to afternoon and evening receptions with wine and finger food, accepting the hospitality of those who seek your company. A few sad souls do.

Some politicians have been caricatured by their appearance and eating habits. Eric Pickles accepts the nickname of 'Spudulike'. The sketch-writers delight in his excuse for the failure to declare, as the ministerial code demanded, a five star Savoy Hotel dinner that he enjoyed at the expense of a lobbyist: on that day he was not eating ministerially, he was eating privately. The distinction was too subtle for the guffawing public to appreciate.

Advice on alcohol is simple. Don't drink at Westminster. Dennis Skinner argues faultlessly that he never drank when he was on duty down the mines – why drink on duty in Parliament? It is not a lonely vocation. There is a large and growing band of Westminster teetotallers. The drinkers soon understand and stop offering drinks. Abstemious Members can still plunge into the full joys of social life by sipping non-alcoholic drinks or by joining in the full delights of après-Parliament activities outside when the House rises.

There is always a good reason for drinking. After a bad day, a consoling swig is essential to rebuild collapsed spirits. After a good day, a celebratory glass is a deserved reward for success. It would be churlish to refuse a drink on social occasions in the constituency at weekends.

That means some alcohol every day – the certain path to softening of the brain, cirrhosis of the liver and political impotence. Happily now the drinks are not subsidised. Prices are similar to those elsewhere in London. Westminster drinkers have the added peril of speaking in the Chamber. Alan Clark is one of the few who have admitted to doing it. He survived, but only just. One notorious Tory soak was packed into a taxi by his friends with instructions to convey him to his Pimlico home. He was so drunk they feared a scandal. They returned to the Strangers Bar and were horrified half an hour later to see the miscreant's name on the annunciator. He had escaped the taxi, returned to the Chamber and was called to speak. Hansard kindly did not attempt to record his incoherent drunken babble. They simply summed it with the word, 'Interruption.'

One unfortunate new MP suffered a baptism of derision on his first late vote. Mark Reckless was so inebriated that he fell to the floor of a Commons bar before the Budget vote in the early hours of the morning. It was the result of a six-hour drinking session that lasted until 2.30 a.m., when the vote was called. A tabloid reported that Mark fell on the floor and had to be helped to his feet. Later, he struggled to open a bar door, repeatedly slamming it on his toe, apparently unaware his foot was in the way. He has not drunk since.

The modern timetable for a happy-eater MP is:

8.30 a.m. Breakfast of toast and tea in the Members' Tea Room. The Tea Room is the cradle of the Parliamentary day. Here the newspapers are read, embryo plots hatched, minor exploratory skirmishes between the parties planned. The day's battle plans are sketched out.

1.30 p.m. Light lunch of salad and oily fish in Tea Room for MPs only (or cafeteria if you have staff or visitors with you).

7.30 p.m. Once or twice a week reward yourself with a quality three-course dinner in the Members' Dining room. Avoid the same company; shuffle companions for quality conversation. Other nights, suffer the penance of character-building, simple meals in the Terrace or the Debate.

Commons eating places:

Adjournment, Portcullis House: Friendly, attentive staff provide a relaxed atmosphere and waiter service. Serves a wide range of sumptuous dishes at good value.

Debate, Portcullis House: Favourite of those working in Portcullis House. Light and buzzy with a good selection. Busy after PMQs. Chance to inspect your food choices in a glass case. Excellent cake provides a sugar rush for afternoon lulls. Great location for people-watching.

Dispatch Box, Portcullis House: Friendly French and Polish baristas run this very popular coffee destination. Often a queue but worth the wait. Great for informal meets.

Annie's Bar: Is gone. It died with its last remaining customers. No doubt the ghosts of sages past haunt the place it occupied. The unique ambience of comatose decrepitude is gone. No more ancient warriors raking over the ashes of fires that are long dead.

Bellamy's Bar: Once a popular haunt of Tory researchers is now a successful crèche.

Bellamy's Restaurant: Cafeteria of good quality and value. Good breakfast spot. Favoured by the security guards. Friendly staff. Often crowded.

Churchill Room: Sumptuous and most expensive food. Stuffed with foreign visitors and celebrities. Tables are decorated with overly large plates that are removed before the food arrives.

Westminster Hall Jubilee Cafeteria: Gothic arches welcome the hordes of visitors. Good place to rest weary legs after a tour of Parliament. Open all week including Saturdays. Marked up prices for the tourists.

Members' Dining Room: Now interchangeable with Strangers' Bar; they are served by one kitchen. Friendly staff, consistently good quality food. The Members' Dining Room was lightly used at lunchtime by MPs and now is well used by MPs with guests.

Members' Smoking Room: Mélange of gentleman's club and geriatric residential home. Refuge for alcohol addicts. Whisky-stained air. Someone could die in the plush chairs and not be noticed for days. In spite of the name, smoking is not allowed.

Members' Tea Room: The most popular place for Members' breakfasts. Divided into two rooms: Labour and Lib Dems/Tories. Probably did not go down well in Devizes.

Moncrieff's Bar and Restaurant: The habitat of the press lobby. Known for 'Fish and Chips' Friday.

Pugin Room: Sinfully comfortable for pre-meal drinks. Great view of the Thames from window seats. Champagne-rich atmosphere. Popular for romantic encounters, the religious plotting holy campaigns and for fat cat stroking. Best for celebrations. Staffed by the superbly attentive Mustafa and Keith, who have worked here for two decades.

Sports and Social: Used to be known as the 'Sports and Socialists' but with the demise of Bellamy's Bar it has seen an influx of Tory researchers. An old favourite with staff, doorkeepers and a sprinkling of North East MPs. Quiet refuge at the start of the week. Lively on Thursdays and Fridays when MPs have left the building. Many a parliamentary staff romance has started in the Sports and Social. Watch out for Karaoke night, which is taken over by Tory researchers and American interns. There are darts, golf and pool competitions. Winners get their names on the honours board. And a cash prize. Feels like a real pub in spite of its exotic location in the bowels of a palace. Newt-congenial ambience. Entry is through Central Lobby, reminiscent of a 'speakeasy'.

Strangers' Bar: A popular drinking hole even though it's a remodelled corridor without charm. Low ceiling claustrophobic. Air is breathable following smoking ban. Regulars kiss each other a lot. Staff are friendly and have worked here forever. Becomes tolerable in the summer with transfusions of fresh air and access to the Terrace.

Terrace Cafeteria: Refurbished to Victorian splendour in pre-expenses extravagance that's impossible now. High-quality, pleasant cafeteria divided into sections for staff and MPs. Extends to the outside embankment in the summer for Parliament's greatest delight, tea on the Terrace. Rightly loved by visitors and villagers.

Terrace Pavilion: Purpose-built marquee used for private buffets and receptions. Open for lunch during June and July with a set menu. Buffet of delights for starter and dessert. Advance booking recommended.

For those wanting to escape the parliamentary estate there are two pubs an arm's length away:

The Red Lion, Parliament Street: Located midway between the Palace and Downing Street. It's a well-known stomping ground for journos and researchers. The pub has a division bell and the main TV is tuned into the parliament channel for those keen not to miss a thing.

St Stephen's Tavern, Bridge Street: Also has a division bell. It disappeared for years behind building work but has been lovingly refurbished in traditional style. Mainly tourist customers, but it still gets a regular mix of staff and MPs who want to blend into the background. The staff say they attract 'journalists, paparazzi and lesser-known backbenchers to drink with us, as well as Neil Kinnock!' One of Churchill's old haunts.

How to be Comforted

The comfort stations at Westminster dominate many of the place's anecdotes, ancient and modern.

Female MPs had few until recently. There is now greater equality. A major concession was changing the signs on the men's loos from 'Members Only' to 'Male Members Only'. Also inviting ribaldry, the Lords' are still called 'Peers Only'.

However, attempted equality has not provided female Members with anywhere as opulent as the Members' Cloak Room above the Cloisters. It's hardly changed since Asquith or Churchill popped in. The stalls and basins are a minor triumph of Victorian marble and earthenware art. Someone should slap a preservation order on them. The airy opulence is redolent of an exclusive gentlemen's club, complete with individual hand towels and clothes brushes. Alas, combs are no longer supplied – possibly an overreaction to the expenses scandal.

The subject of toilets dominated an adjournment debate in 1997. It was a serious constituency issue for Michael Fabricant. He chose the subject of Sanitaryware (Flushing Standards). A threat to local jobs to Michael is a chance for mockery by the media.

The minister Angela Eagle responded appropriately:

> Mr Fabricant's knowledge of, interest in and unashamed enthusiasm for the British lavatory and its siphonic flushing mechanism appears to know no bounds. My ministerial desk was full to overflowing yesterday with a display of toilet flushing mechanisms of every conceivable kind. I would have treated the House to that display had I not been mindful of the very strict rules preventing the use of visual aids in the House.
>
> Mr Fabricant has let his fertile imagination run riot. I simply do not recognise the nightmare scenario that he has painted... The House might be excused for thinking that he is completely potty for such lurid fears.
>
> Before I resume my seat, let me emphasise he has lifted the lid on the worries that exist in the industry.

There is a room for the exclusive use of female Members opposite the old (non) Smoking Room. It is a comfortable furnished refuge from the all-pervasive maleness of the Palace.

The Family Room, off the lower lobby, is a useful starter crèche for the children and a safe haven for the spouses of MPs who fail to get tickets for Question Time. It is comfortably furnished with settees, armchairs and a changing room, plus an array of children's toys and books.

How to Avoid Bad Language

George Orwell said in 1946, 'Prose consists less and less of words chosen for the sake of their meaning, and more of phrases tacked together like the sections of a prefabricated hen-house.'

MPs are duty-bound to be jargon busters. It must be rooted out even to the point when the rules of courtesy may be strained. Jargon derails trains of thought, clogs reasoning, buries understanding, wastes time and is designed to baffle and bamboozle.

It is a defensive weapon of the Executive to maintain their omnipotence. We are meant to be seduced by cute word pairings – 'train to gain', 'patient pathways' – that are offered as solutions to problems. They are not solutions. A fresh cliché distracts the brain from the absence of solutions. Flash adjectives are not alternative policies, they are vacuous words.

Lord Birt transfixed a Select Committee. The language he used was clearly derived from English, but was incomprehensible 'Policy is a sub-set of strategy' with 'three-to-five-year horizons' that 'improve system outcomes' and 'forward strategy'. No backward strategy? He continued, 'Some embedded strategies are rooted in incentive structures ... and conventional performance measurement capability.'

Former minister Tessa Jowell kept a 'little book of bollocks' containing instances of Government jargon and gobbledygook: 'I just sit in meetings and I write down some of the absurd language we use. The risk is when you have been in Government for eight years you begin to talk the language.'

Legislators swim through a mind-dulling morass of place shaping, re-baselining, holistic governance, roll-outs, step changes, public domains, fit for purposes, stakeholder engagements, across the pieces, paradigm shifts, multi-layered, multi-focused, multi-discipline, win-wins and level playing fields that are going forward. Michael Gove MP said, 'Since becoming a Member of Parliament I've been learning a new language... No one ever uses a simple Anglo-Saxon word, or a concrete example, where a Latinate construction or a next-to-meaningless abstraction can be found.'

Some terms have been deliberately minted to hide the truth. 'Extraordinary rendition' means transporting prisoners to be tortured. 'Collateral damage' means blowing civilians to smithereens with bombs.

David Blunkett MP explained the meaning of the mealy-mouthed civil servants' assurance that when no action is possible they will 'stand ready'. Blunkett said, 'That actually means: we're doing nothing about this unless we're absolutely forced to do so.' Not standing ready so much as lying prone. Not a dignified posture for a legislator.

Jargon is contagious, pestilential obscurantism. Up and at 'em.

How to Blog

Parliamentary technophobes are being left stranded among the inkwells and quill pens as techno-freaks plunge into the delicious world of fresh communication miracles.

Blogging has captivated a minority of MPs. It's a refreshing new thrill, like learning to ride a bike for the first time at an advanced age.

Blog Pope Iain Dale has said, 'Most MPs think that MPs who blog are clinically insane.' Those are the average, timid, career-hungry, boring MPs who are terrified of saying anything interesting. They hold that thinking is optional and originality dangerous for MPs. Recording original thoughts is dangerous. They can boomerang back later and bite. Nadine Dorries was taken to task for alleged inaccuracies on her blog. Her defence was odd. 'I rely heavily on poetic licence,' she admitted, 'and frequently replace one place name/event/fact with another.' Dorries later posted on her blog that 'any individual with a smattering of intelligence [could] see that everything on the blog is accurate, because

it is largely a record of real time events. It was only ever the percep-
tion of where I was on any particular day which was disguised.'

It's a choice between the thrill of being damned, praised and
excoriated or the safe, boring wait for the silent to inherit the
ministerial jobs. The nostrums of the blogosphere demand a daily
epistle. This is a welcome chore for incurable communicators
who are restless to put the world right.

However kind the press is in conveying your every thought,
there are frustrations in trying to push complex, serious arguments through the needle's eye of the news editor's judgement.
Here, the exchange of views is exhilarating and instant. Blogs
provide the space to present detailed arguments with added punch
and colour. They can liberate politicians or enslave them. MPs can
talk to constituents and the wider world unedited, un-spun and
unabbreviated. To stodge-brained mediocrities the daily writing chore is drudgery. They give up. But hooked bloggers soon
discover the web skills to stroke the constituency's erogenous
zones. Orthodox opinion can be challenged by an audience that is
both local and worldwide.

The Commons authorities tried to extend to the blogosphere
the Commons rules on courtesy. They objected to comments on my
blog, including 'Lembit Opik's ability has been eclipsed by the bril-
liance of his semi-scandals, clowning and odd enthusiasms'; 'In her
first parliament Ann Widdecombe was everyone's favourite ogre.
Sour, unattractive and humourless, she spat her puritanical venom
at friend and foe'; and, on Nicholas Soames, 'A serious politician
has long been struggling to emerge from the globular mountainous shape. He is remembered as an amiable buffoon.' The situation
of two Labour MPs who took cash from industry was described as
'cash for comrades'. There was no question of political bias because
my comments applied to all parties. This was a pointless attempt at
censorship – trying to impose ancient rules on a modern media. The
Commons were content with anaemic, flaccid blogs that nobody
read. I declined to take down the comments. They were no stronger

than those that are acceptable in newspaper sketches. I continued, privatised the blog and paid my own expenses.

Political blogging is still in its infancy here in spite of stunning successes in the USA. There was very little interest in a political election blog I set up in 2002 and I have not used one since.

To a dwindling small number of MP bloggers the addiction continues. The instant interaction with individuals or groups is a joy denied to politicians of the past. It magnifies the experience of direct personal contact and reaction. Technology will open new channels but blogs, twitter or social networks will increasingly set the agenda and lubricate the processes of political debate. I take a decent camera along when I visit centres of interest in my community. The pictures enliven the blog and are of permanent interest.

The process of merging the coalition parties in the Welsh Assembly was lubricated by Welsh blogs. Ways forward were suggested at a time when parties were not talking directly. Possible areas of agreement were floated on Plaid Cymru MP Adam Price's blog. They were basis for the Labour–Plaid One Wales coalition that was a startling and brilliant success.

Blogging adds immediacy and zing. The obligation to write creatively every day is a welcome discipline to jump-start the synapses into daily callisthenics.

How to Disperse Swarmers

Come the new technology, come the new pestilence.

The web is a playground for the obsessed, the wildly deluded and angry conspiracy theorists. Individuals can be swiftly swatted but sometimes they hunt in swarms. A thousand angry e-mails are dispiriting. It's a hard choice. Reply individually and sinfully waste time or ignore them, reinforce their delusions and face accusations of being undemocratic.

Swarmers have all the characteristics of cults – an exaggerated view of the importance of their issue, a reluctance to challenge their own prejudices, a mistaken sense of victimhood, plus a fanatic's lack of proportion and common sense. Most active are Christian fundamentalists, global warming deniers and opponents of the smoking ban.

The sheer size of e-mail assaults disguises their Lilliputian influence. The anti-smoking ban lobby amassed a mere 0.38 per cent of the vote in one by-election.

The lobby against *Jerry Springer – the Opera* claimed to have sent 50,000 complaints to MPs and the BBC. In my case it was one complaint sent thousands of times: lists of members of chapels and churches were used to top and tail identical e-mails. That is futile.

A full, detailed response to swarms is the most efficient way of dealing with the mass messages. It won't satisfy them but they will get the message to buzz off.

There are a few parasitic ones that exist only to feed on my postings in their debased Tourette's language. They are very helpful to me even though I now never read them. They usually quote a few sentences from my blog, distort them and then attack the absurdity of their creation. Curious surfers then drop into my blog and read the original versions.

How to Tweet

Tweeting is a new art form. Compressing a complex, intelligent argument to 140 characters is a splendid discipline. Brevity is all. Character-losing is character-forming. A barbed tweet with throbbing adjectives delights and excites. Parliament has long suffered abuse from time-thieves who pack out their disorganised, random thoughts with verbal bubble wrap. Each tweet needs a mere few seconds of attention to be understood and enjoyed.

Great thoughts, rumours, insults and prophecies can be broadcast instantly and re-tweeted to an expectant nation. It's Nirvana for compulsive communicators. Constituents can enjoy a constant communion of ideas and inspiration with their Honourable Member. It's lazy to use abbreviations. They pollute the purity of the prose. Strive to find the best words to create a striking aphorism or a haiku.

This demands heavy-duty, concentrated thinking. A happy tweet can be recycled in speeches and can be a model for a Chamber oral question. The 'After Bercow' era is the epoch of the tweet. He has encouraged pithy, one-sentence questions. Tweet examples that have been recycled as questions or interventions in the Chamber include: 'Isn't the Big Society badger slaughter spree a combination of bad science with animal cruelty created by the nasty party?' and 'Did the hollow threat of 65,000 UK swine flu deaths waste £1.3 billion, distort NHS priorities and scare the country witless?'

Some MPs have had problems with unwise tweets. Sending out messages when overtired and emotional is never sensible. It is certainly never to be attempted when a Member is as relaxed as a newt.

Tweeting is overtaking blogging as politicians' best channel for contacting press and public. The press releases that were once the basic means of communication with the media are dropping into clunky irrelevance. Alert journalists will follow up newsworthy tweets.

As all news stories about MPs must be negative, there was a wholly misleading report on the trivia of many MPs' tweets. Tom Watson, Chris Bryant and Louise Mensch kept Twitter enthralled with updates on Hackgate; Liz Kendall tweeted updates on the committee stage of the Health Bill; Ed Balls regularly uses Twitter to push his economic arguments. None of this was mentioned in the news report, which highlighted instead that Ed Balls tweeted his recipes! In the present climate it's not wise to tweet trivia. It exposes MPs to ridicule. But criticism should not deflect MPs from using our most convenient and efficient tool. In 2011 the number of MPs tweeting went from 100 to 300. The non-tweeters are a likely future minority of backwoods people.

Kerry McCarthy writes: 'The best MPs use Twitter to argue and debate with people they might never have met but whose ideas and opinions are interesting and important (and sometimes idiotic and obnoxious, but that's democracy). We should be encouraging more MPs to tweet.' The modernisers won over the dinosaurs. The use of hand-held devices and iPads are now permissible in the Chamber. Communicating from Member to Member in the Chamber adds unpredictable spice to parliamentary discourse. The main debate is enriched with a Greek chorus silent babble of micro-debates among the twitterati.

The crown for brevity has passed from Tam Dayell for his question 'Why?' to Charles Walker for his speeches 'If not now, when?' and 'Fixed-term parliaments: constitutional vandalism.' There should be no hesitation or delay in a mass imitation of Charles's example.

If not now, when?

THE PARTY

How to be Whipped

The nature of the party whips has metamorphosed recently. Their name is taken from the hunting field where whips were used to goad dim animals to do their masters' bidding, and frightening tales are whispered about overpowering bullying by the honourable thugs of yesterday. I witnessed a cowering, tearful young MP pinned to a wall of the 'No' lobby by the fat gut of a sixteen-stone whip yelling his charm-offensive message: 'I have two words to say to you – fucking coward.' The whip then waddled off to share the same potent words with half a dozen other Tories who had disobeyed the whips' instructions.

Today's MPs are made of tougher stuff and the whips are more lobby savvy. They swirl round in a Never Never Land of smiles, illusions, threats and whispers. Against the ambitious their power is boundless. Omnipresent whips in the Chamber and committees perpetually catalogue the strengths and weaknesses of Members' speeches. A favourable report can give novice MPs their first hoist up the greasy pole.

Their mission is to bind the party into compliant unity. Whips allocate offices, control pairing and heap ashes on the heads of unorthodox Members. No formal vows are demanded but their idea is to conjure up the peace, chastity and obedience of the monastic life. Except that to them poverty is not a virtue.

What Dennis Skinner called the 'organised truancy' of pairing collapsed in January 1997. Pairing had long been the emergency balm applied to heal the wounds that the job inflicts on family life – even the longest suffering spouses are outraged when family life is disrupted in order that the party can win or lose a division by fifty-eight votes rather than fifty-nine. Without it, the whips' power was castrated.

It soon became unbearable, however. The addicts returned to their old ways and pairing reappeared in a slightly mutated form. There has been a gradual change. The increasing influence of female MPs has lightened the burden of unreasonable hours. Members now boldly and rightly desert the Commons to shore up family life. Pairing still happens but rarely and discreetly. The tentacles of the whips' patronage are losing their gripping power.

Newspapers delight in perpetuating the fantasy that whips discipline Members with smarting 'raps across the knuckles'. Occasionally it is true for MPs whose pride is enfeebled by ambition. For the wise and self-respecting majority, a haranguing whip is harangued back.

Expulsion from Party

On the occasion when I almost reached the point of rupture with my party, discussion with the whip was quiet and civilised. Only puny sanctions could be applied to a rarely pairing MP who had rejected the patronage of the whipping system. The direst threat was possible expulsion from membership of European Standing Committee B. During much of the previous year I had been my party's sole representative attending that desolate body.

Chief Whips know their only power is to swap a Member's seat on an invisible obscure committee for one in the studios of the vastly influential *Today* programme or *Newsnight*. Whipless MPs are no longer pariahs exiled to a forgotten world of silent solitude. They are welcomed and fêted by the press, and their audiences and influence are hugely magnified.

The whipless Tory Europhobes under John Major were immensely more powerful without their party's whip. The press were excited by the line-up that they described as escapees from

'Broadmoor Ward Ten'. Their whipless fame was brief. They disappeared back into obscurity when it was restored to them. Their
2011 counterparts were not disciplined. The whips are now wiser.

There were some disgraceful episodes when party leaders
panicked over expenses revelations. Some MPs were expelled,
not for the nature of the alleged offence, but because of the space
allocated to it by *The Telegraph*. These moves were backed by party
apparatchiks who were ignorant of Commons procedure but
inflamed by passion to punish alleged miscreants, major, minor
and minute.

The whips are powerless against substantial numbers in their
flock. Some parties rubbish their rebels in reports to constituency
parties, but I know of no instance when a sitting MP has been
punished for independence. The 2010 elections prove that Labour
MPs who rebelled against unpopular Government decisions such
as the Iraq War and the 10p tax were rewarded by their constituents in the ballot box.

In every parliament there are many whose ambition is dead,
who have unassailable majorities or who are in their final term.
Others have ideals and convictions that surmount personal ambition or the need to survive. No discipline can be imposed on them.
The only thing that works is self-discipline.

How to Befriend

Jerry Hayes tells me that the best advice he would offer a new MP
is to develop friendships with a few MPs who can be implicitly
trusted.

The waters of the parliamentary world are infested with the
sharks of competitiveness, malice and envy. A circle of close
friends is a great survival buoyancy aid.

Some Members bond like swans for their entire parliamentary
lives. New MP Andrew Brigden said the MPs he met in his first
few days in Parliament would probably be friends for life. Small

groups of the same MPs are seen eating, debating and drinking together. Some friendships are enforced by party loyalty or geography, others by subject interests. School links are still strong among Tories, although few want to dine in the company of their 'school fag' or the sixth former who bullied them.

MPs with shared interests flock together. The value is not merely social but a defence mechanism against the general hostility or indifference of a Commons community who do not share the same enthusiasms.

There is practical value in having a list of colleagues who will allow their names to be added to EDMs and motions without a prior say-so. They can also come to the rescue when the Member is double-booked to receive visitors, short of passes to the Chamber or needs to swell an audience for a visiting dignitary. Friends are vital voices that tell the truth when MPs make fools of themselves.

Avoid being trapped in ghettos of people with identical mindsets to your own, however. Getting elected provides the admission ticket to some of the best-informed and most stimulating company of any village in the country. Go forth and socialise. Don't stick with those who shrink the boundaries of parliamentary life.

How to Grow a Shell Back

Parliament is not a place for susceptible souls.

Sharp, wounding attacks will come from many quarters. Most full-time politicians soon grow a shell back. Those barbs that penetrate deeply are the rare criticisms that are true or that come from friends.

Some MPs are shaken to the roots of their being by a whiff of critical comment. Depression sets in for long periods, especially after a clever insult delivered by a parliamentary sketch in papers read by MPs. Simon Carr, Simon Hoggart and Quentin Letts are the most feared scourges. A verbal lashing or even a sneering adjective throws Members with insecure egos into early morning gloom – especially when they provoke guffaws from friends over breakfast in the tea-room.

There is a certain resilience to jibes of incompetence, immorality, bias or political incorrectness. Yet searing grief is experienced when an MP's personal appearance is mocked. An accusation that one frontbencher looked like a serial axe killer prompted recourse to the lawyers – from the MP not the axeman. A gibe challenged, however, is usually a gibe quadrupled. Complaints rarely do any good. They give wider currency to the original insult. It's best to accept it with a shrug as part of the territory. Not many goals are scored on the defensive. Attacks are best mounted from selected forward positions. Adjectives should be sharpened for an incisive retort and stored in an armoury of insults.

The ones who bounce back quickly from toe-curling revelations about their private lives are those who tough it out. Instead of quitting the goldfish bowl and disappearing home to hide their heads under a pillow, they take charge of the crisis. Many have appeared in the Commons and deliberately asked Oral Questions hours after the publication of lurid accounts of shaming events in their private lives. In one case the disgraced MP told me he refused to read his old love letters when they were printed by a tabloid. Self-induced amnesia was an effective antidote. The scandal was ephemeral.

Some sketchwriters irrationally home in on blameless victims. The splendid work of Barry Sheerman as a Select Committee chair was defamed by *The Times*'s Ann Treneman, who called him 'a perennial favourite for creep of the year', while the *Daily Mail*'s Quentin Letts wrote: 'He's not so much a greaser as a Channel swimmer ... smeared in whale fat.' Neither of the sketchwriters were disturbed by the wholly fictitious nature of their word assaults.

The tormenting of Michael Fabricant by Simon Hoggart is eternal. The relationship between the two has become a minor parasitic industry. Is candidate Fabricant sponsored by Hoggart

Enterprises Plc? Has the *Guardian* shares in the future volume *Fabb, The Twilight Years*? Who is the host and who is the parasite? Who is feeding off whom? Hoggart has revealed that his name is an adopted one. Is he a closet Fabricant? Are they twins? Will we ever know the truth?

THE MEDIA

How to Handle the Press

These are the guaranteed ways of gaining publicity if you are a devotee of the discredited canard that all publicity is good for you:

- Make a total public prat of yourself.
- Echo popular base bigotry and prejudice.
- Attack a loved national institution, elderly royal, cricket, a national war hero.
- Marry someone forty years your junior/senior.
- Get kidnapped/arrested/shot at/or get publicly drunk abroad.
- Make a pass at anyone who is not your partner.
- Attack your own party.
- Die in mysterious circumstances (preferably involving sex).

Dealing with tabloid journalists is like wrestling with cobras. They all have cruel, small eyes and twisted mouths. Their trade is treachery. Cultivate a permanent state of trembling fear in their presence. A witness at hand plus a running tape recorder are worthwhile defence weapons. Never expect 'off the record' pleas to be respected. After long and bitter experience, Tony Benn records all his conversations with them. Their stories are dominated by the political priority of their proprietors and editors and only marginally influenced by the facts.

It's like sex. Nobody tells the truth.

Broadsheet journalists follow the theme of the day. By a process of osmosis they jointly decide the issue and the line of the moment. The process is irrational, driven by herd and lemming instincts. The motive is self-protection. Brilliantly, they all reach the same conclusion. Nobody is left out. Nobody is wrong. If the conclusion of the day suits you, babble away. If not, don't waste time. They will not be convinced that there is an alternative truth.

Local journalists need their local MP, especially in the present hard times. The Member needs them in an inverse ratio to the size of the majority. The best relationships are founded on shared trust and respect. It's worth working together for both sides.

Recently, many quality local papers have plunged down-market. Their tabloid front pages repeatedly carry harrowing pictures of dying children, scarred crime victims or nuns with cheques for a bleeding heart cause. Tailor your press statement to appeal to their new tabloid standards. Some new regional journalists are reared in special veal crates in an alien land. Their restricted diet contains no nutrition for brain development. One hack relates how his eye-witness story of the start of the Gulf War was interrupted by a request from the news editor of a south Wales paper: 'Not bad Mike, but what is the connection with Gwent?'

The demands of the electronic media are all-embracing. MPs should strive to do interviews on their own terms. Be grateful when 5 per cent of listeners or viewers get the message. But they all will notice if you are out of breath, have untidy or dishevelled hair, or a twisted tie or dress. There is no time to be professionally made up for all Westminster interviews. The well-organised, modern MP of either sex packs a handy make-up kit. Those who are colour-blind or have eccentric tastes should ask a friend to match their tie, shirt and suit.

Drag adverse criticism of media performances out of friends. Irritating voices, constant repetitions of meaningless expressions, distracting gestures – all must be identified and corrected. Trade Minister Jonathan Evans in a brief interview on *Newsnight* used the vacuous phrase 'In point of fact' to bridge the gaps between his thoughts six times. It was hypnotic stuff. The nation, deaf to his message, waited for the seventh boot to drop.

I was given my further education in media relations when I employed a researcher who had previously worked for megastar Tony Banks. Unexpectedly, I was in great demand on a Tuesday morning. In commanding style she marshalled the interview slots. She bullied the press to do her bidding to get maximum coverage for the campaign message. 'If you want an interview you must bring a crew up to Westminster,' she told BBC *Breakfast Time*. 'No, he cannot possibly come down to White City. If you want him that's what you have to do. There was no trouble fixing things with GMTV.' It worked. A crew and live link were sent at the peak viewing time of 8.10 a.m. as demanded.

That episode almost washed from my memory a day ruined by an inexperienced researcher. She booked me a rambling interview with an obscure hospital radio station. Many of the maximum of 100 listeners were asleep, too infirm to remove their headphones or dead. The following day she said that someone else wanted an interview. Compassionately, she had given precedence to the hospital radio: 'I think the other one's name was Jon Snow, from a television programme.'

Lacing humour with a serious subject can be ruinous. A joke by Labour's spokesperson on women, Janet Anderson, that women would be more promiscuous 'under Labour' went nuclear. In a tedious, hour-long interview in Welsh about drugs, I said that magic mushrooms could be legally cultivated and exported when fresh, but became a Class A drug if stored over-night. The comment was never broadcast but was press-released a month later by the producers to suggest I was advocating new drug-exporting entrepreneurs. Understandably, the media were hooked and hysterical.

On another occasion, I thought I had a landed a small coup when I was seated next to Tony Blair's blue sky thinker at a dinner, but I ended up upstaging myself. Lord Birt had been forbidden to give evidence to PASC while he was working for the strategy unit. 'Now that I've retired,' he told me 'I can come along.' I was eager to question him on Blair's rejection of the strategy unit's condemnation of the Government's drugs prohibition policy. Alas, his appearance taught us nothing. He gave a master class in jargon-clogged obfuscation. I read him some extracts from a leaked report on drugs. There was no worthwhile response except to confirm that the Government lacked the bottle to back the strategy unit's conclusions. In some desperation I asked, 'If Blairism ever becomes a religious cult, do you think you will be its Pope?' None of the press reports mentioned drugs. All reported Blair's papal ambitions. It was my fault for upstaging my serious purpose with a flippant one.

How to Write for the Papers

The *Votingham Argus* may well appreciate a regular column. It can be a very useful conduit to the constituents but secondary to other media.

It does not always work. Nicholas Bennett (Pembrokeshire 1983–87) wrote probably a record four weekly columns for constituency newspapers. Nevertheless, he lost his seat with a huge swing against him. Overexposure may have incited anxiety among his constituents.

Ask for payment, even a microscopic one. Otherwise bread is taken out of the mouths of underpaid local hacks. Personal tax must be paid on fees. The rest should be channelled into a local charity or a fund for charitable donations. The cash must be declared in the Members' Interests book. Pocketing it is not worth the resentment aroused. It is helpful to explain that there is no personal profit from the articles. Genuinely cash-strapped papers sometimes claim they cannot afford the pittance demanded. I was paid for many years for a column I wrote for a paper in a neighbouring constituency. They passed the job over to an MP who represented their city and promptly ended the modest payments on the grounds of poverty. I strongly advised the Member to continue the link with his flock and make clear to the journalists the basis on which he was working.

David Taylor wrote columns weekly for three local papers. He wrote engagingly and skilfully on national and Leicestershire life. He won an enviable rapport with his constituents. He always refused payments. David had a winning technique: he selected a readable formula. He avoided a slab of words and worked on the assumption that while all newspaper readers take in the headlines, only 1 per cent read the thousand-word features. He divided the contributions into word morsels of minimum length. Four or five short items of less than 150 words were perfect.

There are other ways to make columns worthwhile. Insist on an attractive format on a well-read page. Push for illustrations and write with an eye for photo opportunities. The Commons supplies dozens of chances for a newsworthy picture every week. Even a picture of a visiting school party or pensioners' group is of interest in Votingham. The most unattractive pictures are those with a line-up of smiling faces. Do something that's visually interesting. Jump up in the air, climb a tree, sit on the top of a post box. If a boring line-up is unavoidable, it's worth taking the far left position with a small group. That will give prominence to your name as papers invariably list names left to right. This is dangerous in large groups, though, where the extremities may be cropped.

Always be alert to your surroundings. An election campaign for London Mayor with Frank Dobson serves as a cautionary tale. A cunning new Labour wheeze had been planned. Tony Blair was to be photographed flanked by the candidates for Mayor and Deputy Mayor, Frank Dobson and Trevor Phillips, in front of a statue named *London Pride* – the work of a sculptor also named Frank Dobson. Tony Blair panicked, sensing a potential gaffe. He refused to allow the salivating photographers to take any pictures with the statue in the background. The photographers protested. They had their stepladders in place. Tony moved the photo shoot to the nearby tube station. *London Pride* is a bronze nude with full breasts at head height to the trio. Blair feared that the tabloids would caption the picture: 'Blair and his pair of tits.'

A creative photographer once conned John Redwood into moving to a precise spot for a portrait taken from knee height. 'A little to the left sir, now to the right, that's perfect. Hold that. Click.' The result was a beautifully composed Redwood head with two curved street light fittings projecting from his head like the antennae on the creature from the planet Zog.

An MP's column that is a weekly diet of party political diatribe will be as unwelcome to the editor as it will be indigestible to the readers. Confine columns to a maximum of a fifth hard political argument. The bulk of the pieces should be irresistible tasters of parliamentary gossip, jokes, consumer items and news of Votingham events.

Rarely is it worthwhile to write speculatively for the national press. Nearly all articles are pre-arranged with the features editor. If an idea for a feature is rejected, it is sensible to accept an offer to print a letter instead. The letters pages are well read. Many national papers employ letter editors who canvas for letters to balance reporting. It's worth building a relationship with them. They will e-mail their subjects and deadlines and an e-mail by return will guarantee 100 words of wisdom that will be widely seen. It's quick, instant and will be read by millions.

Papers with political agendas court MPs who are at odds with their parties. The *Daily Express* and the *Sun* invited me to write articles on education when I had a disagreement with my party. Never before had they shown even a vestigial interest in any of my views. They both refused to give me any control of cuts in the article or of the illustrations, pictures or headlines that would accompany it. They could and almost certainly would have distorted my words by their presentation into an attack on my party. Money was offered. It was no deal without my control.

The *Sunday Times* has repeatedly trapped the innocent or Parliamentary wannabes into writing self-damaging articles. Their technique is to persuade someone on the right or left extremes of the parties to write something outrageous. MPs on the opposite wing are invited to be provoked. The paper then has an article inside and a front page story on a new party split. Some recent pieces have been placed after being written by anonymous researchers, then topped and tailed with a sentence from a would-be rising star.

For three successive Saturdays, a political hack at the *Sunday Times* invited me to rage in pieces on Labour being 'no longer socialist' and 'no longer taxing the rich'. I declined to give them a story about party splits. Others did not. A variation in January 1996 was an invitation for me to write an article on Midwitch Socialists. It was a 'Fable for our Times' that I had previously described in a column in the Welsh language magazine *Golwg*. They sent a former editor of the 'Insight' feature to Parliament to persuade me. I asked whether they would contact Labour's spin doctors on the day before publication and invite them to denounce me and my fable. His dumb response confirmed that the *Sunday Times* were playing the same game as ever. Beware.

Usually the role is reversed and it is MPs seeking outlets for articles. Hundreds of specialist magazines are readily accessible markets for campaigning material. They should not be neglected.

The painful labour of creative writing is never wasted. There is no better method of organising thoughts. Unpublished tracts can be recycled as questions, letters and speeches.

How to Broadcast

Availability is the key to success. BlackBerries or iPads that silently vibrate and alert have now become essential for contacts.

The instant needs of broadcasters are met when they can lasso the meandering Member anywhere.

In answer to the increasingly defensive and evasive skills of politicians, interviewers have grown more aggressive. Try a trial interview with a friend beforehand, preferably one with journalistic skills. Explore the weaknesses in your case and prepare defences.

Ask how long your broadcast contribution is expected to be. Divide the answer by three. Pack your message into the resulting number of seconds. Ten seconds of a quietly delivered sentence in which every word glows will hit the spot. A whole minute of rushed, garbled generalities will miss the target.

Number Four Millbank and the Atrium in Portcullis House are now the temples of Parliament's electronic media. It spreads itself into the adjoining green areas when weather permits. The Central Lobby is a superbly accessible, all-weather location, grudgingly provided by the Commons authorities. Parliament is still reluctant to give greater access in the palace to studios, which would be a boon, especially to Members with disabilities.

The time values for electronic media:

15 secs on main television news bulletin =

40 secs on the Radio 4 *Today* programme =

3 mins on *Newsnight* =

10 mins on networked BBC/IRN local radios =

30 mins on *Radio Five Live* =

60 mins on single regional television station =

1 hours on Talk Radio/Radio One =

6 months on single local radio =

2 eternities on Votingham Hospital Radio

Try to do a less important interview first. Your message will sharpen with each interview.

How to Bargain Fees

Don't, except where MPs' work displaces that of hacks. The media is the binding force between the Member and the constituents. In a modern democracy it is essential that the link is close and constant. The once popular haggling over fees implies that MPs refuse to perform if the fee is too low. There may be justification for this in entertainment shows. For news and information programmes, MPs should not profit for doing the job for which they have already been paid.

Those who argue that MPs' pay needs to be supplemented are often the same ones that vote against any salary increases. Backdoor bargaining demeans the status of parliamentarians and is an impediment to open communication. What is legitimate is payment of small 'disturbance' fees for out of pocket expenses, and fees for items where scripts need to be prepared.

Politicians do tout for cash. When I took part in Channel 4's *The Great Pot Debate* one of the MPs on the panel of four parliamentarians told me that he had refused to appear without a fee of £100. 'You'll all be getting the same – thanks to me,' he boasted.

Andrew Roth reported that a senior MP's secretary had demanded £160 for two broadcasts on LBC. Roth quotes her as saying, 'He only undertakes interviews for payment and certainly the BBC, ITV and Sky pay up.' That may explain why he was rarely seen on the box.

BBC fees are often immutable. From 1986 to 1994 I took part in a BBC Radio Wales programme called *The Critics*. A fee was sensible. A few hours' work was involved in researching three subjects and preparing a script. For eight years the fee remained the same at £44. Producers' control of budgets mean that the BBC rarely pay fees at all for new items and sometimes pay a small amount when scripts are necessary. To rebuild public trust it's unwise to use fees for personal purposes.

A reliable gauge is the bigger the audience the smaller the fee. Radio Four's *Today* programme is top for influence and pays nothing. No fee is paid for the *Jeremy Vine Show* or the main television bulletins. Curiously, the last fee I received in 2011 was for a religious programme. The wages of virtue.

How to Dress

Unobtrusively for males. Your clothes should not upstage your words. A 'besuited image that's male, pale and stale' was Billy Bragg, the pop star's, verdict on the image of MPs.

Kevin Brennan asked the Leader of the House if he could institute a dress-down day for all MPs. He was advised that it was 'open to Members to come to the Chamber in whatever attire they choose, provided it is seemly and decent and consistent with the Chamber'. Brennan arrived tieless for his first dress-down Thursday and Michael Fabricant, in a point of order said: 'I notice … for the first time in my experience, an MP spoke in the Chamber without a tie. I thought we always used to have to wear a jacket and tie at least.' Dress advice from Michael Fabricant is a bit rich when he wears a dead cat on his head, but the Speaker agreed with Mr Fabricant. Kevin ruefully commented that the Dutch Parliament impressed him with 'their informal atmosphere with no strict dress code.'

Young fogey Thomas Docherty complained that some female MPs had been 'rocking up in a mixture of denim and knee length boots'. Women have always been allowed liberated rules on dress. Docherty must be aghast when Members trot through the lobbies having rushed from the gym or the hairdressers. He opposes a drift to smart casual but has not demanded a return to top hat and tails. Yet.

The most dramatic illustration of clothing eclipsing a speech occurred with one of Parliament's most sober dressers. Toby Jessel was a strictly three-piece suit man and frequently wore a tie with red and green diagonal stripes. It looks like a regimental or an old school tie. His usual dress fault is that his stomach swells to expose a white shirt midriff between his waistcoat and the top of his trousers. He told me he wore an ill-fitting brown suit because he had inherited it from his father.

That is nothing compared to his day of sartorial ignominy. His speeches were delivered in an excited red faced bluster. But it was not his face that riveted the attention of the television audience. The voice-over commentator in hushed tones explained that the speaker was 'Toby Jessel, Conservative, Twickenham'. A few moments later the commentator found it necessary to explain that the object poking out of the flies of Mr Jessel's trousers was the end of his tie. Some of the viewers had never seen a red and green one before.

I asked David Taylor if he was colour blind. He was not. There was no explanation for his wearing a multi-coloured vivid tie with a deep purple shirt. He was unfazed, puzzled at my interest in trivia.

When the TV cameras first appeared in the House, red ties were recommended with blue suits. Led by the late Eric Forth and Austin Mitchell, ties have blossomed into an orgy of wild clashing colours. Eric's included a flash of lightning and a psychedelic exploding tomato. Austin peaks with national flags and a *Baywatch* special. When either spoke there was a murmur of interest. The ties were the topic, not the speeches. The House was far more interested in the flag of Borneo or the artist's wipe rag around their necks. Austin has reverted to sober ties for his twilight years or perhaps he is seeking extra gravitas.

Dennis Canavan intrigued the House with an oddly cut suit that married the styles of Armani and the Nicaragua Sandinistas. It looked like the current uniform used by urban guerrilla warriors. Two stubbornly proletarian jackets were worn for years by Dennis Skinner and Rhodri Morgan. Rhodri wilted under criticism and dumped his mud-spattered effect tweed when he moved to the sartorial elegance of the Welsh Assembly. Dennis is soldiering on with the longest surviving garment in the Chamber. It has become a symbol of unchanging working class solidarity.

Women MPs' clothing raises little excitement even when their colours are audacious and startling. Edwina Currie once sported a heavily shoulder-padded yellow costume indistinguishable from surplus Romanian Securitate uniforms that were on sale in downtown Bucharest at the time. Teresa Gorman had a scintillating yellow and black costume – nature's danger signals. Did this subliminally inspire her nickname of 'Jewelled Wasp'?

Theresa May's eloquence was up-staged by a remarkable outfit that may have been bought from a NASA jumble sale. It was a space outfit although she never wore the helmet. It competed deliciously with her spectacular shoes of many colours. Not all of the 2010 intake are so flamboyant. It's a puzzle why a tiny minority of new Tory MPs, seeking the common touch, dress as Bulgarian street-sweepers.

My spouse questions my qualifications for advising on how to dress. She was once involved in a homeless charity that distributed clothes to rough sleepers. Most of them were looted from my wardrobe. She kindly informed me there was no danger of the rough sleepers being mistaken for an MP. The reverse remains a real possibility.

How to Get Real

A new opportunity to contact the masses or a career-destroying embarrassment? Invitations to take part in TV reality shows are new temptations for the famous or notorious.

Few politicians have benefited from the over-exposure. But I was wrong in the sage advice I offered to my friend Ann Widdecombe. On my blog that was reproduced in the *Mail on Sunday* I pleaded with her to reject the invitation to *Strictly Come Dancing*: 'Throw a sickie. Write a new book. Become a shock-jock. Get thee to a nunnery. Take a holiday. Anything but dancing. You will be patronised and humiliated.' She was not. She became the nation's favourite maiden aunt.

Labour MP Austin Mitchell has said he regrets taking part in a TV show, *Tower Block of Commons*, which he claimed set out to 'humiliate MPs'. The politicians were asked to survive for a week while spending no more than £64.30 – a week's jobseekers' allowance.

After spending only one night in the flat it emerged that Nadine Dorries broke the rules by hiding a fifty pound note down her bra. Dorries's defence was, 'I brought it to get things for the kids. I've got no intention of spending it on me.' Of course.

Living down to their reputation of never being able to escape political bias the *Daily Telegraph* reported,

> While Mrs Dorries explains that she broke the show's rules as an act of charity, Austin Mitchell, the Labour MP and another participant, refused to attempt to live by them. In the first episode viewers saw him bring his wife with him for his council estate stay, demand to keep his wallet and mobile phone, and host a dinner party for his new neighbours with home-made fish pie, red and white wine and a dessert of fruit with creme-fraiche.

Austin Mitchell scoffed at the idea of living on benefits for a week. Mark Oaten was also on the programme. The *Southern Daily Echo* reported a moment Mark was confronted by a group of young people on the estate. The youngster shouts, 'Ain't you the one that got done for rent boys?' Mr Oaten tries to walk away but the youth yells, 'You've got AIDS.' The Winchester MP became distraught.

A Cornish MP defended her decision to follow in the footsteps of fellow MP George Galloway by agreeing to take part in a reality television programme. Lib Dem Julia Goldsworthy said her parliamentary duties would remain 'top priority' during Channel 4's *The Games*. Ms Goldsworthy raised money for Cornwall Air Ambulance during the nine-day show. 'I hope I'm leading by example, showing it is possible to fit a healthy lifestyle into a very busy life. Anything that makes MPs appear more like human beings has got to be a good thing.' She said the show was 'not comparable' to *Big Brother* as she would not be cut off from the outside world. Maybe. But she lost her seat in 2010.

Who can forget George Galloway, when he was still an MP, on *Celebrity Big Brother* – pretending to be a cat in a Lycra all-in-one costume? No one heard the hours of earache he gave to his fellow housemates on serious political issues. They were drowned out by the sound of purring. Lembit Opik's stated purpose in his jungle stay was to help his chances of winning the Lib Dem nomination for the Mayor of London election. His weak attempts at humour failed to win over his jungle buddies or the viewers. He was the second to be thrown out. In the vote for the mayoral candidate he was voted fourth in a list of four.

Too much reality.

How to Say No to the Media

The agendas of hacks and MPs often overlap. But they are still separate. So demanding of the time of MPs is the media that it can seriously detract from the work of a Member. Important as they are, their interests are subservient to those of constituents. The perils of media entrapment and treachery are more severe than ever before.

The late John Straddling-Thomas was an affable raconteur who found life as a minister difficult after happy years as a whip: 'I like to kick arse, not to have mine kicked'. As a senior MP he had a long relationship of trust with journalists. He gave an interview to a tabloid hack and entertained him in a Commons bar. At one point the room emptied, then filled up again fifteen minutes later. John explained that they had been to hear Prime Minister's Question Time but that he did not bother any more. The journalist wrote a piece under the heading of 'Britain's laziest MP'.

There were many other MPs who were far more deserving of that epithet than Straddling-Thomas. But he made the mistake of saying 'yes' and dropping his guard. His career and life of considerable service ended ignominiously. A female journalist once questioned me closely on my practices of securing the first EDM of each session. It meant an early morning. The sneering piece that she wrote painted me as a boring nerd.

One very optimistic television company made me an offer I could refuse. UKTV Gold wanted to kit me out in a suit of armour. I was asked to wear it in the House of the Commons. There is a fourteenth century law that prohibits the wearing of a suit of armour in the Chamber. They could not come up with a single reason why a serious sober MP would justify this piece of tomfoolery. 'It would prove whether the law is still in force,' they suggested. This is not high on the list of priorities of the people of Votingham. I recommended them to a couple of media tarts who might wish to play.

The political agendas of many papers send hacks scurrying in search of damaging quotes from garrulous politicians or those who are off guard. Their techniques are usually crude and obvious but recently they have become more subtle. The hackettes are skilled in incipient honey traps. One young female television interviewer sought to persuade me to say something that was indiscreet, damaging and untrue about Members' expenses. She asked me to imagine that she was a new young female MP asking me as a senior MP how the system worked. Her questions were accompanied by simpering while she sensuously wiggled her rear end. Just a reflex action, I'm sure.

There are no limits to the vanity of the male ego especially when confronted with beautiful women who flatter with their attentiveness. There was probably a look of adoration in the eyes of the *Telegraph* journalists who trapped the canny operator Vince Cable into lacerating indiscretions about the secret weapon he had in his pocket. Six months later Vince's leaks on Murdoch appeared far-sighted. But Vince lost a key role and the relationship between MPs and constituents was damaged. Some have argued that the sting was a breach of privilege because of confidentiality. But, the confidentiality of constituency surgeries exists to protect the constituent, not the MP. Vince Cable spoke for all MPs when he said, 'When somebody who isn't a constituent falsifies their name and address and comes in with a hidden microphone – it completely undermines the whole basis on which you operate as a local MP. All my colleagues, of all parties, feel very strongly that some great damage has been done by this.'

Challenging the mighty *Telegraph* with their expenses-revelation halo glowing would be unwise for MPs deep in our bunker of suspicion and guilt. Hackgate was a new low for the crude newspapers stings. It undermines trust and makes life more irksome and anxious.

All are now on guard against hackable voice-mails and seductive reporters who come bearing flattery.

THE CONSTITUENCY

How to Please Constituents

The best bit of advice I have had so far was to keep a file of all the thank-you cards and letters where I and my team have, through our efforts, helped a situation or a constituent and to look at the file when things don't go the way we would want it to or when we can't get the best result we would like. The worst professional moments are witnessing the pain of others and being impotent to help.

MPs should bond closely with their constituents. The relationship is that of a priest and parishioners, solicitor and clients, shepherd and flock, shop steward and workers and friend of many friends. The MP should be the living embodiment of the constituency, tirelessly promoting and defending the territory with the ferocity of a mother protecting her offspring.

A modern MP must be a creature of the local habitat. Only by living, shopping, sharing local schools and entertainment can the Member fulfil the increasingly vital task as the constituency's ambassador to the centres of power.

Expectations of what an MP can do vary widely. Some constituents write on a weekly basis with their latest thoughts. Others apologetically ring once a decade on matters of life and death. Happily the great majority are reasonable and are satisfied if the Member has tried to help even if there are no improvements to report.

Confidence is built slowly between MP and constituents. Hacks are constantly seeking examples from Members' casebooks to illustrate their stories. Any personal matter raised by a constituent should be protected with the secrecy of the confessional.

How to Allow Ventilation

While MPs are not therapists, we have a clear responsibility to assist the mentally ill constituents who seek our help. We should certainly avoid adding to their anxieties by insensitive rejections or perceived indifference. Deeply embedded delusions may be nourished by an MP's brush-off. It's a godsend to have a staff member with skills in dealing with the mentally ill. As far as practical, they should be allowed to ventilate their fears in harmless ways.

My office fondly remembers one constituent whose illness led to persistent infuriating phone calls and visits. He was highly intelligent and often made serious points. But he believed that his concerns should occupy hours of staff time. On occasions his ramblings had to be firmly brought to a halt because of other pressing work. When his sad, brief life came to a tragic end, we were all relieved that we had listened patiently to his most recent calls and not interrupted him. We were absolved from the responsibility of driving him to his final despair. The many long hours spent dealing with his tortured fears were not wasted.

How to Hide the Address

Most MPs now live in their constituencies. Concealing a home address is entirely legitimate. Even MPs are entitled to reasonable privacy. Their families certainly are. If the address is well known, constituents will call in at any hour of the day. It is not much fun when the neighbourhood arsonist, rapist or a weirdo drops in for a chat late at night. Even less amusing is when the call occurs during the week when the MP is in London and the spouse and children are home alone.

Complaining constituents are often angry and violent, as Jobcentre staff testify by insisting on grills and anonymous name badges. One woman brought her six foot gorilla of a boyfriend to my home and explained to my wife that he had been falsely accused of rape 'again'.

If the home address is well known before the election, there is one choice only – move. Then never tell anyone the new address. Almost daily there will be requests for details of the new home. Many are from people late sending mail trying to steal an extra day in the queue for action. Always refuse. They can gain time by e-mailing.

There is a serious security risk. MPs are still liable to receive letter bombs or other offensive objects from a range of zealots. At Westminster mail is screened. If the new address becomes known, divert all your letters to Westminster. Even during the recess there need be no delay because urgent mail can be e-mailed or faxed by staff.

The only occasion where there is a legal obligation to publish your address is on the nomination forms for your election. It is legitimate to use your London address or your party office in the constituency to circumvent this.

How to Convince Voters that the MP Never Stops Working

Never stop working. The alternative is to organise the day to give the impression of a perpetually-working MP. Offices should be organised to respond immediately to letters and phone calls. Backlogs should be cleared with overtime and no self respecting MP's office has a pending tray. Some staff feel reassured, wanted and indispensable by a pile of un-answered letters in their in-trays. Delaying work is the enemy of efficiency and a 24-hour turn round of all correspondence is attainable.

Modern technology amplifies MPs' work. One letter to the readers' letters page of the *Votingham Argus* can be effortlessly reproduced and sent to hundreds of other papers through the wonders of a database. Constituents with specialised concerns can be clustered into computer nests that can be called up instantly for an update letter on their subject.

Be ubiquitous and ever present in the constituency. The drip feed of blog, tweets, early morning radio interviews that are repeated throughout the day, widely advertised surgeries, and attendance in the Chamber in a camera-exposed position, all propagate the message 'Busy MP'.

Some skilled Gullivers are adept at organising staff to e-mail their views to papers while they are sunning themselves and finding heaps of new facts in a sun-kissed exotic foreign location.

Fallow spells of holidays and rest are essential to maintain and restore *joie de vivre*. MPs are entitled to enjoy family life, especially when the children are young.

How to Run Surgeries

The telephone number, e-mail and House of Commons address should be the only contact points for constituents. Setting up 'Drop in' offices for complaints is a temptation for novice MPs. Few are successful. They attract swarms of complaints that cannot be dealt with by MPs. Inevitably they disappoint those who need help from the Citizens Advice Bureau, Council Office or The Samaritans. So overwhelmed did one high profile MP's town centre constituency office become, the staff lost control and complaints were delayed for months or lost.

There has been a distressing increase in the physical attacks on MPs and staff at surgeries, including the death of one member of staff and the serious stab wounds suffered by an MP. Advice is available from the police on common sense precautions that should be taken. Accusations of molestation or assault is always a possibility and it is dangerous to hold a surgery alone. A witness to your words and action may be required later.

How to Say No

Even the most devoted Member has to reject some requests. Otherwise campaigners, the obsessed, third parties and students will swamp the work of the office and make it unmanageable. The late David Taylor's biography is titled *Clockwinder who wouldn't say no*. He was a great MP whose extraordinary industry built an expectation that attracted a volume of work that came close to being unmanageable by David and his staff. In 2008 he announced that he was standing down because of the 'volume of work'. He was unhappy because he could not live up to his own impossibly high standards. He had taken on the workload of three MPs. It was admirable but ultimately self-defeating.

Expectations have to be damped down. The limited role of the two- or three-person MP's team must be understood by constituents and outside groups that share campaign objectives. Productive relations will collapse if either make unreasonable demands on the other.

A tiny number of constituents and campaigners can hi-jack the attention of the office with a relentless flow of letters and calls. Often they have genuine grievances or are pushing fine causes. Sooner rather than later they must be told firmly that they are destroying goodwill and exasperating staff. Often they have a single all-consuming problem and fail to understand the mass of daily demands on a MP's time.

Only accept complaints from third parties for reason of disability or language interpretation. Data Protection rules require direct consent to be sought from the constituent. Solicitors, agents in ethnic communities and relatives must be told that constituents must contact the MP directly. Tell them that information received second-hand is often inaccurate and incomplete. Some third parties charge for passing cases on. Services provided by an MP must not be subject to a charge of any kind. Even under the iron rule of IPSA, it is still legitimate to spend on publicising as widely as possible the Commons address and all other contact details.

The demands of students for interviews, articles and information are now insatiable. Some ring for a half an hour chat in the middle of a fraught day. Others expect their essays or theses to be written for them. They send lists of questions that would take an hour to answer. A practical policy is to try to answer fully 'seed corn' constituency students and those sympathetic to current campaigns. Articles and Hansard debates should be mass photo-copied and filed in anticipation. They can be easily dispatched.

There is no hope of dealing with non-constituent general inquiries on unfamiliar or exotic subjects. You are the MP for Votingham not the United Kingdom. Say so.

More difficult is refusing invitations that say, 'You've been babbling about it. Come up and see for yourself.' After I had an adjournment debate about the increasing numbers of hip opera-tions that went wrong, a surgeon from Wigan, Mr Wroblewski, invited me to visit. The planned programme was:

9.30 a.m. Watch a hip replacement operation.
11.30 a.m. Watch a revision operation.
1.30 p.m. Lunch.

Lunch? After that lot! Pressure of work forced me to unselfishly delegate the trip to a researcher.

Blackmailing charity invitations are the most difficult to turn down. 'Well, what would you have done?' John Marshall asked me, 'if they said they would give £200 to your favourite charity to do it?' when I pulled his leg about a picture of him. 'Reach for your cheque book, John,' I suggested.

That morning there was a glorious photograph of John on the front page of the *Independent*. He was wearing a sunflower hat, a flower patterned hooped dress, carrying a parasol and holding a lead attached to a sheep named Gwendolyn. The deal was cash for charity if John dressed up as Little Bo Peep and walked across Tower Bridge with Gwendolyn. MPs can make fools of themselves without the help of outside bodies. It is not part of the job to be a hired clown even for good causes.

As Lembit Opik discovered, humiliation sticks.

How to Be a Conduit

A central task is to be the channel through which the fears and hopes of all constituency groups are directed to Government.

Industry, the NHS, the Police, charitable bodies, community groups, all rightly claim that their cases must be heard at the top level. There is no discretion. Their best interests must be served.

Every sizeable organisation in the constituency deserves at least one visit per parliament. The resulting detailed knowledge is essential. Mutual trust and confidence should be built. The products of local firms must be vigorously promoted in every parliamentary arena. Local life should be celebrated. Most success owes a great deal to hype. All facets of life in Votingham from local charities, local government successes, pop groups, innovative products, tourist locations, any aspect of local life of quality or distinction, must be shamelessly and tirelessly sold. Before the visit, prepare to discuss issues where the MP can provide practical advice. Wide ranging social discussions are enjoyable, but hard facts and detailed briefing equip the MP for future crises.

The conduit must be wide open for immediate two way contact with telephones and e-mails, to deal with unexpected events.

How to Find the Silent Voices

A widespread delusion of many MPs is that the concerns of constituents are fairly represented in messages received or day-to-day contact. They are not.

MPs resent being told that they should 'get out more and meet ordinary people'. Aren't they always out meeting everybody? Yes, but they far more likely to meet the police chief than a constable, or to be on buddy terms with the editor of a local paper rather than his van drivers or paper sellers. The chair of the NHS Trust writes regularly but no word from a hospital cleaner. Meals are in the directors' suite rather than the works canteen. Seductively, the single patrician dominates our thoughts to the exclusion of the hundred plebeians.

Never visit a school, police station or business without talking to the canteen workers, the cleaners and the caretaker. They deserve more time than the headteacher, the managing director or the chief of police. They have more to say and are more likely to be truthful. Those who write, phone or attend surgeries are predominantly the well informed, the articulate or the fanatics. Usually the voices of the fearful, the downcast or the illiterate are silent.

Half a million pensioners in Britain do not take up their welfare benefits. Often because of ignorance of the system. They are weakly motivated. There are also many others who never contact their MPs. It's essential to undertake a rigorous regular stock-take of office priorities. Has a disproportionate amount of the time and energy of the MP and team been hijacked, bullied or pressurised into wrong directions? Has reacting to invitations, requests and media demands distorted the workload to the detriment of those in greatest need of an MP's work? Has the value of the activity advanced or retreated because of hostility from vested interests, the media or cowardice?

Falling into a reactive routine enfeebles and demoralises the work of Members and staff. Ideals must be rediscovered. New contacts initiated. Ideas refreshed and invigorated. Shock therapy must jump start the paralysis of routine.

One morning, I received an invitation to a luxury, champagne-drenched bash from lobbyists for British Airways. That day's headline in the *Western Mail* was about abused children in a residential home. They said: 'We didn't know who to complain to.'

How to Sympathise

A highly successful councillor in my constituency was taken to task by a constituent. He said that his vote was going elsewhere. The reason was unexpected. 'You didn't come to my father's funeral,' the constituent complained. The councillor expressed his sympathy and asked whether he knew the deceased. 'No, you didn't know him but neither did the other candidate. But he turned up at the funeral.' This was perplexing. Are council candidates expected to haunt funerals with feigned regret at the deaths of complete strangers? The councillor did not change his habits. He was elected. His opponent lost.

In 1962 I received a message of congratulation on my marriage from the late Raymond Gower, then MP for Barry. He was renowned as a diligent constituency MP with a large personal vote. By today's standards the message was woeful. It was a crude impersonal Gestetnered pro-forma offering 'Congratulations on your birthday/anniversary/birth of the baby/marriage/examination success/bar mitzvah.' The MP had made the appropriate deletions and signed the form.

The information had been gleaned from the 'Hatched, Matched and Dispatched' pages of the local paper. He had an alternative pro-forma expressing sympathy for bereavement. The process was universal but sometimes poorly targeted. The evidence is that these notes worked. Raymond Gower's personal vote was genuine and large. Similar tactics now would be mocked as amateurish. They are also accident prone. Lists of ex-patients from local hospitals were sent 'Get well soon letters'. Some had been in for operations that they wanted to keep quiet. Others had died.

Nevertheless, when sympathy is heartfelt MPs should pass on their thoughts. Sincerity will shine through, especially with a handwritten message. When the family or the deceased is known personally great pains should be taken writing an individual letter. It is an important part of the job and can also aid the healing process for the bereaved.

When other terrible events occur that have a political dimension, deference and restraint must be paramount. The relatives should be approached, if at all, with care and tenderness. Those MPs who leap to wring political advantage from tragedy are the vultures of Westminster.

How to Nourish the Seed Corn

For unfathomable reasons loyalty is given at a tender age to favourite football teams, pop stars and political parties. Often the devotion is life-long. Part of the job is to ensure that Votingham fledglings are attracted to the correct causes.

Schools welcome visits from the local Member. Least useful is a booming stage presence at prize day, spraying pompous pieties to resentful fidgeting audiences. To clear the conduit of information from student to MP and back again, there must be an exchange of ideas.

Vocabulary is a prime obstacle. The difference between primary school talk and House of Commons talk is comparable to the gulf between Oxford English and rap. Big variations in language and understanding exist even between year groups.

The best way of connecting with the children is to induce them to talk freely. Then try to join in on their wavelength. A good format is to play House of Commons. Find out what issues divide them. Which pop group is best? Is fox hunting OK? Should animal experiments be allowed? Should polluters be jailed?

Select a talkative advocate for and against and set up a mini debate. The MP grabs the theatrical role by acting as Speaker and booming 'Order, Order!' frequently. The pantomime of baying and grunting in Commons style instead of clapping is quickly learned and enjoyed.

Table a simple motion, allow a free debate from the class after the main speakers. Insist on a vote. This is a fine lesson in democracy plus the chance of dropping embryonic political truths. The kids love it. A benign message is taken home to the voting parents.

Teachers enjoy sending painstakingly prepared letters and pictures from every member of a class. Encourage it as a useful channel of information. They are glorious campaigning and heart winning opportunities. It is worth devoting a few hours to write fully tailored replies to each letter. They will be joyously received and read many times by parents and relatives.

The seed corn is prepared for a future harvest.

How to Switch On Young Voters

To most young people MPs are expenses-fiddling, cynical, rich, antique lechers who hail from the planet Zog. Many young people have long had their brains marinated by rock and hip-hop. They believe politics is a hideous novocaine for the senses delivered in an alien tongue. For others there are promising developments with starter politics of school councils leading to the heights of the Youth Parliament. Tuition fees have politicised a new generation. The over-reaction of the police to their tuition fee demonstrations has heightened that interest into what may be a lifelong passion.

There is still a gulf between the generations that is difficult to bridge. The most absurd politicians are those who preach to the young on the evils of today's drug and drink culture. From the terrace, sexagenarian MPs can be witnessed denouncing the evils of drug use while holding a whisky in one hand, a cigarette in the other and a couple of paracetamol in their pocket for their daily headache.

Few have ever tried to penetrate the youth culture that often revolves around drugs. Most youngsters are extremely well informed on the character of illegal drugs. They know that many are less toxic and addictive than the legal drugs consumed on an orgiastic scale in the Palace of Westminster.

Intelligent communication between MPs and young people is possible only after mind twisting adjustments. MPs first have to undergo disturbing questioning of their own mental omnipotence before alien youthful ideas can be absorbed.

Local pop culture can be usefully hyped through the Westminster publicity megaphone. If it is a promising source of local jobs and pride, the MPs should promote it. It is unwise and dangerous to affect an implausible liking for contemporary music or mores. Sergeant Bilko lookalike, balding Michael Neubert told Parliament that he swapped places with his daughter for a day. She worked as the MP. He pranced and yelped as a disc jockey at the local rock club. It's hard to imagine a less convincing DJ. The Lib Dem MP Norman Lamb is an unconvincing devotee of a musical extravagance called 'grime'. By far the most entertaining Commons link with popular music is the magnificent group MP4 which stars the multi-talented Kevin Brennan (Labour, guitar), Ian Cawsey (Labour, bass/vocals), Pete Wishart (SNP, keyboards) and Greg Knight (Conservative, drums). They have become the acceptable, fun face of Parliament, unrecognisable from the current stereotypical sour image.

That continues to be the high point. The lowest ever was a filmed chorus of MPs who had been press-ganged into singing 'Stand by Me', backing real superstar Ben E. King. Alan Meale was the gang-master who pressed us into service on the Terrace. Our version of the song went viral. Radio One rang me saying they were thinking of broadcasting our MP chorus. They asked me to sing a few bars. I obliged. 'We'll let you know,' they lied.

I developed a mutually mocking relationship with a Newport hip hop group Goldie Lookin' Chain. They gained vast publicity for their brand of outrageous chutzpah. They are engaging, literate and clever but also verbally outrageous. I rejoice in the title of their Spiritual Father. One member of the group has penetrated real politics and is an aspirant candidate for the local council.

But there other more fruitful links with the young. It is

encouraging to find that enthusiasm for animal welfare is still strong among teenagers and environmental concerns have won new followers in the past ten years. These are still the strongest contacts across the generation chasm.

Middle-aged and elderly MPs should cauterise their nerve endings and witness some youth culture. Without patronising, middle-aged MPs can show that they are familiar with the young world with an intelligent working knowledge of YouTube, Twitter and Facebook. But there are limits. Gordon Brown's misjudged foray into YouTube with his forced rictus smile is an object lesson in communicating a bad impression.

The splendid 2010 intake of MPs has shifted the centre of gravity to the young. There is a wealth of talent and beauty. The new image of politics is the chiselled features of a male Adonis or three plus the beautiful brunette Labour and blonde Tory goddesses. Politics is on the way to becoming attractive and sexy again.

How to Run a Rough Tour

For the coach parties of visitors from Votingham to Parliament, facilities have improved. For the rich, articulate and privileged, the welcome is sumptuous. For the coaches of constituency groups, often pensioners and school children, the visit to their Parliament is a once in a lifetime treat. Only very recently have they been sheltered from the weather in the queue outside. Toilet facilities are better. Smart, friendly tour guides show guests around, and the Jubilee Cafe offers welcoming cups of tea and snacks, albeit at tourist prices. But large parties cannot visit the Terrace. During recess the building is opened up to paying visitors with tours available in a variety of languages.

In spite of all, a visit is a wonderful experience and greatly enjoyed. The MP should ensure that arrangements go smoothly. Prepare a letter to send to all enquirers to blow away some of the illusions and provide some practical advice.

It is a foolish underuse of the time, and more importantly the energy of an MP, to act routinely as a guide on a tour. One MP was advised that pleasing visitors was the best way of winning electoral support. He welcomed the coach parties at the Victoria Tower and photographed them. Often he conducted the tour of the palace. In the afternoon he acted as a guide on the mike on a bus tour of London. He finally distributed copies of their souvenir photographs. Constituents may have questioned whether they had a MP or a tour guide. His enthusiasm may have been counter-productive with voters opting to allow him to become a full time tour guide.

The maximum allowed per guide, including MPs, is sixteen. Two thirds of a coach party of forty-eight will be antagonised when only a third of them have the joy of the five star guide spiel.

Sometimes because of cock-ups or with small parties, the MP or staff must take over. Don't repeat the common mistake of professional guides. They wake up sweating in the early hours of the morning worrying because they have forgotten an historical fact or a date.

Parties of tired, foot-sore constituents need the stimulus of jokes and excitement. Sometimes they are crushed down with slabs of incomprehensible, indigestible facts and dates.

Big Ben

Trips up Big Ben are oversubscribed and booking requires patience. It's a great experience with thrilling views from the clock face. Tours take place Monday – Friday at set times of 9.15 a.m., 11.15 a.m. and 2.15 p.m. Space is very limited and advanced booking is essential. There are 334 spiral stone steps with only a small respite. The tours are free of charge and one of London's best visitors bargains.

Rough Guide, or the Only Bits People Remember

While tours are normally run by the trained guides, an MP is occasionally called on to do the business.

The proper name for this marvellous place is The Palace of Westminster. It is divided into three parts.

Up above this massive stone ceiling is the Victoria Tower. It dominates the first part, the Royal Chambers. The middle part is the Lords and thirdly, the Commons. Remember the three parts. Royal, colour Gold; Lords, Red; Commons, Green. You'll notice when we pass from the Lords to the Commons, even the carpet changes colour.

Robing Room. We are following the footsteps of the Queen when she opens Parliament. This magnificent room has one purpose only. It is used once a year by the Queen to change her dress. All the interior was designed by Augustus Pugin. Everything. The ceilings, furniture, ash trays. He went completely mad and died at the age of forty.

The sharp-eyed can spot the Queen's lavatory. It's the door hidden as part of the panelling in the top right hand corner of the room. The door handle is visible. The lozenges in the ceiling (that's really what they are called) have the initials VR on them. This is the first evidence that Queen Victoria's Consort Albert chaired the committee responsible for the redecoration of the place after the fire in 1834. He seized every chance to give his wife a plug.

Gallery. This Royal Gallery is used as a corridor for the Queen when she is kitted out for the procession. She walks down the middle here, with some unfortunate in front of her walking backwards carrying a big key on a cushion. I believe he's called the Silver Stick-in-Waiting.

The other purpose of the room is to embarrass foreign visitors. The two paintings are of Waterloo and Trafalgar. When the President of France visited, he was received here. It was to rub his nose in the memories of our two British victories.

The artist Daniel Maclise had a bit of wife trouble when he was painting these huge pictures. 'Not off up to Westminster again

tonight, with your old painting, leaving me on my own with kids.'
To console her he painted her into the picture. She's the nurse.
Her name 'Polly' appears on the seal of the water pitcher.

The Lord's Chamber. All the gorgeous red and gold in the Lord's
Chamber has grown even more gaudy over the years as their
powers declined. A good rough guide to understanding this place
is that the more glorious the decoration the Chambers have, the
less the power is wielded there.

When the Queen delivers the speech the Prime Minister has
written for her, she, and her family and the Lords sit. Members
of the Commons have to stand in that tiny sheep pen at the back.
Things have become more democratic. At one time, when the
monarch spoke, the Lords stood and Members of the Commons
had to kneel.

The short red curtains in front of the seats in the public gallery
are recent. They were introduced when the twenties flappers wore
short skirts. The noble lords could not concentrate enough to
legislate. The view of all that bare flesh set off a few heart attacks
among them. It was been even worse in the age of the mini skirt.

Central Lobby. This is the centre of the building – the intersection
of the cross is in the middle of the Central Lobby. Behind is the
red of the Queen's throne in the Lords. In an exact straight line is
the green of the Speaker's chair in the Commons. Here everyone
is entitled to come to 'lobby' their MP.

The best part of the Central Lobby is the ceiling. The quickest
way of getting to know the place is by remembering the reason for
the location of the pictures of the four saints.

St Patrick for Ireland is over St Stephen's chapel which is the
main exit from the building. He is there because the Irish have
long been uncertain whether they want to stay in this Parliament.
The English suffer from the delusion that they are better than
everyone else. So St George is positioned above the route to the

Lords. St Andrew for Scotland is placed over the road to the Strangers' Bar, the Smoke Room (Bar) and the Peers Bar. St David (Dewi Sant) bestrides the line to the Commons Debating Chamber because all Welsh people speak so beautifully. There are other versions of this story.

Members' Lobby. The Members' Lobby is the forum of Parliament. When divisions are being held, it is full of hundreds of chattering MPs. During the day journalists and MPs group together, to gossip, plot and tell tales usually about other journalists and MPs. Anything said here is on lobby terms and its source must not be revealed.

The mark on the door is where Back Rod hits it after it is slammed in his face when he summons the MPs to 'attend the Queen in the House of Peers'. In the attendant's box nearby is a shelf where a box of snuff is placed every day. No MP has been a regular user since the late Nicholas Fairbairn in 1997. The cost then was eighty-seven pence a year to the exchequer. It remains as a neglected relic.

Commons Chamber. The first thing we see as we go into the Commons Chamber is this huge bag. Petitions are put in when the House is in session. Hence, the expression 'It's in the bag'. It is locked when visitors are going through because the attendants are tired of fishing out the crisp packets and chocolate wrappers passing visitors dump in it.

That huge spreading wooden canopy on top on the Speaker's chair is no accident. The reason it is that shape is because there was once a rail with curtains running around the woodwork above the chair. At that time there was only one Speaker, and he had to remain in the chair for very long periods. If he (and it was always 'he') was absent, the House was no longer in session.

The Speakers will tell you that the curtains were drawn across for privacy when the 'Speaker's Chop' was brought in. In those days he certainly needed to eat on the job. But the sight was unlikely to have distressed the Members. They were not that fastidious. The real reason for drawing the curtains was so the Speaker could use the commode that was then built into the chair. On those occasions, it was customary to cheer.

Anyone crossing these two red lines in the carpet when speaking to the House will be howled down with shouts of 'Order'. It's a nasty experience. The lines are two sword lengths plus one foot apart. They were necessary when Members were all armed with pig stickers. The green space in the middle is still the parliamentary battlefield's no persons' land.

The little dent on the Prime Minister's Dispatch Box was supposed to have been made by Winston Churchill – banging his fist down and knocking the wood with his ring. The same story was told about Asquith.

St Stephen's Hall. This was once a chapel. That is the reason MPs bow in the direction of the Speaker, even when he's not in the chair. They are bowing to the Blessed Sacrament that was kept in the same place in the chapel. The crack in the sword and the missing spur on the Falkland statue shows the damage caused releasing a suffragette who had chained herself to it.

Westminster Hall. This is the oldest and grandest part of the building. The walls were built nine hundred years ago. It was saved twice from fire while other parts of the palace were left to burn.

Charles I was tried here. He suffered an extra cruelty at the trial when his spaniel lap dog was taken away from him. It was his comforter. Without it he stuttered. Charles II took his revenge by digging up Cromwell's body and displaying his head over the great North Door. It stayed there for eighteen years until it was blown down in a gale.

In the last century, a Fenian bomb was carried by a policeman from the crypt steps into the middle of the hall. It blew out the

South window and made a crater in the floor. After the IRA bomb damaged the wooden roof in the seventies, workers discovered leather tennis balls in the beams. They are thought to have been lost by Henry VIII when he played royal tennis here.

How to See Off Challengers for the Seat

The country is full of aspirant MPs. It is possible to become neurotic about pretenders to your temporary throne. In times of party decline in the polls, fellow MPs nervously plot chicken runs. Boundary changes are a constant threat. They destroy majorities and break umbilical links with well served constituents.

It is unwise to expect local parties to act reasonably in their selections. Experience tells a tale of irrational choices. Faithful, talented, hard-working Members have been ditched in favour of slothful rogues.

Working well and avoiding scandal are only the start of becoming superglued to the parliamentary seat. The local party must be subjected to relentless wooing between elections. Last minute attempts to win over neglected, resentful constituents will be brushed off. Good works are not enough. The good news must be immodestly and continuously conveyed to the Votingham party.

Every conceivable boundary change should be anticipated. Neighbouring constituency parties should be cultivated as possible future inhabitants of redrawn constituency boundaries. Aspirant favourite daughters and sons in the constituency should be respected and never underestimated. Sitting Members have been cast into the wilderness as punishment for their delusions of adequacy or permanence.

One Tory association tried to give their venerable Member a gentle heave-ho in 1986. In 1982 he had been selected with a narrow majority promising that it would be his last term. To cement the pledge the party held a valedictory dinner in his honour a full year before the next election.

It was a sumptuous evening. As the whisky and wine flowed the tributes to the gallant and hardworking Member became fulsome. 'Whatever happens, we could never have again such a wonderful constituency MP'. 'Hear! Hear!'. 'Not only a politician, but a distinguished scientist and a brave soldier ... a wonderful, wonderful MP.' 'Hear! Hear! Hear!'

The guest of honour was genuinely moved and deeply inebriated. His was the final speech. Tears ran down his cheeks. 'My dear, dear friends. I had no idea how much you appreciated my work. It would be treachery if I deserted you now. I will not. I promise I will be your candidate in the General Election.' They all cheered.

In the sober light of day the awful truth dawned. They were stuck with him for another parliament. He had to be prised out eventually with a knighthood and a hint of a place in the Lords in exchange for a promise not to stand again. The peerage never happened.

In all parties there are sad cases of Members who refuse to acknowledge the toll of the years on their bodies and minds. Many have to be pushed because their best friend did not tell them that it was time to jump. For all there is a time to go with decorum and goodwill.

How to Stay Married/Single

In the sexual stakes Parliament fails to live down to its image.

Inevitably, there must be some sexual activity. It is unavoidable where several thousands of sexually active people, separated from their spouses, live jowl by cheek for long periods of the day. No doubt there are furtive encounters in parliamentary offices when resistance levels are falling and testosterone levels are rising. Some serial seducers of both sexes roam the corridors. But rampant lechery is still uncommon. Exhaustion is an effective bromide for the great majority of parliamentarians.

The prime motive for parliamentary infidelity is the divergence of interests between partners created by parliamentary work. The good MP must be deeply absorbed in work. If those interests are not shared by the partner, divisions in the relationship appear and widen dangerously.

More relationships are wrecked by the excessive demands of the parliamentary workload than by the insistent demands of the loins. Relationships are secure and strong if there is shared dedication to the work of the MP. Making your spouse your secretary is the best way to avoid the disruption and heartache of making your secretary your spouse.

Rumours abound of pressures on single Conservative MPs to marry. After one messy scandal it was alleged by one inventive backbencher that a planeload of lobotomised nuns had landed at Heathrow. They had been trained to say in seven languages, 'I will stand by my husband however he humiliates me.' It was claimed that the plan was to line them up in the Commons crypt so that unmarried Tory MPs could select their brides. The whips would be standing shotgun.

At least one MP in the 1987–92 parliament bemoaned his loveless marriage which had been urged upon him by puritanically nervous whips frightened that a scandal would imperil his marginal seat. He related how he had been pressured to 'marry at all costs'. Do women really agree to marriage on these terms? In this case, apparently yes. In the event the couple lost out twice because Labour won the seat in 1992.

The Tory whips were the last repository of homophobia in the House. Labour frontbencher Chris Smith and Tory backbencher Michael Brown 'came out' without any harmful results. In the eighties two other openly gay MPs were involved in a mild public scandal in Germany. One of them unashamedly flaunted his homosexuality and regularly entertained young men in the Commons bars. There was no perceptible effect on their successful parliamentary careers. They were re-elected with increased majorities. Both are now dead.

Homosexual ex-lobbyist Ian Greer has claimed that there are fifty homosexual MPs still hiding in the closet. As a mathematical probability that is likely. But who cares? The House is tolerant except towards the gay MPs who hypocritically exploit homophobia as a political weapon. A new 2010 Tory MP Nick Boles announced his civil partnership in the House to universal murmurs and braying of congratulation.

The sweaty moral panic of the past has gone. It was at its worse with John Major's Back to Basics. This is surprising in retrospect after Edwina Currie's revelations. Over-reacting to the prolonged two weeks' shaming publicity for Mellor's indiscretions, Major said that swift resignations should follow any hint of scandal. It was unfortunate, for the most innocent of scandals emerged. The quietly inoffensive Tory MP Hartley Booth was accused of writing a love poem to one of his staff, which she gave to a newspaper. Resignation may have been wise because of the dire literary quality of his verse. But the affair was nooky-free. They had never touched. The two elements of Hartley Booth's name are the jam making company and the Salvation Army. He resigned his minute responsibilities as a PPS. Labour MPs said he went because he was guilty of having coitus non-startus. The Tories called it 'Hartley's seedless jam'.

In my sheltered life, I have always seen the Central Lobby as a beautiful mock Gothic cathedral-style forum at the heart of the Palace. It's an inspiring place in which to meet constituents and now do television interviews in the dry.

A new insight into the role of the Central Lobby was revealed over dinner in the Members' dining room. An MP friend found himself sitting next to a woman in the Central Lobby. She was waiting to see her Tory MP. My friend chatted to the lady 'as you do', he told me.

The following week he had a letter from her saying that she

would like to see him again. She said she hoped he did 'not have a girlfriend.' Gosh! A member of the Cabinet who was sharing our dining table recalled an MP for a northern town who explained the role of the Central Lobby to him. Twenty-five years ago he had advised the Cabinet member that if he was ever 'short' of a bed warmer for the night, the best way to solve the problem was to linger around the Central Lobby and engage a stranger in conversation. The lecherous MP spent so much time pursuing his passions in the Central Lobby, he lost his seat. The wages of sin.

The *Guardian*'s Michael White has a fascinating story on a past event. He wrote, 'Marcia Williams's two children were born at a time when she was Harold Wilson's all-powerful political secretary. It was not widely known in that innocent era. But one of the tabloids got a sniff of it and asked its veteran political editor, Walter Terry, to crack the case. Walter, whom I knew slightly, had to report failure. Odd really, but understandable because they turned out to be Walter's kids'. The advice of having affairs only with those who have has as much to lose as you by revelation still holds true. But there are limits to sleeping with the enemy if they are tabloid journalists.

A tiny number of MPs survive after allegations of reckless promiscuity. John Hemming and Mike Hancock have been exposed to withering publicity on their very full private lives. John Hemming denied a press claim that he had twenty-six past girlfriends. The nation was fascinated and distraught when his wife stole his new love's pet cat. Mike cheerfully confessed to an affair with an employee who was accused of spying for Russia. It was not the first time he suffered bad publicity about his energetic activity in seeking to increase the happiness of women. There is no perceptible reduction in the voters' appreciation of the political value of these excessively liberal Lib Dems.

For some political nerds and groupies MPs have heightened sexual attractiveness. Prepare for renewed attentions from aspirant sexual or marital partners. Don't be flattered. Many Members are secure on the path of the solitary unmarried state. Probably successful deep sea fishermen and all-in wrestlers also have their admirers. Even some of the most ugly in body and spirit, obnoxious in personality and character have extra sexual magnetism. To earth the throbbing allure it's wise to retire alone early to bed with a chaste milky drink and drift off to sleep absorbed with thoughts of death, electoral defeat and the corruption of the flesh.

How to Behave in a Recess

Recesses are as vital to MPs as the fallow period is to the rotation of crops. It is the time to read, think, write, shore up knowledge, sharpen interests, recharge the brain cells and restock the mind banks.

A change of worry is a holiday. Some MPs replace the Westminster routine with intensive study, book-writing or religious retreats. They emerge refreshed. David Lloyd George said, 'With me a change of trouble is as good as a vacation.'

The work of the fully staffed office continues. Recesses are the chance to assuage the guilt of not finding enough time to pursue all possible avenues for constituents' complaints. The pace of life slackens agreeably. Schools, charities and factories can be visited. There is time to read the half-understood reports that were published during the session.

But the two-month summer recess is far too long. The public are understandably cynical about what they regard as a two-month holiday. Most years, Dennis Skinner engineers a vote against it. In 1994 he mustered seventy MPs to vote against. The voters appreciate opposition to months of parliamentary silence that helps only the Government.

The myth that Members enjoy six weeks of sun and sangria was exposed by the full parliament that returned to debate the English riots in August 2011. It was a good safety valve to express the anger and fear of constituencies that suffered. The return of the September fortnight is welcome. Only the Executive is helped by the protracted absence of the Legislature. The long vacations should be modernised out of existence.

OUT OF TOWN

How to Survive Abroad

The annual summer migration follows a ritually ordained pattern. The minion MP metamorphoses into world statesperson. The habitat of small flats in Kennington is exchanged for the pleasant comfort luxury of three-star hotels with exotic names. The car and bus are abandoned for the limousine and economy class plane travel.

Shapeless suits are pressed. Plumage is smarter and brighter for the flight to the sun-warmed, fact-filled destinations. It is facts that they are out to find. One Select Committee adviser, backed against the wall, did confess that the harvest of facts was likely to be thin on one planned odyssey. 'But, not to worry, there are fine nuances of information that can be picked up only by going to the USA.' A 'nuance-finding' trip costing £25,000 for eleven Members was a less persuasive proposition. A sliding scale of futility for foreign trips starting from rock bottom would be:

Commercial Jaunts

Paid for by Greed United plc. Sometimes vaguely wrapped up as study or research tours, their prime function is to stuff large quantities of protein and alcohol into MPs. Ideal for MPs who have decided to prostitute their time to the highest bidder. But it's best to protect the liver and digestion, and quicker and healthier to accept a domestic jolly. Suffering a decline with current transparency.

Tyrant's Trips

Dozens of ugly repressive governments welcome soft-hearted and soft-brained Members. The gullible and greedy have been seduced by heady flattery. Perhaps even a country's President is seeking their advice and help. George Galloway is the supreme 'presidential groupie'. He was on good personal terms with Saddam Hussein, Romania's Ion Iliescu, Benazir Bhutto and Yasser Arafat. Michael Forsyth sneered at George about tripping to Libya. Incredibly Michael chose a county that George had never visited and had to apologise. George has some riveting opening lines, 'The President of Horrorstan told me last week...'. Azerbaijan, Belarus and Equatorial Guinea are the latest favourites for the gullible who are not offended by oppression and tyranny.

Military Invasions

MOD and the forces have a colourful brochure of overseas breaks in countries Britain occupies or to odd fragments of the Empire such as Belize. The Falklands is on the list. Great for twitchers and tank spotters prepared to endure the endless refrain from politicians from small countries that they need bombs not butter.

Commonwealth Parliamentary Association Conferences

Can be worthwhile in establishing links with politicians from exotic countries. Also can be banal and superficial. Spouses can sometimes come along to enjoy the pleasant social whirl, but strictly at their own expense, not the taxpayers'. It's a chance to rub shoulders with fellow international statespersons and learn from their experiences running the governments of Isle of Man or Alderney. Recommended for miniaturists because the total budget of some Commonwealth Member countries is less than that of the Commons Catering Committee.

Select Committee Tours

The process for sharing out the available diminishing funds is decided by a committee of Select Committee chairpersons called the Liaison Committee. The process is similar to gypsy horse-trading. The agreed tours vary in research content. Some are concentrated studies of serious subjects that deliver dividends for taxpayers. Others are shameless jaunts to the far corners of the world to inspect bananas, tourist attractions or techniques of cutting waste in Government spending. Some cynicism is justified. The post expenses scandal visibility has cut abuse. Most MPs now run a mile from any invitation that smells of luxury.

Inter-Parliamentary Union (IPU):

The IPU trips are serious attempts to penetrate foreign cultures and create international bridges. Three quarters of the time is devoted to genuine work. There is a proud record of building international understanding. Far better value in time, and avoiding all that tiresome travelling, is to act as a host to IPU delegations visiting Westminster.

Exchange Funds

Even more worthwhile are the several organisations that use cash for exchanges with parliamentarians from Third World countries. The Mother of Parliaments still has a few things to teach the embryo democracies. No accusations of jaunting will be thrown at Members on trips to Tallinn or Ulan Bator in December.

British–Irish Parliamentary Assembly

This is a uniquely useful body. Under the benign leadership of Paul Murphy, Peter Hain and John Cope, Westminster and the Oireachtas have been brought to a closer understanding facilitated by the lubricants of brogue, blarney and Guinness. The micro-surgery of a myriad of links has eliminated the mistrust that bedevilled Irish–British relations of the past. The Assembly also includes delegates from the Scottish Parliament, the Welsh Assembly, the Northern Ireland Assembly and the Channel Isles.

Character Forming Visits

The splendid John Battle once demanded his share of foreign travel from the whips. Indignantly he protested that he was shouldering Public Bill Committee burdens for frontbenchers who were constantly abroad. The whips promised him that 'the very next trip that comes into the office will be yours, John.' It was. He went to the Arctic, training with the SAS – in January.

Martyr Tours

I was invited to visit the Muraroa Atoll to witness the French nuclear tests. The cost to me would have been Aus$5,000. There was no additional charge for possible nuclear irradiation or the possible experience of being done over by French commandos.

How to Party (Conference)

Party conferences are periods of penance for backbenchers. Listening to a week of speeches from your colleagues and party hopefuls is akin to working a double shift every day for a week in a steelworks. MPs should not speak at conference unless party bosses insist. The delegates hate their only annual platform being taken over by MPs who have many other platforms. The only MP speakers should be those in danger of losing their seats in coming elections, or those recruited to grovel to the leadership on some unpopular issue.

Speaking to large conference audiences requires special techniques. Know your speech by heart. Mark the pauses. Look strong even when the audience does not respond. Check notes only for reassurance, not when speaking. The speaker's eyes should be focused on a fixed point at the rear of the hall. Never hold notes in your hands. A slight nervous tremble will multiply itself when it reaches the end of the piece of paper into a riveting twitching.

Never correct spoken errors by repetition or apology – unless they are disastrous. Keep the voice strong and pace controlled to the final word of every sentence and the final letter of every word.

Don't slump across the rostrum, or hug it. Stand straight. The microphone is adjusted to pick up your words. There is no need to try to swallow it. Use visual gestures sparingly to match the emotion of your words. Craft your original sound bite with care. If successful, the audience for that ten seconds of glory will be the television viewers. Replace the Trafalgar Square Rally voice and style with a quiet intimate tone for the sound bite.

The week is filled with fringe meetings and receptions. They are an inescapable duty and often barely endurable. Many delegates apply the dulling drug of alcohol as a barrier between their inner sensibilities and the exterior hell's pageant.

For the incurable gluttons, free-loaders and winos, receptions can be a joyous spree. There are opportunities for self-expression for the serious politician and the devout hedonist. Dedicated do-gooders can usefully use their round of events as an exercise in the redistribution of wealth. Never eat, but contribute generously to the raffle at the events run by the good causes of CPAG, Greenpeace, Marie Curie and Mind.

The formula for speaking is straightforward. List all sound bites that were applauded in speeches made prior to yours. A glean through previous years' speeches and fringe meetings will produce a good crop. String them together with a little bang start and a big bang finish. All sentences must be simple without sub-clauses. Use words with as few syllables as possible. The overheated, over-alcoholised and sleep-deprived audience can be roused only with simple concepts. A quiet voice at the start will force the amplification to be turned up. The crescendo at the finale will blow the wax out of the delegates' ears.

Fringe meetings can be informative. Try only those in which

the subject is of major interest, where a contribution can be made or a question answered. Avoid the earnest ones in which an unknown is keen to read his thesis on the String Theory or give the solution to macro-economic world crisis. Any fringe meeting with jargon in the title will be an endurance test.

Minority British ethnic occasions should be missed by sensitive souls. Scottish Nights are an affront to those of delicate musical, literary or social tastes. Some of the Scots present are determined to reinforce their national stereotype as Rab C. Nesbitt. You would be forgiven for mistaking the music for the sounds made by a non-consenting goose being sexually ravaged.

Welsh Night persists with the mad illusion that all Welsh people can sing. Aficionados find delight in an evening of raffles, beer and a slow desensitising of the brain. It is impassioned sentimentality by the bucketful.

Mercifully conferences are losing their importance. One Tory Member said that at the 2011 Tory conference, delegates were outnumbered by lobbyists. Pray for the early demise of lobbyists and conferences.

How to Help the Party

A disruptive but essential chore is to work outside of Parliament and the constituency for the party cause. Some attendance at by-elections is mandatory. Most MPs have twinning arrangements with candidates in seats where the party is in a minority. Absence from Westminster delays the work of the office and is inexplicable to Votingham people who want an urgent chat. Acting as a minder for a by-election candidate hideously increases the disruption and confusion.

One MP rashly drank too much in a strange hotel in a by-election and failed to turn up for breakfast. Calls to his room and thumping on the door did not rouse him. He was elderly and his lifestyle made him overdue for a coronary. Alarmed colleagues used the master key to open the door a few inches. It was blocked by the wardrobe that had fallen on the floor. They clambered over the furniture and searched the room.

They could not see him. Sounds of snoring came from the wardrobe. He had got up in the middle of the night, mistook the wardrobe door for the bathroom door, and went inside. No one knows what happened then but in his efforts to get out the wardrobe fell over. Hours later he was still there happily sleeping like a baby. Two Tory MPs told me this tale about one of their colleagues. The moral of the story is never do foolish things in the company of your gossiping colleagues.

How to Avoid/Adore Royalty

Parliament is infantalised by royalty. Strong minded intelligent Members are reduced to quivering jelly at the sight or mention of the Windsor family. Ludicrous thirteenth century rules bandage the mouths of MPs from even the mildest criticism of not only the monarch but all the forty minor royals. Criticism of Prince Andrew was widespread in the media, pubs and blogs in 2011. Three times a Member's speech was halted because he attempted to repeat criticism. The lavish praise of the prince was permitted. The system is negative privilege. MPs are denied the free speech in Parliament that is permitted to everyone outside of Parliament.

Royal groupies have many Commons chances of emitting emetic drivel on major occasions in the life of royals. Birthdays and marriages are pretext for the preposterous sycophancy that would have been heard in the court of King Canute. There is probably a correlation in the volume of flattery and the distribution of royal gongs. The enviable few who refused royal honours are entitled to prefix their names with the words Has Refused Honour or H.R.H.

Royals are of little or no advantage to an MP. Depending on their uncertain popularity either credit or embarrassment by association is possible. Yesterday's picture with war hero Prince Andrew is today's headache with buddy of tyrant Prince Andrew. It's tricky to avoid wasting precious time on royal events while remaining courteous to them. Useful tips for royal etiquette include:

- Be otherwise engaged when royalty next visits Votingham (and on all future occasions).
- Never accept an honour or a job as Deputy Lieutenant.
- Always courteously rise to toast the Queen (*sotto voce* you may toast 'The Queen ... and Freddie Mercury. A Great Group!').
- Royal support for good causes can be quoted usefully but never in the House.
- Royal Garden Parties are best avoided. The queues are long and the weather is either too wet or too hot.
- Keep exploring the costs of royalty.

The royals are feverishly thrashing about to find a role. They are no longer the blue-blooded superbeings that stepped out of a fairy tale, nor the ideal of family life after a triple stain of divorces. The new popularity of the younger royals has boosted the institution. Their spinners advise using good causes. Their present ploy is to soak up through osmosis credit by association with charities. It is not the royals who are selflessly shoring the charities, it is the charities who are shoring up an institution hungry for goodwill.

Royal occasions are a sinful waste of an MP's time and incite emotions of tedium and fury. The sad 'subjects' assemble hours beforehand and wait. The purpose of the event is to reinforce royalty's delusion of omnipotence by abasing the peasantry before them. Security is the excuse for the tedium of queues and protocol. The rules are based on the belief that members of public seeing royalty for the first time will try to menace them. Women are expected to curtsy in the presence of an HRH as an acknowledgment that they are inferior mortals. That's an idiocy too far.

Beyond the needs of good manners. Those who genuinely feel lesser beings to the royals might gain deviant satisfaction from self-abasement on these visits. The MPs' only role on these occasions is to be an untidy background to their photographs. There are always more useful ways of spending time.

On two occasions I have had support for campaigns from members of the royal family. Once Princess Diana sent me her 'warm good wishes' for a debate I had about improving the lot of young people leaving care. Royal approval multiplied the attention the debate had by several thousand per cent. One news agency misunderstood the message and decided that Diana was backing a Labour MP in an attack on the Government. Again there was a wave of attention to a non-existent royal gaffe but also beneficially to the plight of youngsters going from full time care to full time neglect. A similarly useful boost was given by Diana to the anti-landmine campaign.

As royalty is being supported by public funds, it is entirely legitimate that their influence should be used to back worthy causes.

IN THE CHAMBER

How to Pray

Even at prayer the House can be a writhing, posturing political animal. There is a theory that the mood of the country can be gauged by the numbers of Government Members at prayer. They increase in proportion to the deepening mood of national anguish. The Chamber was full for the inspirational Rev. Rose Hudson-Wilkin's call to prayer before the debate on the English Riots of 2011. Perhaps the reference to 'chariots of fire' was a tad ill-judged.

Presence at prayers guarantees a seat in the Chamber for individual Members for the rest of the day. A green 'prayer' card is placed, booking the seat for peak attendance later. There are full congregations for budget days and other major occasions.

Opposition MPs rarely use prayer cards, though Dennis Skinner's seat under the gallery is sometimes claimed by the usurping MPs. Dennis is the only Member I have seen who sits during prayers to assert his atheism.

Members of the House stand facing each other for the first prayer then turn to face the back of the Chamber for the rest. There are two rival theories about this. It is perhaps a relic of the days when Members knelt on their seats to pray. The Serjeant at Arms still does. The other explanation is that prayers were once a shambles. Members made faces at each other in order to provoke laughter. This is more plausible and sounds like the Chamber we know and love.

Once prayers were interrupted by a devout Catholic MP denouncing the hypocrisy of praying while so many people outside were unemployed. There was no known response for an interruption of this kind. The House cannot be suspended if the sitting has not started. But the Member concerned refused to be quiet. Instead he contented himself with making a little history.

Prayers are not witnessed by the public or recorded in Hansard. Many Members wait outside the Chamber until prayers are over. Frequently their chattering is heard inside and attendants call them to Order.

Under Speaker Weatherill's reign he let it be known among the religious organisations of MPs that he was unhappy that few Labour Members attend prayers. Reversing the usual practice, the late Donald Coleman took to dropping in for prayers then usually absented himself from the Chamber for the rest of the day.

There is an unprovable belief that Speakers are more likely to 'call' MPs for questions and speeches if they are in for prayers. Possible with past Speakers, definitely not with Speaker Bercow.

How to Speak

It is not true that Members can sit anywhere in the Chamber. A third of places are occupied by the same individuals or party groups.

Not only will a new Member receive hard looks for sitting in territory that belongs to a veteran, there is danger of being sat on. Even where there is no room between two Members a veteran will insist on occupying the usual place. The technique is to aim the bottom at the non-existent space between two Members, bear down heavily while wiggling the posterior vigorously from side to side. By a phenomenon that puzzles physicists a space appears where there was none before. The bottom of the MP with ancient rights hits the green leather.

The maiden speech is a potentially nervous occasion. The secret of great speaking is not to change the speech but to change the audience. Use the stories and phrases that have gone down well over and over again in Votingham. The words will flow easily and comfortably through familiar waters. Be magnanimous to the previous Member especially if the voters have chosen a new MP by election and dumped a long-serving one, their virtues hailed, sins absolved. Abandon the venom of the election campaign even if the wounds have not healed. Opponents are now dead meat.

The tradition of uncontroversial maiden speeches has been ruptured so frequently that it is no longer obligatory. But a ferocious attack on opponents entitles other MPs to disregard the tradition of hearing a maiden speech in silence.

The first speech is a daunting hurdle. Ignore advice to postpone it for months. Delaying it increases the trepidation. Put a request in to the Speaker immediately after taking the oath. The likelihood is that a slot will be found the following week, in the Queen's Speech debates.

The House will be largely empty, a doughnut of friends may assemble and the Chamber's intimacy will quiet jangling nerves. Once that hurdle has been surmounted the Chamber becomes your friendly habitat.

In theory maiden and all other speeches should not be read. Most are. Notes are permitted and Members frequently read every word. Quotations are now allowed.

Backbench debate speeches have plummeted in importance. Whips are often hard pressed to persuade anyone to fill the empty dog hours between 6 p.m. and 9 p.m. The main excitement of peak events of the day is between 2.30 p.m. and 4 p.m. In the evening hacks and MPs have other things on their minds.

The best hope is that regional media may be interested in a parish pump speech or that *Today/Yesterday in Parliament* might quote a golden sentence or two. It is rare for either of these programmes to use any but the first or last sentence in the oration.

But they like a bit of colour. John Marek delivered a lengthy, scholarly speech as a frontbench spokesperson on Treasury matters. Alan Beith intervened, 'I have been listening to the

Honourable Gentleman for twenty-five minutes and I still don't know whether he is for or against this bill.' Marek sighed heavily and replied, 'I will come to that later.'

That exchange was the only part of John's splendid, carefully prepared homily that was broadcast in *Yesterday in Parliament*.

A lesson to us all.

How to Address

Everyone has done it, at least once. The universal error is to misuse the word 'you'. The occupant of the chair alone is 'You', everyone else is addressed in the third person. That is the only bit of the archaic verbal rituals that modern MPs should respect. Punishment is swift with howling from opponents and a correction from the Speaker or chairperson. The other forms of address are flummery against which progressive MPs should be subversive. As a concession to the sensitive all Members can be addressed as 'Honourable'. It is the least accident-fraught address for all. Even if you never use the word, Hansard will insert it into their printed report.

There is no point in finding out who is 'Right Honourable' and who is 'Honourable'. The tags are always changing and Members constantly get it wrong. Why bother? It is positively beneficial to avoid the antiquated forms of address such as 'learned', as in the 'Honourable and Learned Member for...'. Outrageously the only 'learned' Members are senior barristers. An MP who has won a Nobel Prize for science is 'un-learned'.

'Gallant' is another snobbery based relic that is half buried but sometimes rises from its dishonoured grave. Its use is confined to past commissioned officers in the Forces. A private who had won a Victoria Cross is not 'gallant'. The sprogs of the aristocracy, the sons of dukes or earls, are entitled to the courtesy title 'the noble Lord, the Member for...'. Now it is only used by Members out to get a mention in a newspaper diary as 'creep of the week'.

Jeremy Hanley helpfully innovated a new form of address at a committee meeting. He forgot the Great Grimsby constituency of Austin Mitchell and referred to him as 'the Member with his own face on his tie.' Wrong, Jeremy. It was definitely Mick Jagger's face. But he may have started something. The 'one in the blue pullover' or the 'lady with the pink dress' is much easier to remember than the rest of the antiquated, confusing mumbo-jumbo.

There is no chance of making mistakes when Members refer to 'the last speaker in the debate', 'the Member below the gangway', or 'the Lady opposite'. By a magic process your words will expand in Hansard to 'The Right Honourable Member for Cwmscwt (Mr Llywelyn)'. I have never used any of these titles but the record says otherwise. Hansard are the last defenders of an archaic system that reinforces the class-ridden mores of an earlier age.

While there is no list of forbidden epithets that are out of order, objection has been taken to the following: coward, hypocrite, git, blackguard, hooligan, rat, swine, stool-pigeon, traitor and shit (when used to described a minister). George Foulkes was forced to withdraw the word when he described Douglas Hogg as an 'arrogant little shit'. During Hogg's perform-ances on food safety George has been tempted to request that the word be reinstated as a fair and accurate description of the minister.

When Tam Dalyell said that the Firth of Forth Bridge was 'encrusted with seagull shit' it was allowed. 'Lickspittle' is not allowed when applied to Members but can be used to describe non-Members or strangers. In a ground-breaking event in January 1997 Ian Pearson used the word 'crap' to describe job schemes and was not challenged. In 2008 Greg Mulholland stormed out of Westminster Hall after insulting Ivan Lewis. In Hansard it was reported that he called him an 'a-------'.

Mysteriously the Hong Kong Legislature forbids the use of this piece of oriental wisdom: 'Foul Grass grows out of a foul ditch'. The Dáil Éireann has ruled that it is disorderly for a TD to describe another as a chancer, coward, brat, buffoon, communist, corner boy, fascist, guttersnipe, hypocrite, scumbag, fatty, rat or yahoo. In December 2009, Paul Gogarty, TD, apologised in advance for using 'unparliamentary language' prior to shouting 'fuck you!' at an opposition chief whip. This phrase was not one of those listed explicitly as inappropriate, prompting calls for a review.

The British Parliament does not yet reflect the vanishing taboos on bad language. The day will come when rude Anglo-Saxon brevities will be preferred to ugly newly minted jargon.

How to Recover from Crash Landings

Inevitably there will be disasters. The key fact disappears from memory in mid-speech. Simple words become unpronounceable or come out backwards. The punch-words will be spoken in the middle of the oral question, leaving a floundering feeble final sentence.

An impassioned plea will be interrupted by the Speaker explaining that the question has already been answered ten minutes earlier. An opportunistic question to the Prime Minister is halted because it is a closed question. Worst of all, there will be no words at all. The mind and lips freeze up. An Oral Question may be disastrously untrue and comprehensively flattened by a minister. There are countless ways to suffer humiliation in Parliament.

Crash landings strike novices and experienced Members. Cultivate a state of constant nervousness. Fear will enforce thorough preparation. The spectre of failure will discourage rash risk taking when unexpected opportunities arise. Claire Curtis-Thomas suffered the ultimate nightmare because she was sitting in the wrong place. In 2000 she sought to change the Transport Act, giving Merseytravel power to push up prices without the need for a public inquiry. She sponsored the bill but it failed in its first hearing when she sat in the wrong part of the Commons and the debate collapsed. She tried to 'move' the bill but the Speaker refused to see her. She was in a seat under the gallery and technically was not 'in the Chamber.' It was expensive for the bill's sponsors and the bill was delayed for four years.

Work is the best material to use to bury the memory of embarrassment. It is futile to endlessly repeat the incident in your mind, finding dozens of ways of getting it right – next time. Many politicians waste energy perfecting the speech they made yesterday, not the one they will make tomorrow. Obliterate the memory by refusing to read about it, listen to it on the radio or talk about it. That only deepens the wound. Time will heal and dull the pain. Then laugh at it.

Tony Lloyd now cheerfully recalls what must have been an excruciating experience. His question to Mrs Thatcher was based on an evening paper's claim that Peter Walker had been rebellious in a Cabinet meeting earlier in the day. Confidently Tony taunted Thatcher on this Cabinet split. His confidence was shaken by Thatcher's cheery smile and the giggles from the Treasury bench. Tony was then pulped by Thatcher's answer. Peter Walker was not only not present at the Cabinet, he was in China.

The House judges everyone by their last performance in the Chamber. Make sure that a stunner is delivered very quickly to smother the nagging memory and restore an impression of competence.

How to Avoid Language Lapses

Choice of language is tricky in communicating with voters and Parliament. To avoid excessive pomposity and increase intimacy I usually drop titles, especially aristocratic ones. Lord Stevenson was happy to be called Mr and in return called me Citizen Flynn. God-botherers in the shape of an Archbishop and a senior Rabbi were unfazed when addressed at a Select Committee as 'You guys...'

A path between expected formality and received familiarly should be sought. Ignorance of changing word use is dangerous. A local paper asked for a comment from Caerphilly MP Wayne David on 'increased dogging' on Caerphilly Mountain. He said 'I welcome it. Should be more of it.' Luckily the reporter did not thank Wayne and click-brrrr off. Quite fairly he could have published the shock news that 'Local MP calls for more open air sex between strangers in constituency.' Unworldly Wayne thought 'dogging' meant corralling stray dogs.

Dari Taylor had occasional lapses. She tried to cheer up John Prescott when he was mired in a sex scandal by congratulating him in the Commons Chamber on his 'hands-on approach'. She provoked a radio interviewer into giggles when she complained that her morning chores as a new MP included 'handling six inches of mail'.

Hansard recorded laughter when Michael Fabricant said, 'It is not much fun standing on a platform and a high-speed train sucks you off because of the turbulence.'

Keith Hill suffered an excruciating moment because of ignorance of street talk. The diminutive, smart Hazel Blears is an incongruous figure straddling her custom-made motorbike. Her worst parliamentary moment came when the usually hip Transport Minister Keith tried disastrously to praise her.

In answer to an oral question from Hazel on the floor of the Commons Keith brightly replied, 'My honourable friend has asked so many questions about motor bikes, she is becoming known as Blears the Bike.'

Keith was totally innocent of any double entendre, he paused in answering the question, aware of the mounting murmur and giggles provoked by the expression 'Blears the bike'. He might also have noticed Hazel turning puce.

To add further insult to injury, Tory MP Michael Fabricant asked in a loud whisper, 'Did he say, "Blears the dyke"?' Hazel said afterwards, 'One side of the House thought I was promiscuous, the other thought I was a lesbian.' Keith later said that it was one of his three worst parliamentary moments. Get with it.

Another of Keith's worst moments was late at night before an empty Chamber. He had to read a speech prepared for him by a civil servant. Laid back, he had not troubled to read the speech beforehand. Panic overwhelmed him when he read the first sentence. There was an accident-fraught expression he had to read eighteen times. He summoned up all his courage and slowly said 'Short Sea Shipping'. Fear and nerves produced giggles then laughter. Not once did he fall into the obvious wordtrap. YouTube has had 53,000 hits since; for educational purposes, I put this classic example of parliamentary corpsing on the site. It is strongly recommended as a lesson to all.

How to Survive the Speaker

The changes that Speaker Bercow has introduced are profound. In the future parliamentary history may be divided into years BB and AB – Before Bercow and After Bercow.

I have served under four Speakers. Speaker Weatherill was a principled kind man. He made an offer to abstain in the vote of no confidence in 1979 because of a rule on pairing with a Labour MP who was on his deathbed. That could have finished his career. He was his own man. He limited Points of Order to its present 3:30 slot. It has been a mixed blessing.

Betty Boothroyd was distinguished as the first woman Speaker. She annoyed a predecessor George Thomas by declaring 'Time's Up' at the end of business 'like a barmaid.' She stamped her authority on the House and was impartial and independent of the Executive.

Speaker Martin was not the strongest candidate for the job. He was elected because of his crafty lobbying among Labour MPs. He was forced to resign, not because of snobbery, but because he had misjudged the allowances scandal and made a bad situation worse.

Speaker Bercow has set his own high standards for his role free of the tyranny of the stultifying traditions that have blocked past reformers. Jacob Rees-Mogg said Bercow is 'supporting the Legislature against the Executive'. This is the job of the Speaker, to represent Parliament and to challenge Government when necessary. He has more pioneering courage than all his three predecessors.

He has promoted the feeble rights of backbenchers against the overweening powers of the Executive. Contriving to call a record number of urgent, oral and Topical Questions has liberated back-benchers and multiplied our chances of holding the Executive to account. He has reduced the loquacious garbage that clogs the parliamentary word machine. Bercow has been the scourge of the verbose, the self-regarding, boring time gluttons. He has been the friend of those whose contributions are brief, pithy and substantial.

One oafish MP said that Bercow is not 'effing royalty'. No he is not. Unlike them, he was elected on merit by his peers. He and his office are entitled to respect as the most innovative Speaker for a generation. One tabloid attacked him before he was elected, when he was elected, after he was elected and before and after he was re-elected.

No Speaker can increase parliamentary time but John Bercow by repeated imprecations, body language and occasional light mockery has reduced the time-wasting verbal Polyfilla emitted by self-indulgent boring backbenchers. It was a rarity in the past for all PMQs, Oral, Business or Topical Questions to be called. Now it's routine. In the debate on the English riots all MPs who wished to question David Cameron did so. The PM was at the Dispatch Box for a record two and a half hours. Bercow granted the SO24 request for the Hackgate debate that allowed full parliamentary scrutiny.

Only the foolhardy underestimate Speakers. They have earned great powers through winning the respect of the Chamber. Head-on challenges from backbenchers will strike solid rock.

A rare occasion of a Speaker being humiliated was when Eric Heffer insisted on being called to speak. Speaker Weatherill refused. Heffer stood in protest before the mace. Weatherill surrendered but said that it was 'an abuse of the House'. His authority was diminished.

Many others ruefully recall the wounds of other encounters. Unforgettable was a blood-curdling telling off delivered on a Friday morning by Speaker Boothroyd to Labour's Ann Clwyd. It was several minutes of detailed accusations and threats. Her crime? Ann had parked her car in the Speaker's Court. But it was early in Betty Boothroyd's Speakership. We all got the message and understood who was boss.

Suspension from the Commons is now almost always contrived. Once it made headlines and could be damaging to individual MPs. Now it is used to make a strong point. John McDonnell in 2009 seized the mace and placed it on the Labour benches. He said, 'My job is to represent my constituents. Today I was reasserting the values of democracy and the overriding sovereignty of Parliament.' He was protesting against the expansion of Heathrow. The ceremonial mace rests on the table in front of the Speaker when the Commons is sitting and is a symbol of its authority, technically delegated from the crown.

Defying the Speaker is itself an ancient tradition. Twenty-eight MPs have been suspended from the House since 1949 for failing to obey orders. Bessie Braddock, a Liverpool MP, was the first woman to be thrown out for using bad language. She famously accused Winston Churchill of being drunk in the Chamber, to which he retorted, 'and you madam, are ugly, but I shall be sober in the morning'.

But perhaps the most unjust suspension was that of Dale Campbell-Savours, who branded Jeffrey Archer 'a criminal' in 1995 for his role in the Anglia TV shares affair. Refusing to retract, the Labour MP said, 'I believe it is criminal activity and I will leave.' Future events justified Dale's judgement.

Dale Campbell-Savours probably holds the record for being suspended the most. He is convinced that it did him no electoral damage and was helpful in highlighting important issues. So frequently was it used in the nineties, it lost its force. The media remain unimpressed. Speaker Boothroyd skilfully side-stepped confrontation. Instead of complaining provocatively that Members should wind up because they have spoken too long, she deployed her considerable charm by saying, 'I am sure the Honourable Member is about to wind up his interesting remarks'.

Only two MPs have been expelled from the House in the past 100 years – Horatio Bottomley (1922) and Peter Baker (1954). Baker was sentenced to seven years in prison for forging signatures on letters to guarantee debts when his companies ran into financial difficulties. Bottomley was a serial fraudster who was served with sixty-six bankruptcy writs during his life.

Antagonising a Speaker is a kamikaze ploy. Backbenchers can swiftly become invisible, ignored in debates and passed over for opportunist questions. Imposed silences are bitter fare for professional communicators. Only slightly better, is being called late in a debate and cramming a lovingly-prepared thirty minute oration into a breathless five minute gabble when time has run out.

There is now a scientific pecking order of precedence on the Speaker's database. Criteria include seniority, knowledge of subject, frequency of speaking and immaculate behaviour records. Still, as always, most Members are convinced that they are treated unfairly.

Prize a good relationship with the Speaker. The rewards are thought to include:

- Called early in questions, debates.
- Included on trips abroad.
- Invited to Speaker's dinners/receptions.
- Allowed to break minor rules of debate.

- Allowed to make mini-speeches under the guise of Points of Order/Business Questions.
- Given latitude on questions of uncertain relevance.
- Generosity on orderliness of groundbreaking Written Questions.
- Expanded time allowed for Oral Questions.
- Have urgent questions accepted.

John Bercow strengthened his support for backbenches when he said, 'I would like inscribed on my tombstone, "Here lies John Bercow, the backbenchers' Speaker".'

How to Dilute Boredom

Hours of mind-sapping boredom are the inescapable lot of legislators. There is no escape from enduring other backbenchers' speeches while waiting to be called in debates or committees. Erudite, witty and well-informed contributions are rare in the vast dross and dribble of the meandering streams of verbiage. Speakers are called in accordance to their seniority or knowledge of the subject of the debate.

The eternal fate of junior backbenchers is to endure hours of emptiness before their names are called. These should be productively filled.

Rework the speech. Silently voice it to spot weaknesses and verbal trip wires like difficult pronunciation. (Don't do this while doughnutting in the camera's view. Silent goldfish mouthings will be taken as proof of incipient insanity in Votingham.) Eliminate accident-prone words that knot the tongue: pluralism, statistical, proliferation, similarly, remuneration, mayoralty. Some easily spoken words become unpronounceable when preceded by others. Familiar expressions have a habit of coming out upside down. Bill Cash once mentioned 'the prodigal son on the road to

Damascus'. Norman Lamont denounced his own party opponents as the 'Flotsam and Bobtail' of politics. John Wilkinson said we must continue to sell arms abroad so that we do not 'cut off our noses to spoil our throats'.

Write a five minute and a two minute version of the speech. There must be strong opening and closing sentences. Often that is all the time left for the last MP in the queue of speeches.

Work. Long-neglected reports can be read. Write Parliamentary Questions on subjects that suggest themselves by the debate. Collect mail and hand write replies. Write a haiku.

Play. Low spirits and exhaustion will kill the work impulse. To avoid permanent brain abuse from the corrosive boredom, try playing. The most deadly speech by other MPs can be entertainingly analysed. Write down:

- Grammatical errors.
- The most stupid sentence.
- The longest/most platitudinous sentence.
- The largest number of repetitions of the same point.
- The most self-admiring comment.
- The contrast between the words spoken with underlying meaning.

Fantasise. One MP confided to me that much of his empty time in the Chamber agreeably speeds by in dreams of the Hansard writers or 'goddesses' as he described them. They perch on high above the MPs in the gallery hanging flatteringly on their every word. When press and public have deserted the Chamber they are loyally ever-present to raise drooping spirits.

The new miracles of technology have come to the rescue. BlackBerries and iPads are godsends for multitasking, answering the mail, writing speeches or articles while enduring the wait to speak. Some Members productively tweet from the Chamber with a running commentary on the debate. This can be a useful extension of democracy, doubling the output of the workload and prolonging the sanity of Members.

The technology averse must still endure the boredom.

How to Doughnut

The MP speaking is the hole in the doughnut. The doughnut is the circle of faces, knees and bellies that surround the speaker in the television frame. The doughnut is a living thing, yawning, scratching, dozing, chattering and, just occasionally, listening attentively. Half a dozen MPs make a doughnut. Uniquely Cyril Smith, past Member for Rochdale, was a whole doughnut in himself.

An unruly doughnut is fearsome. It fascinates and hypnotises the viewer. One Cabinet minister had the misfortune of having a backbencher perched above his left shoulder during a critical speech. The backbencher was obsessed with his nose. First he scratched it. Then he blew it noisily with energetic flapping of a handkerchief. Then rubbed it. The performance eclipsed the minister's words.

Roger Stott suffered a similar fate. He was earnestly addressing the House from the Dispatch Box on the serious matter of Northern Ireland. Emanating from Roger's head a shoe appeared. Then disappeared. Appeared again and bounced up and down rhythmically. It was Tam Dalyell sprawled lengthways in the seat behind. He had his legs crossed performing some energetic footwork. Roger should have saved his breath. No television viewer listened to a word.

The Dispatch Box is the least flattering spot from which to address the House. The doughnut is exposed and the camera angle is cruel especially to bald heads. The foreshortened bird's-eye view makes MPs look like pygmies shouting from the bottom of an untidy green pit.

The prime perch is now the back bench. There the background is handsome oak panelling that never distracts or walks out. Attention is concentrated on the speaker at the most favourable camera angle of eye level.

Elsewhere, dedicated doughnutting can be an asset. A lacklustre speaker can sound like Cicero with a skilled group of adoring friends. Their attention to the speaker must be constant. Cultivate the absorbed stare of a worshipping angel in an El Greco painting with a tear in the corner of the eye.

Body language should be that of a reverential supplicant. No folded arms, legs crossed to the speaker, perpetually expecting jewels of humour and erudition. The gestures of nodding heads, jaws dropped open aghast, slapping thighs, head in hands in despair are useful when used sparingly and with caution.

Vocal backing from the growled braying of the Dalek-like parliamentary 'Hear, hear' is basic. Skilled support comes with judiciously intoned 'Ooohs!' that can express shock, amazement or disgust. Variation is vital in one word exclamations of 'Disgusting', 'Scandal', 'Exactly', 'Of course', and 'Absolutely'.

The sound bite that is likely to be relayed to the masses is contained in the final words of any speech. However banal or fluffed the last sentence is it must be buttressed with loud heartfelt 'Hear, hear'.

Negative doughnutting is a subtler art. Body language and facial expressions should express rejection, contempt and derision. If the speaker turns for support, a shake of the head or eyes imploring the heavens in despair are confidence-sapping. Hyperactive twitching and writhing will destroy the television viewer's concentration on the speaker. During the final sentence of the peroration slowly stand up, stretch and conspicuously walk out.

How to Nickname

Name-calling is the lowest form of parliamentary invective. But nicknames are devastating in undermining the confident speaker and destroying the nervous.

It is not a decent or honourable way to behave, but it is as hallowed a relic of parliamentary discourse as our elaborate courtesy. If politics is war, nicknames are the small hand grenades. The deadliest are brief, true and wounding. They hit their target by highlighting a weakness in the victim's character, appearance or history.

Reminders of unfortunate past incidents hit the spot. A popular one was 'Gorillagram', cruelly applied to one Member who is said to be the only MP who could earn a living delivering gorillagrams without the aid of monkey suit.

Sheep noises torment as reminders of discomforting incidents. An MP once slipped in some droppings while loading sheep into the back of his van. He removed his stained trousers and drove off. A faulty rear light led to a police check. They were surprised that the driver was wearing Wellington boots and no trousers. To the delight of the tabloids he is Welsh. The hilarity about Wellington boots and sheep was long-lived confirmation of apocryphal fables. After about thirty or forty years the incident will be forgotten.

The most startling hair in the Chamber is the blond profusion of Michael Fabricant, which fascinates sketch writers. The Table Office refused to accept a question asking what the Government intended to do to improve the standards of wig making in Lichfield (his constituency). They said it was tabled in the spirit of mockery.

One rural Tory wore dreary country suits. They looked like recycled agricultural detritus. He was dubbed the 'Talking Grow Bag'.

During his period as Transport Minister the weighty Robert Key earned the title of the 'Colossus of Roads'. The pale pallor of veteran Member Dr Alan Glyn suggested the epithet of 'The Stalking Hearse'. A spell as Minister of Food left the gargantuan Nicholas Soames nicknamed 'Butter Mountain'. During John Redwood's leadership bid his resemblance to Mr Spock of the planet Vulcan damaged him. There had been rumours that the reason that, as Secretary of State, he never spent a night in Wales was because he was beamed up to another planet where he slept hanging upside down from the roof of a cave.

Ann Widdecombe had a penchant for wearing all black outfits with little crucifixes dangling from various parts of her anatomy. That earned her the title of 'Doris' (Karloff). She delighted in the name and answered her phone with 'Karloff here'. She also absorbed with pleasure the name 'Marilyn' that Tony Banks called her after a change of hair colour.

Margaret Thatcher benefited from her Iron Lady image and Peter Mandelson was more interesting as the 'Prince of Darkness'. David Cameron could benefit from his Flashman image.

It's best to draw a veil over many other unkind and ribald epithets. They are fit only for use by consenting MPs and hacks in private.

How to Cultivate Enemies

Having a close circle of enemies is not as vital as having friends. But they are important. There are Members whose views and prejudices are the antithesis of everything you hold dear. They appreciate nothing, worship false gods and are reliably perverse on every issue. Their presence, names and voices set your teeth on edge. They are anti-reason, anti-progress and antediluvian. Your mind races with schemes to frustrate their knavish tricks.

Stalk them. Be in the Chamber whenever they speak armed with piercing heckles or canny interventions. Practise a permanent sneer of mocking contempt. Never laugh at their jokes but be noisily amused by their attempts at sincerity. Try to speak immediately after them and crush their thin ideas with reason and ridicule.

Crawl over their EDMs to find a weakness that can be extracted with a powerful amendment. Be better informed than they are on their pet subjects. Offer to trump their media interviews by volunteering to contradict them.

Your loathing will creatively deepen your knowledge and understanding of a wider range of subjects. Competitive instincts will sharpen. Your mission is to out-think, out-question, out-speak the unspeakable. Your passion to serve your constituents will be topped up with antagonistic venom to destroy falsehoods. Remember: cosiness is the enemy of efficiency and leads to a lazy brain and a lack of thinking and inventiveness. Maintain a fertile bubbling anger.

Edward Heath's *raison d'être* for the final period of his life was his detestation of Margaret Thatcher. He glowered at her from his seat a few feet away from her, poised, waiting for signs of weakness that he could exploit. Dennis Skinner and George Osborne have an electrifying antagonism. George frequently tells Dennis to retire; Dennis repeats allegations about the use of white powder.

Be constructively and destructively hyperactive, you will learn to appreciate, if not love, your enemies.

How to Insult

Insult is a desperate tactic. The injuries to mega-egos often never heal. Michael Foot said that Aneurin Bevan's career was blighted by long smouldering resentments from fellow MPs whom he had carelessly insulted.

There is no fury like an MP scorned. What was probably a unique walkout took place in protest to a litany of insults against public figures in Wales delivered by Rod Richards. All Opposition MPs left their seats and walked to the bar of the House. Many public figures were tarred with Richards' indiscriminate brush. Afterwards shadow Welsh Secretary Ron Davies refused to give way to him in speeches because he does not 'respect the rules of courtesy of the House'. Peter Hain gave Elfyn Llwyd the same treatment in similar circumstances.

Ian Liddell-Grainger was described by Quentin Letts as 'not necessarily one of life's most organised brains but possessed of the boldness of a Jack Russell'. His signature questions are all insults. At a meeting of PASC he asked Dame Suzi Leather, the chair of the Charity Commission, 'Have you ever had a proper job?' On the Charity Board he commented, 'Every single one of you seem to be quango queens.' The Select Committee chair, Tony Wright, explained all. He told Suzi, 'I apologise for the fact that he was excessively unpleasant and personal. He is a public schoolboy.'

With a bold lack of tact Ian went for the chair of a committee that was about to give all MPs a great deal of grief. Talking to the new Standards chairman, Christopher Kelly, Ian enquired, 'You strike me as a very boring man. Are you a boring man?' Kelly offered to bring a couple of board games along to the committee on his next visit to liven things up. No doubt Kelly forgot the remark and it did not influence his future austere treatment of MPs.

Insults from the Dispatch Box are usually rare. Unwisely Simon Burns *sotto voce* described one Member as 'a stupid sanctimonious dwarf'. On the back row of the other side of the Chamber I clearly heard the jibe because the minister's mic was live. The object of his scorn was unconcerned but the Walking with Giants Foundation was livid. They represent those with primordial dwarfism.

Michael Howard attacked Tony Blair over tuition fees: 'Let me make it clear: this grammar schoolboy will take no lessons from that public schoolboy on the importance of children from less privileged backgrounds gaining access to university.'

The inspired Tony Banks was allowed more latitude than others because Speakers have shared in the fun of his audacity. Once he accused Margaret Thatcher of behaving like 'sex-starved boa constrictor'. He got away with it. John Major was forced to withdraw when he said that Tony Blair was a 'dimwit'. Later Tony Banks had another go, this time at John Major. He said, 'He is so unpopular, if he became a funeral director people would stop dying.' Michael Portillo also felt the lash of Tony's tongue, 'At one point Portillo was polishing his jackboots and planning the next advance. And the next thing is he shows up as a TV presenter. It is rather like Pol Pot presenting the *Teletubbies*.'

The most deadly recent insult was the brilliantly conceived Vince Cable comment that Gordon Brown had gone from 'Stalin to Mr Bean'. It hit the bullseye of collapsing public confidence in Gordon. Brief, visually memorable and accurate. Brown was wounded and never fully recovered.

How to Out-Tech

In spite of the opposition of old and new fogeys, technology has invaded the Chamber and transformed debate. Instant research is possible on BlackBerries and iPads.

As shadow Welsh spokeswoman Cheryl Gillan came a cropper in the Commons St David's day debate when she chose a Newport Community Councillor as an example to emulate as 'a good man, in touch with the people'. Proudly she quoted this exemplar's words of devotion to the high principles of Toryism.

Alas for Cheryl a Labour MP checked the MySpace site where the newly discovered paragon had been unwisely frank. A septuagenarian MP suggested Cheryl should curb her enthusiasm. She retorted, 'This sounds like a case of young versus old. I think that it is just jealousy because he is so young at nineteen, and obviously very much in touch with people.'

As the young man has been cited as typifying the brave new world of Conservatism it was fair to quote his own words, 'I've evolved from a little whining pussy to a thrill seeking wreckhead to a Conservative who still loves the wreckups.' He said he wanted to go into politics, for 'the power, the flash suits and the money.'

Cheryl may rue the day that her research was limited.

How to Prepare Impromptu Remarks

All MPs can make speeches. The special terror of the Commons at all levels is intervention. It is not enough to read a prepared script or to give a straight from the shoulder rant. An MP must answer 'interventions'. There is no respect for those who refuse to 'give way'.

The simplest interventions are the deadliest because they rob the speaker of thinking time. The only form of defence is to painstakingly prepare an array of 'impromptu' answers. Many of the interventions can be intelligently anticipated and apposite quips written. Often answers that are slightly off target can be anticipated.

A study of regular attendees on the subject of the debate being discussed will suggest killer retorts against them. They can be irrelevant to the subject of the intervention if they are personal to the questioner. A good riposte will be appreciated by the House, long after they have forgotten the original question.

On committees it is much easier with a limited number of a dozen or so MPs. The Register of Members interests can be easily searched through Google or theyworkforyou.com. There are some delicious details in everyone's past speeches, electoral history or previous incarnations that can be used to boomerang back on them. If a smart response to an intervention doesn't spring to mind, hit out with an insult. Have a quiver full of lambasting sound darts, ready to throw.

George Foulkes was a model Commons performer. He and I were locked in animated private conversation during Oral Questions one afternoon when the voice of the Speaker broke through our argument. 'George Foulkes' he called for the next oral question. George jumped. He tore the Order Paper from my hand to check the number and shouted 'Number six, Mr Speaker?' He had forgotten that he had tabled a question.

The minister's one word reply allowed no time for George to find out the subject of the question. Powerfully he gave his omnibus supplementary that is good for all occasions. 'That's exactly the sort of heartless answer that I expected to have. It proves again the total incompetence, indifference and lack of compassion of this awful Government. Isn't it time for them go? Let's have a Labour Government?'

We all cheered. Mostly for George's recovery from the brink of humiliation. That supplementary question had been lodged for years in the recesses of his mind ready for that occasion. Government backbenchers similarly caught short would say 'I am most grateful to my honourable friend for that encouraging reply, that proves again... (the rest is the reverse of George's question).' All purpose omnibus fallback questions are an insurance against embarrassment.

The resourceful create stinging responses to every conceivable situation. The daily bloggers can build up a rich stock of aphorisms, wisecracks and insults that can be instantly drawn on from the memory banks and sprayed around the Chamber.

How to Be a Hooligan

Rowdyism is a hallowed Commons tradition. Compared with previous centuries the house is seemly and courteous. The cameras have helped. Votingham disapproves if an MP bearing their town's name behaves like an oaf. Misbehaviour is now furtively out of sight of the camera or communal, where numbers obscure identity.

John Major, Tony Blair, Iain Duncan Smith, and Gordon Brown have been targets of organised yobbery. The weapons deployed to destroy their composure were noise, body language and gesture. The ambient noise is often deafening but is diminished by distance sensitive microphones that enlarge the Dispatch Box speech and reduce the background bedlam. Many leaders have been silenced and paused forgetting that even though they may not be clearly hearing their own voices the listeners and viewers can clearly hear them above the yelling in the background.

PMs and opposition leaders face a daunting mob. Hundreds of MP opponents facing the Dispatch Box project body language rejection contortions that are formidable confidence sappers. Dismissive synchronised gestures undermine composure. A new ploy is to mirror the gestures of the leaders in a mocking pantomime.

John Major was greeted with mysterious Woody Woodpecker noises. Quality hooligans waited for Major's pauses to dynamite his argument. He often blundered into the quicksand of rhetorical questions. His staccato delivery left second long gaps in his flow that were filled with shouts of 'Wriggling', 'Pathetic,' 'Boring', 'Resign'. The hazard of sedentary yelling is to push the Speaker into fury.

The first rule of professional yobbery is to hit and shut up. Repeated catcalls are dangerous because the Speaker's radar might have homed in on the first shout and if repeated, attention will be sharply focused on the offender, ready to zap. Rod Richards, a few days before he was made a minister by Major, shouted 'Liar' when Peter Hain was asking a question. He repeated it a few seconds later and was forced to apologise by the Speaker, twice – first to the House, then to the Speaker.

He also broke the second rule. His mouth was not shielded from the Speaker's view by an Order Paper or the bulk of another MP. On a rare lapse when I once unwisely shouted some monosyllabic advice to the Prime Minister I was shielded by the frame of George Foulkes. The Speaker 'named' the aghast, dumbly protesting George. He was having a rare quiet afternoon. The Speaker was unrepentant when I confessed my guilt. George's previous fifty offences had been taken into account.

Speaker Bercow has used some withering put-downs to recidivist offenders. A favourite is to remind the Children's Minister that he does not have to behave like a child.

How to Intervene

One of the glories of the British Parliament is the open door backbenchers have to question and humble the mighty. The most obscure backbencher can intervene in party leaders' speeches on almost any occasion. The more obscure the Member the more likely the speaker is to allow the intervention. All Prime Ministers and Leaders of the Opposition have had speeches wrecked by interveners who have hit a bull's-eye.

The most difficult for speakers to handle are interventions that seek answers on matters of fact: 'Could he explain what his Government did about earnings disregards in 1964?', 'What was the level of employment when his party was last in office?' A tedious repeated question is 'What will the Opposition spend on this if they ever get into Government?' It wears down speakers tired of their own repeated answer.

Increasingly interventions are scripted by the whips. Lists of single sentence questions are distributed to backbenchers. They are designed to trip up frontbench speakers on big occasions. They are useful but dangerous. Never be the first one to use one. Both Major and Blair have pummelled interveners because they have had copies of their opponent's questions that have been left on photocopiers. For original questions the best time to intervene is early.

The speaker is allowed a few minutes grace. Stand during a natural pause or when the speaker is moving to a new theme. Others will stand a second later in synchronised intervention. The cry 'Will the Prime Minister/minister/Hon. Member give way?' must be immediate, loud and authoritative. If rejected, keep standing at intervals, especially if a promise has been made of giving way later.

An obvious failure to honour a promise is worth a Point of Order if the mood of the House is sympathetic. The times when all speakers will give way is when they appear distracted. They may have lost their way in their speech, have a frog in the throat or are otherwise discombobulated. They will welcome the break to recover.

The crippling interventions are those that are apposite to the theme, quote a killer fact or ask an unanswerable question. The spirit of many politicians is sapped by embarrassing incidents in their past. John Major was disturbed by any mention of 'O' Levels; John Prescott was unhappy with taunts about his life as a steward. These are cruel but legitimate weapons in the political arsenal.

How to Legislate

Even though executive power is ballooning in our elective dictatorships, backbenchers still have a legislative role.

Since 1948, 728 bills have been brought onto the statute book through the work of backbenchers. There are three ways of initiating legislation.

Presentation Bills are introduced behind the chair. The process is swift and simple. Notice can be given to the Public Office as late as the preceding day. All that is required is a long title that outlines the purpose of the bill. It is then printed on the Order Paper and the Member has to be present to hand it to the Clerk of the House when called to do so by the Speaker. Most presentation bills are going nowhere on the legislative conveyor belt. They are for publicity or act as embryo ideas for future bills. Nevertheless one hundred and thirty of them are now law.

The fortunate dozen Members a year who win high places for Ballot Bills have succeeded on 439 occasions. Success or failure is often determined by the choice of bill. Seeking genuine reform is hazardous. Major successes were achieved by Leo Abse who challenged the prejudices of his time on homosexuality and divorce. He was a backbencher by choice, operating from a secure constituency base with a network of cross party contacts. Triumph here depends not on having many friends but having few enemies.

The fate of all Private Bills is in the hands of Government. Reforms can only get through by compromise. Government whips are always ready to blow them out of the water. Outside bodies are now almost essential in campaigning beyond Parliament to build support and put constituency pressure on MPs.

Small victories are the rewards for bills that have Government support and enjoy a smooth passage through the House. Most of Michael Shersby's bills provoked little opposition. He has put a record eight on the statute book. He told me that it needs 'two years hard work' to succeed. Most of it is in persuading ministers and backbenchers of Government and Opposition to give the bill a fair wind. Winning friendship among political opponents usually mean adopting an ineffectual party political role.

The Lords have chalked up 117 bills and even the undervalued Ten Minute Rule Bills have had fifty-three successes. Diligent and intelligent planning and luck can secure committee time for Ten Minute Rule Bills.

But Private Bills are a gargantuan thief of time. Instant success is rare. Apparent failure is reversed by later bills by other Members.

Rewards may come – in heaven.

How to Use Ten Minutes

Ten Minute Bills are a prime weapon in the backbencher's armoury. They always deliver a captive audience of the House and the live television audience for a topic of the Member's choice. At best a new law could be placed on the statute book.

The success rate is not brilliant. Only sixty-six have been successful since 1945, and only seventeen since 1970. I was surprised to read that my modest Animal Health Amendment Act is one of the last three enacted. That was in 1998. It was a surreal experience. Both Alan Clark and Eric Forth supported it although neither of them understood its real purpose. Eric was a fearsome bill assassin. My final speech at third reading was curtailed to two minutes of vague generalities. I did not want to antagonise anyone by revealing the real purpose of the bill. It then sailed through the Lords and provided a minor improvement on the laws on animal quarantine.

Securing a bill slot prior to 1997 entailed queueing all night at the Public Bill Office. A minor crisis developed in December 1996 when I turned up at 4 a.m. and found two sleeping bodies. There were four slots on offer that day to be allocated at 10 a.m. Daylight revealed that in addition to two sleeping Labour Members, Tory Elizabeth Peacock and another Member had 'bagged' places the night before. Then they went off to sleep at home. Peacock had left a teddy bear behind, garlanded with the message 'I am Elizabeth Peacock's research assistant queuing for a bill for LIFE.'

Elizabeth Peacock argued that it was not reasonable for her to have to spend the night with three bearded Labour MPs in order to get a bill. John Heppell and Paddy Tipping were a little hurt. I magnanimously declined to press my claim and Peacock had her bill. The whips gave me the next slot. The horrors of the possible fate of Elizabeth Peacock and three bearded MPs was too much. The incident accelerated reform to a less open but more civilised allocation of slots by the whips.

When a place is won, the procedure is simple. All that is needed is to provide the clerk with a long title of the bill stating its purpose. Pack information into the title to intrigue and excite the hacks. The form is that the Member 'begs leave to introduce a bill to abolish the monarchy/to introduce daylight saving/to reform the electoral law'. Add the coda 'and for connected purposes' to include all the extra ideas that will crop up in the fortnight's wait before the bill is presented to the House.

Heaven is starting the speech precisely at 3.30 p.m. with a full house present, inherited from Prime Minister's Question Time and perhaps waiting to hear a vital debate that follows. Hell is having the slot delayed by a sensational Government statement on a juicy scandal, followed by an hour of questions. The hacks have their story for the day. They and the MPs will have deserted the Chamber by the time for Ten Minute Bills.

Ten minutes is an ocean of time for those skilled in squashing arguments into three brief sentences. The perfect ingredients for the speech are a riveting start, a punchy finish, two or three good jokes and persuasive middle that makes a positive case and demolishes any reply from your opponents. Time the speech for eight minutes to allow for rhetorical flourishes.

It is fatal to try to cram too much in and garble the denouement. Often a division is useful but is best organised with (unofficial) co-operation with the whips. On the day the Public Bill Office will prepare for the Member a Dummy Bill and a copy of the choreography. It is a surprise to read the details of the rigmarole for marching from the Bar of the House to the table. 'Five steps and bow, another five steps and bow.' Quaintly, it concludes, 'Then hand your Dummy to the clerk.'

Opposing someone else's Ten Minute Bill is tricky. Intelligent research on the mover's part will almost always explain the line of argument that will be used. Give notice to the Speaker as early as possible of the intention to oppose. There may be a queue. Listen intently to the speech. The House always appreciates a good debating speech that could not have been rehearsed.

The opposing speaker must shout 'No' when the Speaker calls for those for and against even if a vote is not wanted. Explain to the Speaker what is happening and make it a whispered shout. A futile or an abortive vote will drag hundreds of Members away from their desks, will anger friends, delight enemies and may shift votes against the bill. An unwanted vote can steal the time available for later important debates.

Penny Mordaunt refreshingly broke with tradition and introduced what she called a 'five minute bill'. That was all the time she needed for a striking speech on improving special education. She deserves to succeed. Voluntarily reducing a ten minute allocation of prime time is almost unknown but very progressive. Vast quantities of luck, arm-twisting and guile can get Ten Minute Rule Bills into committee and onto the statute book. It happens rarely, but that is not really the point of Ten Minute Rule Bills.

How to Petition

Petitions have been re-incarnated as e-petitions.

They are really repackaged old petitions that are likely to repeat the unhappy fate of the existing system which represents centuries of wasted efforts. Their history is arcane and extraordinary. Petitions to Parliament have always faced hostility. One presented by the Mayor of Salisbury in 1640 was ordered to be burnt. The Chartist petition with two million signatures was ignored. Not much has changed since.

In the last century ten thousand a year arrived. Twenty years ago the number had slumped to about forty a session. Recently they have picked up twenty-fold. Single issues, particularly on disability or animal welfare, have excited new epidemics of petitioning.

E-petitions are the weak third link in the otherwise admirable Wright reforms. Constituents should be warned of the limits of the value of this approach. They mobilise opinion and create publicity. But that is all. In the past an archaic wording was mandatory. The first page had to be handwritten and the petition began 'To the Honourable the Commons of the United Kingdom of Great Britain and Northern Ireland in Parliament Assembled' and ended 'and your petitioners, as in duty bound, will ever pray, &c'. The procedure has been greatly simplified. A modern form of words is now permitted, alongside the more traditional form above. A petition may now be handwritten, printed or typed, but there must be no erasures, deletions or interlineations in it.

The tradition of minimal interest inside the House continues in spite of the recent revival of extra-Parliamentary enthusiasm. There is an Act still in force saying that no petition can be presented by more than ten persons. It is quaintly called the Act Against Tumultuous Petitioning, passed in 1661, and could still be invoked to block any petition that was likely to be taken seriously. I have been tempted frequently, but no one has invoked this Act in living memory. Very surprisingly another very useful Standing Order 134 has also not been invoked for fifty years. It states that that Petitions 'complaining of some present personal grievance, for which there may be an urgent necessity for providing an immediate remedy...' may be discussed, though opposed.

Only MPs can present petitions, either by dropping them in the green bag behind the Speaker's chair while the House is in session or verbally presenting them on specific occasions. Prior to the second reading of the Alton Bill and at other times multiple petitions have been used as a time-wasting ploy to delay discussion. This is no longer possible. The only historic relic still operating in their favour is that, uniquely, petitions can be sent to the House post free as long as they are unsealed. Some constituents still believe that letters to MPs are post free, as all Members occasionally discover to their cost.

E-petitions are a reworked Blairite gimmick. He embraced Downing Street petitioning as a glittering, epoch-making weapon of mass communication. They are nothing of the sort. Experience has shown them to be clumsy, time-wasting ramshackle devices for telling Government what they already know. The dream from two governments was of a Brave New World of mass e-discourse from which fresh ideas would bubble up to inspire and inform a listening Legislature. The Cameronian 'false gold' offers a parliamentary debate for petitions of more than 100,000 signatures and the enticing possibility of a bill drafted to match the public's demand.

The Government already has its antennae focused on shifts in public opinion. Little new will be revealed. E-petitions will confirm the tabloid-aroused and fed prejudices of the masses. Governments rarely abandon entrenched position but a false dawn of hope was grudgingly provided to cheap fuel campaigners. This chimed with their stance in wooing Jeremy Clarkson bigots. More disillusionment and resentment is guaranteed if no action is taken to match the public's demand for restoring capital punishment, withdrawal from the EU or for cutting benefits.

The world experience of similar initiatives is not encouraging. But there is one exception. Public opinion forced the introduction of euthanasia in Oregon. The unhappiness about the right-to-die is shared by many MPs but it remains a taboo subject. The House Leader George Young is wandering down this parliamentary cul-de-sac of e-petitions.

MPs should limit their enthusiasm for an idea whose time has probably already gone.

How to Win Prizes

There is little tangible evidence for backbenchers to prove that they are doing a good job.

No one admits to being interested, of course. But in the small hours of the morning many MPs secretly live out the fantasy of being acclaimed as the 'Parliamentarian' or 'Backbencher' of the year. Prizes are a balm for sorrows of the wounded ego, a bolstering comforter for under-loved toilers in the Parliamentary vineyard. The chances of success are minute.

Trying to win disqualifies. Once canvassing was fatal since winners are chosen by parliamentarians. But now e-mail 'reminders' arrive. They are probably counter-productive.

In the past, right-wing journalists picked the winners. Dave Nellist candidly acknowledged when he was named Backbencher of the Year that the prize was intended to embarrass the Labour Party. The same party later expelled him for his connections with Militant Tendency. John Redwood and James Callaghan got their awards as proof that backbenchers could make it after spells on the front line.

Tam Dalyell had a unique mention as 'Troublemaker of the Year'. The most prophetic choice occurred in 1991 when the 'Member to Watch' was David Mellor, just before the nation's attention became riveted to his love life.

The steaming climate of jealousy at the Palace of Westminster is hostile to prize winners. Parliamentarians/Backbenchers of the Year can expect a chilling of friendship. It is better to secure the Parliamentary Campaign for Freedom of Information award, the Parliamentary Friend of Small Businesses prize or the Greenest MP gong. Yvonne Fovargue has been named Citizens Advice Parliamentarian of the Year 2011. The Inland Waterways Association has made its 2011 award for 'Parliamentarian of the Year' to Alun Michael. Minor awards agreeably boost stature in

Votingham but are not prestigious enough to incite envy. They harmlessly make Members big fishes in a few tiny ponds.

Constituents have ways for assessing the worth of their Member. The flood of information from the House of Commons databases provide insight into Parliamentary activities. League tables are compiled of the numbers of divisions attended, speeches made and questions asked. Attendance registers at committees exist that identify the habitual truants. The measure is quantity not quality. Sadly no one can assess the value of the contributions in the league tables. They are a crude guide to activity. It is a sore embarrassment to the inactive Members who record *'nul points'* for parliamentary work.

Paul Murphy was feeling very hard done by late one Thursday night. He was one of the few Members left in a deserted House. His day had been spent slaving on a Housing Bill long after most MPs had gone home. He was told in a telephone message that local television had produced a league table of Welsh MPs, analysing who was doing the most work. The sad news was that he was almost bottom as the least hard working MP. The worst news was that the only two Members below him in the table were both dead.

Increasing publicity for these league tables sometimes has a galvanising effect. A shame list of non-speakers in one session prompted most of them to break their silence within the following fortnight.

Theyworkforyou.com has become the most accessible account of parliamentary activity and expenses claims. They provide a useful service in alerting friends and foes to oral contributions in the Chamber. The voting record is infuriatingly misleading because it attempts to judge the strength of MPs passions against votes cast only and not by all other activities. Their expenses figures have sometimes been misleading. Many MPs were named as being top of the table of ignominy for being the highest claimants for most expensive stays away from their main home. Later it was pointed out that 183 MPs had shared top place. They had exceeded the allowance and were guilty only of spending their own money.

These tables have had a beneficial effect of exposing the lazy MP with comatose activity records. Some have been aroused from their slumbers to active life because of unfavourable publicity. The site was the creditable work of volunteers who have served the public interest. But there are niggles. Curious comparisons on the use of alliterative phrases seem pointless. Their methods of assessing speed of e-mail replies is wildly unreliable. After the demise of Parliamentary Profiles, theyworkforyou.com is the best mirror to parliamentary activity in spite of occasional distortions.

How to Apologise

Apologising to the House can be one sentence of regret for using unparliamentary language or a humiliating confession of career-wrecking greed.

Peter Lilley, James Gray and Rod Richards apologised for using an improper word in calling a Member a 'liar.' Gray also apologised for not confessing immediately. It's wise to end the misery swiftly.

Some apologies have been so misjudged that Members have been asked to apologise for their apologies. They should be unconditional and demeanour is as important as the words chosen.

The words of Derek Conway's personal statement accepted full guilt for employing a relative. But his confident smiling demeanour showed no evidence of remorse. The press were irritated and they pursued Derek. Harry Cohen was clearly upset and contrite at his shortcomings. The pursuit was less fierce.

The most ill-judged apologies in recent years were from Jonathan Sayeed and Keith Vaz. In his first apology Sayeed suggested 'there were a few errors' in the Committee on Standards conclusions. The committee disagreed and 'invited' him to make a 'fuller apology' which he did without further demur.

Keith Vaz made a very long statement of apology which included several quibbles. Chairman of the Standards Committee George Young replied that Vaz 'had made matters worse by his subsequent behaviour which in my view has been aimed at undermining the entire investigative process.' He also criticised Vaz for holding a press conference where George Young said that Vaz was 'unwise to criticise the punishment as "disproportionate" and the report as "misled"'.

Brief informal apologies were made for minor offences. Claire Perry apologised for inquiring in the Members' Tea Room, 'What have I got to do to be called by the Speaker? Give him a blow job?' A letter of regret was sufficient because it was treacherous colleagues and a newspaper that put her private remark into the public domain. Tom Watson said sorry for calling Michael Gove 'a miserable pip-squeak' and Harriet Harman expressed regret for calling Danny Alexander 'a ginger rodent'.

There is an obvious lesson. Conclusions of the Standards Committee should be fully accepted. Most recent apologies have involved expenses that have been wrongly claimed.

In 2011 I had grounds to call Defence Secretary Liam Fox to the House for an allegation he made about me, which I demonstrated was completely untrue. Liam wrote to me in generous, helpful terms. Not only did he admit his mistake but he praised my parliamentary work in sentences that may well grace a future election leaflet. Little useful purpose would be served by a Commons' apology for Fox's remarks made in the heat of debate. In the area of Defence there are far more important issues to concern the Chamber.

That was two months before Liam was forced to resign and apologise for what he called a 'blurring' of the ministerial code. He used the passive tense in his confession, which suggested that some mysterious unknown forces were responsible for all the errors. For 'blurring' read a flagrant abuse of the ministerial code. The House is generous and accepts contrition even when it is blatantly counterfeit. The press and country judge more harshly.

ADVANCED STEPS

How to Get it Wright

The greatly admired Tony Wright created reforms that attack the impotence and infantalisation of the House of Commons. He said of the role of backbenchers: 'In a way it is easy when we can blame the Government for everything, but from now on we shall have to attend to ourselves and take responsibility for ourselves.'

Leader of the House George Young agreed with Speaker Bercow that 'this is a 'truly wonderful time to be in Parliament. We are both reformers at heart'. George Young said the Wright reforms meant MPs would 'never again be forced to plead for more time from the Government in order to debate its own business'.

Tony Wright's three major reforms are the election of chairs and members of Select Committees by secret ballots, to give backbenchers a significant control of scheduling business in the Commons and to give the public a say in setting the Commons agenda. Although the third element is the weakest, all the reforms will strengthen the power of the backbenchers over the whips, the Legislature over the Executive.

The endemic weakness of the House of the Commons, George Young says, is that, 'Over recent decades, it has simply become too easy for the Government to sideline Parliament; to push bills through without adequate scrutiny; and to see the House more as a rubber stamp than a proper check on executive authority.'

The Backbench Committee has had a successful year in achieving the aim of the Wright Report to 'create new opportunities for all Members, giving them a greater sense of ownership and responsibility for what goes on in their own House'. The committee's chair Natascha Engel insisted on public meetings for the Backbench Committee to ensure it did not become 'our own hobby horse'.

Full debates on subjects that the Government wanted to avoid have taken place, including Afghanistan, immigration and votes for prisoners. There is some evidence that Government is lightly whipping for these debates although they took a strong line on the Afghanistan debate.

Natascha's stewardship of the committee has been praised by fellow MPs. The weekly bidding sessions, held on Tuesdays at 1 p.m., when MPs queue to persuade the committee to allocate debating time. The Backbench Committee has full control of thirty-five days during each parliamentary session, twenty-seven of which are in the Chamber. A leap forward in the powers of Select Committees was taken by the Public Administration Committee (PASC) in 2011. PASC had pioneered pre-appointment hearings. First blood followed a hostile interrogation of the recommended candidate for the job of chair of the Statistics Authority. The committee complained because of the strong establishment character of the appointment panel, the reduced wage and working week. PASC emphasised the supreme importance of independence from Government in the role of the appointee. The recommended candidate withdrew.

The committee suspected an attempt by the Executive to dumb down the statistics watchdog's role. The Government caved in. They added an MP to the appointment panel, increased the salary and number of days worked.

The Treasury Select Committee was also given an effective veto over appointments to the Office for Budget Responsibility, including its director. The Liaison Committee, comprising the chairs of all Commons Select Committees, want MPs to have a greater role in choosing holders of specific posts which either uphold standards in public life, defend the rights of citizens or exercise direct control over the activities of ministers.

These profound changes have moved power significantly from the Executive to the Legislature.

There's fierce competition for time.

Getting it Wright is the prime opportunity for today's backbenchers.

How to Go to War

Voting on joining Bush's Iraq War in 2003 was probably the most important decision that MPs took in the last century. For the first time, MPs decided. Previously these judgements were part of the Royal Prerogative exercised by the Executive.

Most military interventions by the UK have enjoyed the support of the overwhelming majority of the people. Suez and the second Iraq War were different. They were fiercely opposed. In the almost certain knowledge that he had a majority in the House, Tony Blair surrendered to demands for a vote. MPs decided. 139 Labour Members defied a three line whip. Eighty Labour MPs who had previously expressed doubts were bribed, bullied or bamboozled into abstaining or voting for war. Sixteen Tories rebelled against Iain Duncan Smith who was even more gung-ho for war than Tony Blair.

The majority for war was 179 – the exact number of British soldiers who later lost their lives. Had the majority been smaller, Britain would not have joined the war and 179 British lives would have been saved. The outcome would not have altered had Britain not contributed our blood and treasure. The monster Saddam Hussein would still have been killed. One rotten Government would have been replaced by another rotten Government.

Many MPs judge the value of their entire political lives by the decision that they took on that March day in 2003. There is bitter regret from the majority of Labour's eighty doubters. They are haunted by the belief that they failed their sternest test. The whips tried everything including the threat that Blair would resign and call a General Election. The prospect of P45s on the horizon is a potent fear. Many were persuaded that advice from the secret services was infallible. 'After all,' one told me, 'the Prime Minister would not lie.' The slow revelation of the truth of the 2003 decision is slowly being revealed.

The UK did not need to join Bush's war. Tony Blair was elated by successes of British military actions in Sierra Leone, Bosnia and Kosovo, none of which were approved by Parliament. Leaders are more prone to megalomania and the need to carve out their personal place in history than rank and file MPs are. Warfare should be decided by the Legislature not the Executive.

The constitutional situation has not been finalised. In 2006 the UK blundered into Helmand province in the hope that 'not a shot would be fired'. Then only two UK soldiers had died in combat. It soared to nearly 400. The incursion was debated in Westminster but there was no vote. Parliament did not vote on the war in Afghanistan until 2010. MPs voted on Libya with an overwhelming majority the day after our armed forces were involved. A precedent is set but not yet ratified.

The chair of the Political and Constitutional Reform Committee, Graham Allen, called for a clear statement of Parliament's role on decisions to go to war. He said: 'The Government has said that Parliament has a role, but there isn't an agreed position on what this role is, certainly not one that Parliament has ever agreed to.'

Formalising the role of MPs and votes on future wars are crucial matters of life and avoidable deaths.

How to Squirrel

Odd sums of money arrive in the post. Cheques from media interviews, for writing or from market research companies are not really earned. They are usually paid for doing the job for which MPs are already paid.

If they lie heavily on the conscience, they can be diverted into a fund for excess income. Set up a proper charitable trust with defined aims and trustees, into which the full sums can be deposited. A simpler course is to pay tax on the cash, then deposit it in a separate charitable account with independent signatories.

Either way the sums quickly accumulate into substantial amounts for worthwhile giving. They help to avoid dependence on outside money and ensure that work priorities are not distorted by financial temptations. Always insist that any charitable giving is anonymous. It absolves the giver of the insulting charge of trying to buy votes and it reduces the calls on the fund from unworthy causes.

How to Survive Unpopular Causes

Voters now are more tolerant and respectful of MPs who display independence. In the first year of the 2010 parliament there were more rebellions from MPs of all parties than ever before. The biggest avalanches of mail that have threatened to overwhelm the Commons' efficient Post Office in the past decade sprang from the highly contentious issues of abortion, the Hunting Bill, capital punishment, the smoking ban, the sell-off of forests, police pensions, and the Iraq War.

Many angry constituents' letters have a sting in the tail threatening not to vote for the incumbent MP in the General Election. In most cases this is a vacuous ploy. There are few issues that determine voting habits in General Elections. Mostly they are decided by how the national policies of parties serve the material self-interest of voters. On issues of conscience a firm position should be taken as soon as possible. Expressing uncertainty invites furious lobbying from all sides.

Factions are quick to identify those with strong opinions that cannot be moved. They concentrate on the waverers. I received letters, petitions and calls from ten per cent of my constituents on the Alton Bill because I had expressed genuine doubt. On hanging I had fewer than a dozen letters because I had long said that I would never vote for the restoration of capital punishment. Voters soon recognise an immovable object.

British contemporary politics has slid into the same pit of political cowardice as the USA, where legislators can use their vast allowances to measure voter opinion on all issues. Their votes can always be trimmed to the current prejudice and bigotry of the masses. No doubt, this is a great way to secure an election majority and swell the incumbency factor. But this is not the way for politicians to operate unless their highest ambition is to be an automaton. A computer could vote slavishly in line with opinion poll results.

Some MPs are mesmerised by the ebb and flow of their majorities. That is the measure of their self-worth. A healthier view is that a bloated majority could prove that the Member is not challenging the baser views of the local constituents.

A progressive MP should charge the barricades of ignorance and bigotry. No worthwhile reform has ever been achieved by obeying the lowest common denominator of public opinion. There will be a loss of votes for any current MP backing euthanasia, legalising illegal drugs, modernising royalty, cutting unnecessary NHS operations and drug prescription, or arguing for humane treatment for prisoners, sites for gypsies, and immigrants' rights.

Supporting any of these subjects will cause eruptions of fire and brimstone from local press, party and voters. With a majority of 1,000 such a course would be perilous. With a comfortable majority it is a positive duty to lead on issues regardless of their popularity. An adjective that has followed me in Parliament is 'controversial'. Short term, it's problematic. Long term, it's beneficial. Being controversial means that everyone agrees with your views twenty years after you have expressed them.

It is electorally hazardous to be identified with a single

unpopular cause. Causes with popular support and constituency issues must be laced into the cocktail of work to create an acceptable brew for the constituents.

Voters loathe hero-worshipping Members. They much prefer to say, 'My MP is round the twist on some issues but otherwise a great constituency MP'. Sometimes there's a modest pride in having a highly individualistic character of an MP. Minor eccentricity and notoriety are generously tolerated and preferred to obscurity. I have proof of that.

How Not to be Spun

Spin doctors strive to control the parliamentary web. Employed by the party leaders, their gossamer is used to clog the brains and bandage the mouths of backbenchers. Their 'plot' is to stun into a state of continuing manic exaltation of the leader and all his works.

Nothing must be allowed that will slow or divert the majestic progress of the 'plot' of securing General Election victory. The next one and the one after. Their concentration is needle-point focused but its span is that of a retarded earthworm. Nirvana to them is a happy headline in the tabloids tomorrow. The day after tomorrow and the rest of the future is invisible, far over their time horizon.

They can help. Their inventive minds produce venomous, inspired quips for the sluggish-brained backbenchers short of a retort at Prime Minister's Questions. Slothful reporters are supplied with the glowing heaps of words that build and promote the plot of the day.

There are few intellectual giants among the spinners. Their judgements often lead to hell. In the week of the Littleborough and Saddleworth by-election I felt the hot breath of their wrath. For months I had tried to get a debate on legalising the use of cannabis for medicinal reasons. My chance came dangerously close to the date of the by-election for the spin doctors' comfort. Their strategy was to paint the Lib Dem candidate as a drug pushing libertine and canonised the Labour man as an immaculate hermit.

The Lib Dem candidate had advocated a Royal Commission on illegal drug use. Panic broke out when my debate was noticed. I was approached by friendly whips, a creepy spin doctor and an aggressive backbencher. Their judgement had been twisted into a belief that I was about to give ammunition to the Lib Dems. The plight of many thousands of sick people unfairly deprived of a unique medicine was dismissed by all except Chief Whip Derek Foster. He understood the need for a change in the law because of a constituency victim.

The debate was not widely reported. The voters decided that the Lib Dems had been caught in possession of an intelligent argument and elected its candidate. Labour was rejected on the grounds of implausible sanctity. Worse was to come.

The umbilical link between spinners and hacks guarantees that their version of events is reported first. Sometimes to their detriment. On occasions when I have incurred their wrath, their negative briefings have been provocative and damaging to their cause.

At a private meeting of the Parliamentary Labour Party I raged in direct simple language at a piece of party folly. An hour after the meeting, Ceefax carried the spin doctor placed news that I had expressed 'unease'. That word is rarely in my vocabulary, especially that day when emotions were soaring.

The tactic, I believe, was to dilute the true nitric adjectival tirade that they expected me to leak to the hacks. It was counterproductive and gave publicity to the far stronger words that I used. An attack that would otherwise have remained private oozed into the media's agenda.

Now it is unwise to treat the meetings of the Parliamentary Labour Party or the 1922 Committee as private. Leakage from both has become a flood.

How to Ignore Disabilities

Disabilities are of prime interest only to the disabled. There will be superficial kindness and help but the attention span of self-absorbed egomaniacs is limited. How David Blunkett pours tea without over-filling the cup is interesting. Discovering the wheelchair route to the cafe for when Great-Aunt Joan visits is worth knowing. But MPs are sprinters not marathon runners on extreme compassion.

A powerful personality eclipses even the most interesting diseases. Few remember that Churchill was a wheelchair user or that JFK, Roosevelt and Iain Macleod had infirmity problems. The Commons rejoiced in the contributions of Anne Begg, David Blunkett and Jack Ashley. Their triumphs over adversity have been heroic. New MP Robert Halfon has impressed with his energy and originality. His crutches are invisible. He seeks no concessions for a childhood disease that prevents him from standing repeatedly to catch the Speaker's eye. He manages to be a leading questioner by waving an Order Paper. They are inspiring role models for children with disabilities.

In the past twenty-five years the Commons has become an improving habitat for the disabled with several concessions, grudgingly given. Extra allowances and equipment are available to compensate for disability. David Blunkett has an office allowance at three times the going rate to pay for his specialist Braille translators and extra staff. Although the process is lengthy, requiring a vote in the House, funds would be found to assist a seriously ill MP to continue working. More improvements are needed. IPSA was hard-hearted in refusing first class rail travel for Members who cannot stand for long journeys.

Those with spasmodic or minor disabilities should take care. My walking gait is irregular and was a worry when I was first elected. I limped and stumbled. At worst I ricocheted from one side of a corridor to the other. If I had the slightest smell of alcohol on my breath, a fair conclusion was that I was 'staggering drunk'. Such reputations are easily gained in the House of Plots and Rumours. I broadcast that the real reason was arthritis. Soon everyone understood why I walked in that funny way.

There is some limited advantage in appearing to overcome adversity. But the limping wildebeest syndrome of targeting the imperfect is an electoral threat. It is entirely legitimate to make light of private disabilities. It is not fair to lose empathy with those who must cope with similar problems without the gorgeous ego-boosting distraction of parliamentary work. It's wise to negate criticism of possible deficiencies by over-compensating with hyperactive record-breaking parliamentary workloads. The disabled can be brilliant MPs. Almost all the effects of disabilities can be surmounted with ingenuity or modern technology. Standing for speeches or at receptions may be impossible. But alternatives are available.

A civil servant constituent complained to me a few years ago that his promotion was blocked because the place where civil servants sit in the Commons Chamber was inaccessible for his wheelchair. In spite of my entreaties, it still is. There is still no dedicated, redesigned place with microphones at appropriate levels for wheelchair-using MPs in the Chamber.

There is much still to be done.

How to Avoid Murder

Closed communities of monasteries, refugee camps and parliaments breed internal conflicts. Familiarity breeds antagonisms. The MP most likely to be murdered by colleagues is the Select Committee time glutton. Those waiting to pack their allotted time with concentrated interrogation of witnesses smoulder at what is perceived as the aimless never-ending babbling of other MPs with disorganised brains.

One Select Committee member sharpened his act after being

told that his 'bouncing questions' were legendary. Beginning, 'Can I bounce this off you?' he spouted a spiral of verbal ectoplasm that wreathed the committee with wayward, futile words, going on ... hypnotically ... eternally. Not once did he see the homicidal yearning in the eyes of his colleagues for silence, a full-stop or a question mark.

Also at risk are the pitiable Friday morning debate groupies. The thinly attended Chamber allows the junior, the unloved and unnoticed Members to burble and bore. Chances of publicity and a spot on *Today in Parliament* are increased as there are poorer pickings from the Friday dross. Government whips nurture the Friday groupies to block and obstruct bills from opponents. The ammunition is filibuster briefings designed to give ersatz leaden authority to speakers on the topics of the day.

Time is the executioner of Friday bills. The bores congeal, forming a solid blob to jam the hours from 9.30 to the 2.30 limit when bills are talked out and decapitated. The authors of other bills in the queue fantasise a similar fate for the filibusterers.

The doyen of backbenchers Leo Abse gave me a valuable piece of advice forty years ago. 'When you are speaking in the open air, never speak for longer than three minutes'. I have always followed it. Even on a warm day with a sitting audience, three minutes is enough because there are many outdoor distractions. An audience standing in the cold, desperate for a rest or a loo will rapidly lose patience. No one has ever complained that any of my speeches were too short.

In Newport in December 1995 Clare Short spoke for less than a minute and won the eternal love of the audience. Another speaker did not. 'Stop him or there will be a riot,' a friend whispered. It was the opening of Newport's Transporter Bridge and an inexperienced speaker was going on and on:

'...and someone else called Fred made the handrails, well some of them anyway, with a bit of help from Joe. Or was it Bill?...'

He was the third speaker. It was the coldest night in Newport since the Ice Age.

'I'd never been down to Newport before, but the other chap Harry, I think had, but I am not sure. Anyway...'

A shivering desperate voice in the crowd yelled 'Get on with it!' He was wildly applauded. The Speaker misunderstood it as appreciation for his lecture.

'Thank you, very much. Where I work there is a steel works and a river just like Newport's and a little further on...'

The face of Clare Short and those of the rest of the platform party were contorted, frozen in arctic pain.

'And there are sixteen cables in all. Each one of them is made up of a hundred and twenty-seven strands of round wire wrapped together in...'

The thoughts of the crowd were elsewhere. How much cable would be needed to garrotte someone? Which bits of the bridge would make the best gibbet?

After an eternity something made him stop. Maybe he heard sobbing from the crowd. Perhaps the penny did drop. A lesson to all open air public speakers. Shut up when the audience stops looking at you. Don't wait until your tormented listeners are planning to lynch you.

In the bad old days of overcrowded offices, I shared a room with seven MPs plus assorted researchers. Order and tidiness were impossible. Desks disappeared under a tip of papers. To compensate a sign was fixed on the door saying, 'A tidy desk is proof of a diseased mind.' We learned to survive in, and to love our squalor – except Paul Murphy. There was never a scrap of paper on his polished desk. Perpetually, it gleamed mockingly at us. From our squalor, a frequently contemplated remedy by the other six of us was homicide.

Others who incite similar emotions to some Members are those who trample over other MPs' constituencies without prior notice, or muscle in on issues to which others have proprietary rights.

The Commons is a village of peculiar people doing a peculiar job. They are chronically susceptible to jealously and irrational rages.

Take care.

How to Persuade Government

A Government is a vast organism internetted and muscled by bonds of self-interest and self-defence. Insensitive and inert, its reaction to new ideas can be precisely predicted.

The 2010 Coalition Government has been prone to U-turns. Skilled lobbying deploying constituents' e-mails has toppled several announced policies. All governments claim to be listening. Translating public fury into backbench pressure has worked with the Coalition.

Insider and well-connected Peter Bottomley let me into the secret five steps to success. Usually they are divided by periods of about six months.

Send the idea to the Government.
Forever afterwards they will deny ever receiving it.

Send it again.
They will confess they've seen but they have lost it.

Send it again.
The third time they will simply say 'No'.

Send it again.
They say the idea won't work and provide irrational reasons why not.

Send it again.
Finally they will introduce the scheme and announce that it is their own idea.

Records of the first move in any campaign should be treasured. I prize a cutting of an article I wrote for the July 1974 edition of the RoSPA magazine *Care on the Road*. I had the temerity to argue that lives would be saved if speed humps could be placed on public roads. The RAC denounced the idea as 'crazy'; RoSPA ridiculed the idea saying it would cause more accidents than it would avoid. The Government followed the first step above and subsequently the other four. Traffic calming has since saved thousands of lives. The rewards of persistence.

How to Free Information

My greatly missed friend the late Tony Gregory, an independent member of Dáil Éireann, prophetically warned that the UK's Freedom of Information (FOI) act would crucify MPs. The earlier Irish act embarrassed TDs. Jubilation about transparency and FOI in Parliament cooled when Norman Baker sought disclosure of full details of all Members' travel expenses. Heather Brooke's FOI request succeeded and the consequent expenses scandal erupted.

But FOI has also extended parliamentary scrutiny. As MPs can already ask Parliamentary Questions of all departments, why use FOI requests instead? PQs provide short, statistical answers; FOI requests can access more detailed information, actual documents, opinions, and deliberations. But they can take weeks, even years.

Gordon Prentice was Parliament's Sleaze-buster General. He relentlessly pursued Jonathan Aitken. His questions on Jonathan's perjury had an influence. The issue could not be quietly forgotten as many establishment figures had hoped. The absentee status of Lords Laidlaw and Ashcroft and their lavish contributions to the Conservative Party were his constant theme. Gordon used the full armoury of Select Committee and Parliamentary Questions to unearth the truth. But success came from his FOI request. It took two years until a confession of culpability was made and full disclosure was inevitable.

Tory MP Justine Greening campaigned against the expansion of Heathrow Airport. She used FOI requests to access communication between the Department for Transport and BAA. It took eighteen months for the information to be released.

Tory Andrew Tyrie's All-Party Parliamentary Group on Extraordinary Rendition used a FOI request to the Foreign Office to confirm that inaccurate assurances had been provided by the US in relation to Diego Garcia on at least eight separate occasions.

Prentice's triumph was the most impressive and proved the potency of FOI law. His FOI request asked 'What form did Michael Ashcroft's undertaking take to become a permanent resident in the UK in 2010 and to whom was the undertaking given?' The Cabinet Office refused to reveal the information, citing exemptions in the FOI Act about confidentiality and personal information.

But the Information Commissioner ruled that Prentice – and the public – had the right to know and ordered the Cabinet Office to give Prentice the information. In anticipation of this, Ashcroft declared he was indeed a 'non-dom'. The Cabinet Office then released a memo showing that, a decade earlier, Ashcroft had given a 'clear and unequivocal assurance' to the then-Conservative leader William Hague that he would take up UK residence by the end of 2000 and that he would not take up his seat in the Lords before that happened.

The result was a change in the law to limit the role of tax exiles in funding political parties and to exclude non-doms from Parliament.

All governments are secretive. One element of the denial of information policy in the eighties was to end the printing in Hansard of parliamentary answers from 'next step agencies'. This was a serious loss because almost all the civil service is run by the agencies. It was a special problem for MPs and outside bodies who rely on Hansard for news.

Confusingly the questions were printed in Hansard and whetted the appetites. As a frontbencher, photocopying answers to outside bodies grew to be a major office activity. With the help of a grant from the Joseph Rowntree Trust and the great work of researcher Tony Lynes, I published a monthly selection of answers called 'Open Lines'. Copies were sent to all MPs and many outside organisations. In the meantime I campaigned with questions for the Government to change policy. After two years they nationalised my private enterprise venture, and answers and letters from agencies' chief executives now appear in Hansard.

The daily grind of questions, written and oral is essential to prevent future governments slamming shut the door of secrecy. Gordon Prentice, Justine Greening and Andrew Tyrie have scored significant victories for the Legislature over a secretive Executive. More will come as FOI develops as a powerful new investigative weapon for backbenchers.

How to Blaze a Trail

The most widespread talent among MPs is fluency in saying the obvious. Students of Friday debates discover countless repetitions of what is accepted wisdom. It is usually a restatement of shared prejudice founded on ignorance. A Law and Order speech runs: 'Crime is bad, I want to stop it. More punishment please.' After a well publicised accident the same theme is repeated by dozens: 'I am sorry and sympathetic. We must stop an identical accident happening again.' An illegal drugs one goes: 'Drugs deaths are increasing, the best policy is tough punishment, we must be tougher.'

Only rarely during these orgies of mass-deception do small voices try to ask challenging rational questions. Do longer prison sentences reduce crime? Why debate ten deaths in a rail accident and ignore ten deaths a day on the roads? If drug prohibition is working why do drug use and deaths increase every year? It is not working, so don't fix it?

Debates in which opinions were changed in the House numbered one, on illegal drug use. An amendment powerfully argued by Tony Banks and Diane Abbott urged a new policy to end the prohibition of soft drugs. Two North of England MPs and one from London said that the speeches changed their minds. They had never heard the arguments before. Martin Bell said in his book *An Accidental MP*, 'And I have changed my mind, for instance on the legalisation of cannabis for medical purposes because I heard Paul Flynn MP advocating it in the House, and found his arguments unanswerable.' One for the Bouquet File.

There are many trails that can be blazed through the Westminster forests of errors and half-truths. The vast powers that Parliament has of inquiry, innovation and law-making are often used as crude blunt instruments. There is great talent and experience among Members especially in the fields of the law, industry, trade unions and the arts. Knowledge of science is lamentable, and techniques of scientific thinking are embryonic.

There are scientific institutions in Westminster. The most accessible and useful for Members is the Parliamentary Office of Science and Technology (P.O.S.T.). The magazine *New Scientist* is a treasure house of digestible information for politicians, anticipating new trends as it does.

Regularly Parliament congratulates itself on buying technological jobs from what were recently Third World countries. Rarely do we ask why we have neglected the successes of our own inventive genius for scientific innovation.

Major reforms will be initiated by those who work to put right our neglect of science and who challenge the disrespect for objective reasoning. It is certain that one of the reforms of the next decade will be in reducing harm caused by legal, illegal and medicinal drugs. The case will not be argued by the majority gluttons or those climbing the greasy pole. It will come from backbenchers – especially those who are backbenchers by choice.

How to Walk on Water

Regular excessive demands are made on the understanding and knowledge of MPs.

All have to learn to walk on water. Ignorance is no bar to the daily chore of pontificating on complex matters. The act has been described as 'treading on a sea of bullshit'. The danger of sinking is always imminent.

The public rightly question how mere mortals can be expert on everything, today preaching on nano-technology and income support and tomorrow on CSA, Hackgate and Seamus Heaney. That is the duty of the artisan backbencher. Oral Questions on unknown topics are easy. Frontbench teams will provide the three necessary sentences. The library or Google will turn up the latest editorials and feature articles.

Speeches are minefields that destroy the careless. Interventions can puncture aplomb and expose gaping ignorance. On a Public Bill Committee, opposition backbenchers are frequently supplied with gobbledygook notes by specialist 'advisers'. Reading them convincingly is an acquired technique. Sometimes half-way through a speech, understanding dawns. The speaker begins to get an inkling of what he is talking about.

On one social security bill an amendment was selected for debate that puzzled the frontbenchers. An adviser from a voluntary body had asked for it to be tabled. He was not in the committee and could not be contacted. No committee member could remember its purpose or understand it. Sensibly, we panicked and withdrew the amendment.

Only once did David Drew accept a hand-me-down question from a Government whip. It then appeared in a very high position for Oral Questions. The wording was incomprehensible to

David. He demanded the promised briefing from the minister. Embarrassed, the minister explained that the wording had been drafted by a civil servant who had just left the department. No one else understood the meaning of the question. The minister suspected a parting shot from a disgruntled civil servant. David and the minister agreed to exchange complimentary meaningless inanities.

Nobody noticed because no one else understood.

How to Climb the Greasy Pole

Labour has dropped its elections to its shadow Cabinet. The selection is now the same used by all parties. God and the whips whisper the names of the chosen into the party leader's ear.

But elections have increased with votes for Select Committee chairs and members. The seduction offensive is led by e-mails. But that is just the start. Colleagues who usually pass by with a curt nod, develop a keen interest in the welfare of the spouse, the kids, the bad foot.

Aspiring committee members will insist that it is always their round for the tea and carrot cake. Congratulatory notes arrive: 'Your speech on Wednesday was the best thing heard in the House since the time of Gladstone', 'Would you mind if I copy your brilliantly funny question yesterday for my constituency newsletter?', 'Will you send me a copy of the speech you made at conference? Everyone is talking about it.'

The flattery is based on the well founded assumption that there is no limit to the vanity of MPs. For many this approach has long been successful. Edward Pearce once commented that the sycophantic approach of one MP was the most impressive display of begging since the mendicant friars of the Middle Ages roamed the country selling indulgences.

The killer line for one habitually successful candidate was: 'I know I won't win this year, because of the quality of the competition. But you will think about voting for me? You won't see me humiliated, will you?'

In the past some candidates for shadow Cabinet places overdid the outside publicity under the strain. Jack Straw once demonised squeegee windscreen washers as akin to muggers in his now famous 'Kick a Beggar for Socialism' speech. Mo Mowlam puzzled the nation when she suggested building a new palace for the royal family. Most people thought this was a bit unnecessary. They have seven palaces already.

Negative campaigning is in embryo form, but it will grow. Life will be blown into old gossip of candidates' frailties and disloyalties. Poisonous anecdotes will be unearthed, malevolently revitalised and broadcast widely.

While democracy lost out with the demise of shadow Cabinet elections, the Wright reforms elections of Select Committee is a substantial victory of the Legislature over the Executive.

How to Succeed

'When all else fails, lower your standards' was the message on a badge worn by a barmaid in a pub in Marshfield in Newport. The secret of success and happiness in politics is adjusting ambitions to abilities and realistic prospects. For those who get it right straightaway, no lacerating adjustments of standards is necessary.

The belief that all political careers end in failure is based on the myth that all MPs hope to become Prime Minister. They do not. Happiness is keeping as small a space as possible between hope and achievement. Paradise is when they coincide. Here is a scientifically calculated guide to the odds of achieving ambition. Factors have to be applied to the calculation depending on party, age or susceptibility to the seven deadly sins.

Current prospects: odds
Prime Minister: 1,000-1

Speaker: 600-1

Secretary of State: 50-1

Chair of Select Committee: 60-1

Junior minister: 20-1

Disgraced sleaze ball: 40-1

Knighted: 4-9 (Con); 250-1 (Lab)

A whip: 7-1

Good constituency MP 8-1

How to be Honoured

The Welsh writer Ellis Wynne in his *The Visions of the Sleeping Bard* described Hell. A uniquely devilish punishment was used against those who in life had titles and honours that puffed them up above the egalitarian herd. They were to suffer each other's pompous company, in hideous fashion, for eternity.

The invisible lure of a knighthood is a potent force in Parliament. The Labour Party is generally opposed to honours. A few accept them. About twelve years of attendance as MP once entitled every Tory to one. The process was accelerated for dumb loyalty in the whips' office and slowed for any signs of independent thought or action.

The late Robert Adley harangued me for withdrawing the word 'lickspittle' at the request of the Speaker Betty Boothroyd. She allowed me to substitute 'mediocre, talentless and obedient' as a description of Tory MPs who accept knighthoods. Adley never became Sir Robert. He was a great expert on railways, a long serving Member but no 'lickspittle'. In respect of all the worthy un-knighted ones and in the interests of egalitarianism, no titles are recorded in this book.

As Labour Members of great distinction and service to the House refuse them, honours are tarnished. They are seen as the rewards for plodders for services to routine minor duties or to international travel. To the low flyers and the miniaturists they give some consolation and a little distinction especially when they travel abroad. Foreigners still have lingering respect for titles.

A useful subversive ploy is to address all the knights as 'Mister' or all the non-knights as 'Sir'. It creates nervousness. Describing 'Hons' as 'Right Hons' and vice versa distresses those who prize honours. They cannot correct the speaker without revealing their belief in a meaningless flatulent system.

Jacob Rees-Mogg in a point of order asked that I refer to Prince Charles and Camilla as 'Their Royal Highnesses the Duke and Duchess of Cornwall.' I declined, emphasising that calling them 'The Heir to the Throne and his wife' was accurate, in order and pithy. It also avoided sycophancy.

Some new knights are gracious enough to be embarrassed. 'I had to take it, y'know. It's my wife. She's really keen to be Lady Cringe.'

Why knighthoods? Knighthoods are used:

- As a badge of mediocrity for undistinguished long service.
- For malcontent political opponents in order to annoy their leaders.
- To reinforce subservience to royalty.
- To silence aspiring rebels.
- To coax the clapped-out to retire.
- To punish independent MPs by exclusion.
- To reward senior civil servants for survival.
- Because everyone 'likes his wife'.

How to Use Privilege

Privilege is precious and must be used only with caution. It can damage the accused and the accuser, as I know to my cost. An asset enjoyed only by parliamentarians can become a nightmare.

Its apparently casual use by the resourceful John Hemming

in naming a scandal-hit footballer was widely condemned. The persistent use of privilege by Tam Dalyell in revealing important concealed truths was admirable.

Parliamentary Privilege allows Members to speak freely during ordinary parliamentary proceedings without fear of legal action on the grounds of slander, contempt of court or breaching the Official Secrets Act.

Beware. MPs are protected only for their words in the Chamber or in committee session. Even press conferences on committee reports are not protected by privilege. Comments to the media on statements made under privilege must not stray from the original protected words used.

Privilege is a useful last resort threat to name commercial bodies that have badly served constituents. My own experience offers a cautionary example. I have used the threat many times but only three times in twenty-five years have I carried it out. The effect twice was galvanising, the third a calamity. The first was against a man who planned to re-open a power station in my constituency. He had a colourful past which did not inspire confidence that the station would be well run. It was a serious polluter when operated by the Electricity Board. I named him in an adjournment debate. The plan was dropped and the man left the country.

In the second case a person had harassed two of my elderly constituents rendering the flat that had been their home for twenty-two years uninhabitable. His plan was to open a children's play centre in my constituency. He had many previous business ventures. Four of them had failed after their premises had burnt down. In EDMs I said that he was not the ideal person to run a children's centre. He left the town and the project collapsed.

In both cases I had voluminous evidence and I warned the two people that I intended to name them. Both refused to co-operate and drop their schemes. Although newspapers had a great deal of evidence they were reluctant to use it until I had published it under privilege.

In the first case I had a brown envelope of correspondence delivered anonymously to me, I believe, from a civil servant. On the second the Welsh Language television programme *Taro Naw* and the *South Wales Argus* collected the evidence and courageously published much of it before privilege fully protected them. The two cases were happy results of sensible collaboration between press, Parliament and my anonymous informant.

My third use of privilege was a financial and political disaster that cost me a great deal. The accusation I made concerned alleged excessive claw back of compensation from clients using a firm of ambulance chasers. Unfortunately I was not aware that MPs are covered with insurance for legal costs in cases of this kind for sums up to £25,000. Engaging an outside firm invalidated any claim for help from the Commons fund. That proved to be a very expensive oversight. Convinced of my innocence, I refused to back down. In my judgement, this was an attempt to kill a wholly justified campaign against the exploitation of those who are financially unsophisticated.

My legal advisers gave me some encouragement and a few worries. I was advised that I had an eighty per cent chance of winning if the case went to court. But there was no guarantee. It depended on the disposition of the judge and other uncontrollable factors. I could lose. Then the costs could be ruinous, possibly £500,000. The news that I was being sued for '£300,000' was leaked to a local newspaper a week before the 2005 General Election. Libel laws inhibited my publishing a full defence. To avoid financial ruin, I was forced to accede to their demands.

MPs remain vulnerable as a weak link. While I was fireproof on my EDMs and Commons statements, a comment quoted in the *Financial Times* in my name was not covered by privilege. Few MPs can afford to pay for the legal muscle that a national newspaper can employ. We are out-gunned and legal teams are demoralised by barristers in the pay of commercial firms with bottomless pockets.

The Commons Authorities and the Inland Revenue accepted that my costs were wholly, exclusively and necessarily incurred through legitimate parliamentary campaigning. That helped defray some of the costs and the Inland Revenue can also help in certain circumstances.

These risks go with the parliamentary territory. After the event, I wrote to all MPs warning them of our vulnerability. Dozens wrote back. Many had suffered attempts to silence them with libel threat charges. In spite of the present money-grabbing image of MPs, I have a long list of honourable MPs who lost large sums of money in pursuit of courageous and worthy aims. The value of privilege would be diminished if we could be silenced by the threat of crippling court costs. In one instance a constituent asked for an MP's help in a housing matter because he said that he was mentally ill. The MP raised the case with the housing author-ity. He was then sued by the constituent for passing on the infor-mation about his 'mental illness'. The case cost the MP £10,000 in costs. The price of doing his job.

Unfortunately the reputation of MPs was further sullied by a foolish attempt to use parliamentary privilege as a shield to avoid prosecutions. The case involved three MPs charged with expenses offences. It was a lawyer's not a politician's argument. Privilege is designed to give MPs freedom to expose wrongdoing and to defend our constituents, not to protect MPs suspected of breaking the law. This attempted ruse led to accusations of one law for MPs and another for everyone else. The MPs should have rejected the advice of their lawyers. It needlessly prolonged their misery and extended the life of the ugly screaming nightmare of the expenses scandal.

Privilege remains as an ancient right that must be cherished and used sparingly.

How to Switch Off

The Commons has some little known oases of relaxation. There is a gym which offers beauty treatment, massage, sports massage, sauna, sunbeds, physiotherapy and acupuncture. Exotically, it provides a 'cardio theatre entertainment system' and a 'power plate vibration machine'.

In Portcullis House there are well-appointed showers and baths that are well used by staff and Members. The gym supplies personal massages. Once there was a mobile massage service to Members' offices. They were called 'Workplace Energising and Re-vitalising Massages'. The cost was five pounds for ten minutes. That service seems to have gone. The scope for misunderstanding from spouses limits the number of customers. A great deal of kudos was created for one MP in the eyes of his staff impressed by his frequents visits to the gym. A sudden crisis called for the cancellation of an appointment by a member of his staff. She was crestfallen to discover that she was talking to the masseur.

There is an on-call Westminster hypnotherapist who offers sessions to help with 'giving up smoking, stress management, insomnia, weight management, memory, phobias, fears, anxiety and panic attacks'. That lot covers the average MP's day.

Some MPs get inspiration from the buildings. Virginia Bottomley is a devoted fan of Portcullis House: 'I feel even more energetic and industrious – and proud to be an MP. So splendid are the offices that I even come in on Sunday evenings so that I can start each week on top of my work. Many MPs work late at night and one of the many strengths of Portcullis House is that at night it takes on a life of its own.'

Many groups meet to discuss hobbies and interests. There are thriving photographic and painting societies in the House that run annual exhibitions of Members' work. Once a week there are yoga classes. Somewhere in the bowels of the building is a hotly controversial shooting gallery.

The parliamentary choir is eleven years old. Weekly rehearsals are held in the crypt allowing escapes for divisions. They have achieved distinction with a varied repertoire from Verdi's *Requiem* to Songs from the Shows. Members include staff. Performance standards have improved even though new members are not auditioned. A leading voice is the professionally trained Bernard Jenkin.

Although there are no shops in the Palace, some urgent services are available. Vending machines supply four different varieties of tights suitable for all occasions. A mobile ice-cream vendor has been observed in high summer near the Terrace. Multi-channel televisions in Members' office supply live feeds from the Chamber and the main terrestrial and satellite channels. Sky Sports is hugely popular.

The best spot for top quality relaxing is the Terrace in summer. It's a consolation for the most abject moment of political inadequacy in my life. Once I shared an election forum with a yogic flyer from the Natural Law Party. He promised the voters 'an end to war, reducing the incidence of all diseases by half and a world that will be suffused with bubbling bliss'.

All I had to offer was the minimum wage. There have been times on the Terrace in late summer evenings, sitting watching the drama of the moving river, warmed with a drink and the company of good friends that I have had moments when I felt the bliss bubbling up.

How to Stay Sane

Staff and MPs need a refuge from desolate days.

An ungrateful constituent abuses the staff. A strong case to reverse an injustice fails. A tabloid savages a pet cause. The MP bombs in a crowded Commons. A loved constituent dies prematurely. A constituency firm loses hundreds of jobs. A political

enemy wounds with a bull's-eye attack. Vital office equipment
has a nervous breakdown.

The best protection is the strength of the trust and solidarity
of MP and staff. This is the product of mutual respect and shared
hard work to achieve objectives. The MP and staff must all be
prepared to undertake all tasks – pleasant and unpleasant. Staff
should be encouraged to pursue their own ideals and allowed
time for research and collaboration with outside groups. Don't
limit social or online life to the world of politics.

The bouquet file can be a wonderful balancing balm. Re-read
the warm appreciation from grateful constituents for work done.
Take out and wallow in articles of praise from the press. Look
again at reports of good constituency days when new jobs arrived.

When equilibrium is restored a bout of concentrated work is
the most effective bromide for driving the bad thoughts to the
back of the mind.

As always work is the best medicine.

How to Know the Village Folk

Parliament is a village, a lively, living community of several
thousand people. In addition to Members, there are secretaries, researchers, police, cleaners, waiters, contractors, a doctor,
nurse and hairdressers. Within the confines of the palace
they live, socialise, eat, sometimes even sleep, make love and
occasionally die.

Commons staff are a daily link with reality. Performing unpre-
tentious jobs they can be an anchor. Their company and views are
worth cultivating. Some are celebrated as Commons characters.
Both George Osborne and David Cameron are known never to say
hello to police and attendants. They are probably unaware of the
hostility engendered. It can spread in ripples from Westminster.

While many faces come and go in the Members' Tea Room,
Julie Clifford and Noeleen Delaney are among the long-term

survivors. It is a mark of distinction to be greeted by either of them by name. Staff wear name badges. MPs rarely do. Being recognised means that Julie and Noeleen have spotted you on the television. It's an accurate measure of fame. Noeleen has charmed us with her unfailing kindness and her beguiling Irish accent; Julie impressed when she gave evidence to a Select Committee on the poor wages and conditions that the Commons provides.

In the public catering areas two greatly loved personalities toil through the unsocial hours of Commons life. Cathy Walsh joined the catering department in 1987, while Betty Thompson has been serving Members and public for seventeen years. Their pleasant breezy personalities brighten our days and human-ise our workplace. Their loyalty is appreciated, although it is rarely recognised.

One unlamented Commons tradition has gone forever: hair-cuts for males only, executed in the style of the First World War basin cut. The now unisex John Simon is an over-subscribed convenient service for discriminating parliamentarians. For some it may be more than a matter of convenience. They may be seeking refuge, fleeing the ear-bashing they would endure from constituency barbers who store up grievances for the MP's visit. The charges are reasonable and the staff are wonderful.

Security threats have regrettably made the palace a fortress. Armed London Police are stationed on key entrances. They provide reassurance. The unarmed, traditional, unique breed of parliamentary police has survived unchanged. They are an unrelated species to the police on *Vera* or *EastEnders*. Their career paths may have been wayward. Once they planned to bring law and order to the unruly streets of Brixton and Tiger Bay. Perhaps they dreamed of quelling riots or dealing with hard characters. But then they changed. One day their companions noticed they were different. Perhaps they developed a passion for preserving the marsh fritillaries, making dolls out of raffia or even discuss-ing the subtleties of Plato. Dealing with criminals no longer held their interest. They were consigned to the police Nirvana of parliamentary duties. Even those who have had bad previous experience of the Metropolitan Police acclaim the Commons Police as kind, considerate and courteous. All MPs say to other MPs, 'Aren't our police marvellous?'

How to be Re-Elected

Ignore conventional wisdom. Fear the unexpected.

Having won six elections in a seat that was previously held by a Tory, I could immodestly claim that I know something about being re-elected. But other factors determined the results. My victories from 1987 to 2005 were thanks to the Newport West Labour Party, generously helped by the presence in Downing Street of Margaret Thatcher, John Major and Tony Blair.

The local party triumphed in 2010 in unusual circumstances. All advice on how to be re-elected emphasises the vital role of the active daily participation of the candidate in the campaign. In 2010 I was stuck in Geneva, marooned by the volcanic ash for nearly a week at the height of the campaign. It was frustrating for me but, apparently, liberating for my agent and campaign team. Nobody outside of my party noticed or complained. The swing against Labour was smaller than in all the neighbouring seats. Absence made the voters grow fonder.

The unexpected 2010 nightmare of Phil Woolas has profound implications for all candidates in every future campaign. Extravagant language, half-truths, distorted images must be excised from election literature. It is illegal to publish any false statement of fact in relation to the candidate's personal character or conduct, unless he can show that he had reasonable grounds for believing, and did believe, that statement to be true.

Woolas is the first MP to be found guilty of illegal practices by the specially convened Election Court in ninety-nine years. He was banned from public office for three years and was forced to resign his seat. Labour's Deputy Leader Harriet Harman said it was 'no part of Labour's politics to try to win elections by telling lies' and the party would not support any appeal.

It was no defence to claim that other parties make untrue claims in the fever of an election campaign. The Woolas case may end the wild abuse that has been previously tolerated. Almost all negative campaigning is counterproductive. I thought everyone knew that.

Elections results are only marginally determined by the final month's campaign. Canny MPs are campaigning for a constituency loyalist identity from the day they are first elected. It's the drip-feed of consistent valued constituency work that matters, not the final big bang. The rewards are won by the MPs who put Votingham before party.

The 2010 intake of MPs was promisingly independent. A full 36 per cent of the House was newly-elected; including 48 per cent of Conservative MPs. Freshly elected MPs are usually docile and obedient. But the 2010 cohort of Tories was to be the most rebellious ever. Philip Cowley has calculated:

In absolute terms, more Conservative newbies have rebelled (forty-six) compared to Labour ones (twenty-one) or the Lib Dems (seven). In percentage terms, while 30 per cent of new Tory MPs have now rebelled, 33 per cent of Labour ones have done so, with the highest percentage of newbie rebels located among the Liberal Democrats: although there are only ten newly elected Lib Dem MPs, a full 70 per cent have defied the party whip.

But these headline figures mask an important difference in terms of dissent by the new MPs of the three main parties. Between them, the newbie Tory rebels have cast a whopping 249 rebellious votes, compared with a modest twenty-three for Labour, and only a slightly higher number, twenty-seven, for the Liberal Democrats. The top Conservative newbie rebel, David Nuttall, has amassed fifty-four rebellions.

The formation of the eighty-one-strong group of Tory sceptics after the rebel vote for a referendum may be as significant as the establishment of the 1922, exclusively backbench, Committee. While most rebellions are still anti-European Union there is a real hope that the new parliament will be less docile. In Jacob Rees-Mogg's memorable words more 'tiger' than 'Bagpuss'. The Legislature might now beneficially challenge the Executive. There was a startling declaration of independence from Tory Mark Pritchard:

On Monday, in return for amending my motion [on the ban on wild animals in circuses] ... I would have been offered a job. [Hon. Members: 'Ooh!'] ... Until last night, when I was threatened ... I was told that the Prime Minister himself had said that unless I withdrew this motion, he would look upon it very dimly indeed ... I might be just a little council house lad from a very poor background, but that background gives me a backbone, it gives me a thick skin, and I am not going to kowtow to the whips or even the Prime Minister of my country on an issue that I feel passionately about and on which I have conviction ... We need a generation of politicians with a bit of spine, not jelly...

Paranoia is rampant shortly before elections. A *Times* journalist declared, twenty-nine days before the 2010 election, 'Although up to a dozen Labour MPs are expected to announce that they are not standing for re-election on Tuesday, the leadership feels that several are "bed blocking" by refusing to stand down.' One of the bed blockers mentioned was Alan Meale who was at the grand old age of sixty-one. Another six Labour MPs over sixty-eight were named. 'Some may announce their retirement today,' *The Times* exclusively revealed. None did.

The *Times* was suffering from the politician's ailment of Chronic Re-Election Paranoia (CREEP). MPs become more irrational than usual in the final few months. I was pleasantly surprised by the number of distinguished politicians who signed my *cri de coeur* against CREEP in a February 2005 EDM: 'That this House believes that no legislation should be enacted in the three-month pre-election period, which should be used for debating draft bills; notes the lamentable collapse of the courage and critical abilities of honourable Members induced by pre-elections tension.'

A sad spectacle in 2010 was a handful of Labour MPs who had been deselected by their own parties but unwisely stood as independents. One blamed a party conspiracy. Not true – the system is heavily weighted in favour of retiring MPs. Before a serious challenge can be made, half of the constituency's branches and affiliated bodies must ask for a full reselection. Up to that point, the sitting MP is the only candidate. If half the local Members do not have full confidence in the MP, it's time to bow out gratefully and gracefully.

A new neurosis is the right of voters to recall their MP. Where there is a clear sign of wrongdoing, a petition signed by 10 per cent of the electors in the MP's constituency would be enough to recall them.

The expenses scandal culled many in 2010. Oddly it was not the total sums involved that was deadly. Many who were alleged to have wrongly claimed tens of thousands of pounds survived. The curse was the newsworthy nature of the claims made. Those who charged for cleaning a moat or for a duck house disqualified themselves. David Heathcoat-Amory had claimed more than £380 of horse manure for his garden. As a frequent visitor to the Wells constituency it was impossible to miss the graffiti: 'One vote = one bag of horse shit.' It did for him.

A lesson to us all.

FINAL STEPS

How to be Ennobled

The House of Lords is the ideal rest home for the tired, disillusioned or clapped out. The burden is lifted while the comfort and pampering of Parliament continues, along with the power to influence policy. Worriers are freed from the threat of losing their seats and their livelihood. The duty of helping constituents has gone. Tony Banks, for one, spoke enthusiastically of his joy at escaping from his nagging constituents. Of constituency work he said, 'I found it intellectually numbing, tedious in the extreme.' His welcome in the Lords was limited, however. Stuffy rules frustrated his choice of title as 'Lord Banks of the Thames.'

An odd game is played out by MPs contemplating retirement. Most announce their intention to resign in good time for their constituency party to reselect. By doing so, they lose the bargaining chip of securing a passage to the Lords. The Tories have the twin bribes of the Lords and Knighthoods on offer to lubricate the departure of the unwanted.

It was not until the late Roy Hughes had fought two contested reselection battles for his seat that he announced he was prepared to resign. He said they came at him 'like elephants' promising a place in the Lords. Tony Blair was keen to find safe Labour seats to reward Tory MPs who had crossed the floor. Roy was ennobled and former Tory MP Alan Howarth became a Labour MP. He was later ennobled along with other Tory defectors. All major parties have cynically used honours for party political interests. The future is uncertain, it may not continue.

A few months before the 2005 General Election a group of left wing sages at the Peter Pike table in the Members' Dining Room speculated on the likely recipients of the eleven Labour places in the Lords. Based on the assumption that ultra-loyalty to Blairism would be the only criteria the full quota was accurately forecast. The retiring Peter Pike and the independent David Hinchcliffe were not among them. Their cards had been marked because of the company they kept and their flashes of independence. They were unsafe pairs of hands.

The hereditary principle is crumbling and reform of the Lords is tantalisingly close. There are persistent accounts of MPs leaving the Commons certain of noble reincarnation. Promises were unrequited. One MP resigned his candidacy shortly before the 2005 election in the belief that he had been promised ermine. It never arrived. About ten of the departing MPs from both main parties in the 2010 election were convinced that they would be ennobled and said so. They have been disappointed. Places have been filled with talented people from outside of Parliament.

There is little certainty and a great deal of treachery in love and politics.

How to Resign

By-elections are troublesome and expensive for the party and constituents. They consume party energies, empty the coffers and expose parties to the ugly truth of their unpopularity. Leaving for career reasons or financial improvement is forgiven only under very exceptional circumstances. David Davis resigned in extraordinary circumstances. It was part of his libertarian campaign to protest at, among other things, the excessive proliferation of CCTV cameras. The debate he sought with Government did not happen. Only (mostly lunatic) fringe candidates opposed him. The turnout was poor and the election cost taxpayers an estimated £200,000. The stunt ended Davis's hope of becoming Home Secretary. Accusations of an ego-trip and a vanity election at public expense were made. After the English riots of 2011, CCTV cameras have rediscovered their popularity.

Now there are few health reasons for resigning. If Stephen Hawking can be a brilliant astrophysicist with very little of him functioning except his brain, MPs can struggle on. Infirmities of the body and fading mental powers are compensated by reasonably financed staff and equipment. One MP who had a mini-stroke one evening in the Commons dictated a blog the next day from his hospital bed. It was intended to discourage premature hopes from aspirant candidates for his seat. The blog reassured, 'All my bits are still working as well as before. Which is not saying much.'

Staff can do a great deal to keep the work free-wheeling along until an election. Electronic aids allow a bedridden MP to complete work acceptably. In circumstances where the constituency would suffer as a result of an MP's illness, however, there is no choice other than resignation. The long-established procedure for resignation is by applying for a job either for the Manor of Northstead or the Chiltern Hundreds. Retiring MPs apply in turn for each one. With Eric Illsley it was Chiltern Hundreds.

Gerry Adams upset the apple cart. When he decided to leave the Commons he had a major problem. As a Republican, he understandably refused to seek an office of profit under the Crown. There is no other mechanism to resign as an MP. David Cameron insisted he had applied for an office of profit under the Crown. He was wrong. Gerry had sent in a simple letter of resignation to the Speaker. 'It had to be accepted,' a Treasury spokesperson explained. 'Consistent with long-standing precedent, the Chancellor has taken [the letter] as a request to be appointed the Steward and Bailiff of the Manor of Northstead and granted the office.' So even if a retiring Member does not apply for a Crown Office, Government will deem that an application has been received. Another piece of new parliamentary tomfoolery is born, replacing antique tomfoolery. Gerry Adams's precedent has probably ended forever a curious but useless practice. A simple note of resignation will now suffice.

How Not to Revolve

Sinning may have ended, but the occasions of sin remain. There are obstacles in the path to restoring confidence in our battered political system. Practices that were tolerated in the past should be eliminated in order to avoid new scandals.

The 'revolving door' is the procession of former ministers, generals and top civil servants hawking their souls, skills and contact books to the highest bidders after retirement. It's damaging that confidential information of national importance is being sold to Mega-greed Plc. Worse is the corrupting influence of the hope of future retirement jobs on decisions made when top people are in office determining contracts. If the choice is between Company A or Company C for a fat contract, does a nod or a wink or the dream of a hacienda in Spain tip the decision?

The weak system of policing the revolving door is a scandal that is potentially more serious than the expenses scandal and more damaging to the country. Public cynicism is fed by freshly retired politicians joining the nouveau riche.

The group Transparency International suggests a lifetime ban on lobbying to ease public concerns about the way ministers and officials in 'high risk' areas such as defence and health move seamlessly into top jobs.

Under the existing rules, ministers and top civil servants have to notify the Advisory Committee on Business Appointments (Acoba) of any new jobs taken up within two years of leaving office.

The committee is hardly a representative cross section of the nation. It consists of four Knights, two Peers and a Dame. The privileged retired are judging the privileged retired. They are not the solution. They are part of the problem. The committee's recommendations are not binding.

Following the 'cabs for hire' sting, when former ministers offered to sell their souls, former Transport Secretary Stephen

Byers, former Health Secretary Patricia Hewitt and former Defence Secretary Geoff Hoon were all suspended from the Parliamentary Labour Party for 'bringing it into disrepute'. The chair of the toothless pussy cat Acoba was interviewed for 'cabs for hire'. Later he sent his CV in for consideration for additional work for himself. Public mistrust in politicians will deepen unless tough new rules, transparency and a powerful watchdog slam the revolving door shut.

The shining example of how to behave after ministerial life is Gordon Brown. He has devoted the sum of £250,000 to charity from his post PM earnings. All those now exploiting the revolving door are recipients of good pensions. They should not be prostituting the legacies of high office for glutton's gold. Take an unpaid job with a charity, become a beachcomber, enter a monastery, find a hobby, become an armchair politician.

Never hawk influence and contacts for financial gain.

How to Eulogise

Inevitably, calls come to pay tributes to those who have died. Time must be found to prepare thoroughly and find the best balm of words to bring comfort to the bereaved and do justice to the achievements and personality of the departed. Close relatives will advise on anecdotes that they wish to hear and memories that they want to revive.

The eulogy or the obituary must be self-effacing and self-deprecating. David Mellor mentioned himself sparingly in his eulogy to Tony Banks. On the dreadful day when the papers reported that Mellor had made love five times in a Chelsea strip, he was at first delighted to hear Tony on the radio denying the claim – then, crestfallen. Tony continued, 'Not since the great days has anyone scored five times in a Chelsea shirt.' Mellor compared his plight to a minor composer who had written a piece of music for Rossini's funeral and was told that 'from the musical standpoint, it would have been better if you had died and Rossini had composed the tribute'. Mellor confessed, in the interests of a witty oration, it would have been better if he had died and Tony was giving the eulogy.

Tony's beloved wife Sally commented on the day of the funeral that a minke whale had swum up the Thames. The beautiful creature played and cavorted in full view of the Commons Terrace. Exhausted she swam further up the Thames to Chelsea Football Club's home at Stamford Bridge. There she died. Sally was convinced that the spirit of Tony had transferred to the whale. It made great sense. Had he had the choice, he would have swum up his favourite river, cavorted at Westminster, the scene of his many triumphs, and then struggled down to Chelsea's home to breathe his last breath.

How to Die

Dying is impossible in the Palace of Westminster. Some MPs have died there. Officially they have not. The rules say they cannot. There are many well documented cases of 'non-deaths'.

One Welsh MP, convinced he was suffering from self-diagnosed ME, tried the cure of a session in the Commons Gym. He collapsed an hour later on the terrace and died as a result of undiagnosed heart disease. Another MP passed away in his office during excessive exertion involving a female member of his staff. Both deaths were mis-recorded as taking place outside of the parliamentary estate. One explanation is the unsubstantiated claim that dying in a royal palace gives entitlement to a state funeral. It's one of the least pernicious of the absurd royal strictures that Parliament irrationally continues to tolerate.

Tony Banks was concerned that pension entitlements were linked beneficially to those who expire while fulfilling parliamentary duties. Dying on the job was better for the widow's pension, he believed. He instructed his wife Sally, in the event of his dying suddenly in the bath, to slot a parliamentary document in his hands before rigor mortis set in.

The insurance payments made for death in office are odd. To the loved ones of new Members they are generous; for mature Members they are not. MPs have died after serving less than a year in the House. Their dependants were entitled to two and a half times the annual salary as a lump sum. This generosity does not extend to those who pass their seventy-fifth birthday. The rules were drafted in the belief that MPs should have died before then. Changes must be made in future pension and insurance rules. MPs are seen to be in a privileged position, enjoying an index-linked final salary scheme.

Unexpected deaths are immensely disruptive. There is a duty for MPs to take medical and other advice on when to retire. Subjective judgements are inevitably misleading.

In a small number of cases, MPs' deaths have been the most colourful event of their careers, eclipsing their worthy achievements. Avoid death in any circumstances that might interest the tabloids. John Stonehouse famously faked his 'death' in 1974 by leaving a pile of his clothes on a Miami beach. He was jailed for seven years. The talented Stephen Mulligan is remembered for little except the circumstances of his bizarre death.

Under Thatcher the death rate of MPs was twice as high as under Tony Blair. The main cause of death for MPs is stress-related heart attacks, which disproportionally affects Northern MPs. The average age of death of male Labour MPs is sixty-seven and Conservatives seventy-one. For females the roles are reversed. For Tory women it is sixty-four while Labour ones continue to seventy-nine.

Forecasts that the conflicts of coalition government would add to stress and increase the death rate have been unfounded. But the news is still bleak. The traumas and excesses of parliamentary life take their toll, with an average MP life expectancy of sixty-nine compared with the national average of seventy-five for men and eighty for women.

Cultivating inner serenity amid a maelstrom of anxiety is the surest way to delay the arrival of the Grim Reaper. Privately, most MPs wish to have some autonomy in the choice of the time and circumstances of their own demise. But political caution has dominated. That beneficial reform is still awaited. Only a minority have pressed for the most elusive of human rights – the right to die.

THE FUTURE

How to Restore Trust

It will take many years to rebuild trust in politics. Many judge all MPs to be lying thieves. The details are forgotten but the mud still sticks. The sins of predecessors are visited on present MPs.

The tentacles of corrupting corporate lobbyists are sunk deeply into the body politic. Removing them requires all-party microsurgery. David Cameron has correctly warned that 'corporate lobbying goes to the heart of why people are so fed up with politics. It arouses people's worst fears and suspicions about how our political system works.' More MPs than ever are former lobbyists. Many hope to be future lobbyists. The Werritty scandal shocked the Government into refreshing their reform notions. Ominously, the first debate following the scandal was crowded with former lobbyists lobbying for lobbying.

The nature of politics is to exaggerate success, to oversell, to deny failure, to spin – or, as the public interpret it, to lie. Even the giants of the past, Roosevelt and Churchill, lied. On occasions they had no choice in order to serve their nations' interests. Optimistic manifesto promises that are not honoured are also pilloried as 'lies', whatever the reasons for failure. While party leaders must bear the brunt for future disappointments, individual MPs need an alternative strategy for service and survival. Only very foolish MPs lie. Every word we say is chronicled in Hansard or recorded and is instantly available to be Googled now and in the future. Stephen Pound submitted himself to a lie detector test in 2011. He emerged triumphant as a teller of the truth.

The questions were ones where spin or subterfuge were expected. Stephen answered with the unvarnished truth. The age of spin has gone. Unfortunately the Executive does not fully understand. There are worrying signs of backsliding from the zeal for reform. Eric Pickles and Liam Fox used the pretext of meeting 'privately' not 'ministerially' in avoiding declarations. David Cameron delayed his promised reform of lobbyists for three years. Minister Henry Bellingham gave tacit approval of lobbyist-led luxury jaunts by MPs financed by despotic regimes. The inquiry into the Fox-Werritty scandal was rushed for political expediency and bypassed the sole enforcer of the ministerial code.

To maintain or create trust, MPs should abide by the Backbenchers' Ten Commandments and actively build trust. Post-expenses scandal, new precepts are necessary:

- Understate promises, never exaggerate successes.
- Reply within forty-eight hours to all messages.
- Be transparent and puritanical with allowances and expenses.
- Avoid serving commercial or partial interests.
- Generously give time and enthusiasm to local causes.
- Never accept personal favours or advantages.
- Always pay for substantial meals.
- Put all excess income above salary in a charity trust fund.
- Never lie, tell half-truths or mislead.
- Keep constituents informed on key issues.
- Deflect criticism with truth and humour.
- Admit failures.
- Oppose commitments to war made without MPs' consent.
- Redirect complaints that are beyond responsibility or competence.
- Match behaviour to ethical self-image.
- Refresh and re-invigorate ideals.

- Resist immediate political gratification; seek permanent reforms.
- Advance the shift of power from the Executive to the Legislature.
- Strive to give unambiguous answers to questions.
- Choose simplicity and utility over luxury and extravagance.

The private prayer said every day in the Commons is a worthy ambition:

May they never lead the nation wrongly through love of power, desire to please, or unworthy ideals, but laying aside all private interests and prejudices keep in mind their responsibility to seek to improve the condition of all mankind.